Tales of the Old-Timers

The History of Lexington

Tales of the Old-Timers

The History of Lexington

by

Robert A. Carter

All rights reserved. No portion of this book may be reproduced in any form or by any means, including photocopying, recording, etc., (except as permitted by U.S. copyright law) without permission in writing from the author or the original copyright holder.

Copyright © 2007 by Robert A Carter

Second Edition.

All Rights Reserved.

Photo Credits:

- Arlow Stull Collection
- Bud and Tim Corwin Collection
- Chalfant Family Collection
- Cockley Family
- David Foust
- Donna Fuhrer Hoffner
- Elsie Simon Collection
- Ester Hildebrand Collection
- Gene Wirick
- Harriet Koscheiser Curry
- Harry Linton Collection
- Harry Smith Collection
- Linton Family Collection
- Helen Griebling
- Helen Smith Steiner
- Homer Wagner Collection
- Jim Leedy Collection
- John Gledhill Family
- Lana Garverick Sluss
- Lynn Wiles Leitschuh
- Marilyn Linton Miller
- Marilyn Miller Linton Collection
- Mary Kay Gore Leedy
- Mrs. Beverly Bowers
- Peggy Jo Carpenter Collection
- Richard Lewis Collection
- Richland Foundation
- Robert Snyder Collection
- Rollin Cockley
- Rosie Brumenshenkel Hoffer
- Rosie Hoffner Family Collection
- Sid Earhart Collection
- Sid Earhart Collection
- Sid Earhart Collection
- Stevens Family
- Swigart Family
- Tillie Taylor
- Tribune-Courier
- Vivian Van Cura

Tales of the Old-Timers

The History of Lexington

by

Robert A. Carter

ISBN: 978-1-7361884-4-6

2nd Edition, December 2023

TURAS Publishing
4833 Saratoga Blvd., No. 129
Corpus Christi, TX 78413

To Jackie:
You had to put up with a lot of old stuff
...including me.

Table of Contents

Introduction ix
From the Park Bench 1
The Unlikely Delinquents 4
Our Man Watson 7
Fate of the Old Bell 15
Back Down the Road 16
Taverns and Hotels 21
Al Moore – Correspondent 34
Lexington Newspapers 38
Law and Order 43
The Dollar Kodak 53
Fires, Floods and Wrecks 54
Whiskey and Plenty of It 66
The Railroad 69
Tales of the Graveyard 79
Small Places – Strange Names 83
The Doctors 92
Old Soldiers 94
Early Lexington Business 111
William W. Cockley 117
Other Business Ventures 124
Character of the Town 130
Lexington Awakes From a Slumber 149
Growing Problems 159
Post-War Industry 161
Snakes by the Tale 169
The Smith Family 170
Commentary 189
Politics 190
A Business Variety 191
Historic Building Mourned 208
Schools and Education 209
Women Drivers 210
A Little Church History 212
End of the Rails 224
Photographs of Lexington's Past 225
The Gass Family 233
Those Daring Young Men 238
The Future 240
Index 241

EAST MAIN STREET, LEXINGTON, OHIO.

Introduction

Like most small towns, Lexington's history does not merit the erection of bronze monuments on marble bases. However, neither should the adventures, deeds, triumphs, failures and characters of our little town be brushed away and forgotten.

This book is an attempt to record small portions of life in Lexington, Ohio, over the last two centuries. It's a collection of interviews and stories that I've gleaned from old records, newspapers and family letters over the last 45 years. A few of the stories are off the beaten path of what might be expected from a local history. The interesting words of early writers are also often used just as they put them to paper. I feel the book is a more interesting read that way.

This isn't a professional publication by any means. As you read this book, you'll see that it bears the hammer marks of an amateur writer. Nor is it a fictionalized tale with neatly fitting parts, culminating in a thrilling ending. This book is simply based on facts dug up by the author and written down with only his own understanding of times past and the perspective of old-timers used as a guide.

The latter, sometimes supplied from fading memories, were perhaps embellished or remembered incorrectly by the old-timers. As a case in point, several locals told the story of a building, which later became the Minnear Hotel, being won in a card game. It wasn't. You'll have to read the book to find out what was actually won in that card game.

Wherever possible, the donors of photographs are identified. If not otherwise marked, the pictures come from my own collection. Gathered over many years, my memory may have failed regarding the origin of a photograph. So it is possible that errors may be found and a donor slighted. For this, I want apologize in advance.

Much credit is due Bonne Hildebrand, a retired Lexington school teacher, who advised me on manuscript changes and corrected the places where the author murdered the King's English. Also Ed Carter, who is a computer genius, helped fit the pictures and manuscript together and readied the book for publication. Were it not for the talent of these two people you wouldn't be reading this book.

Finally, it should be said that it was difficult to decide which statistics or stories should be included. The limiting factor in these decisions was the cost of publication verses the expected number of books that might be sold. Since few people are interested in local history and much of the area's population is now made up of transplants from elsewhere, it was decided to reduce the book's size wherever possible.

This is not a profit making venture. If the author can break even on the cost, it will be worth the two-year effort. If not, it has been a labor of love and the book will be a donation to future generations.

Robert Carter, 2007

Editorial Note: This Second Edition has been slightly reformatted and reprinted in order to make it available to a wider audience. An Index has also been added.

From the Park Bench

Photo courtesy of Harry Smith Collection

A normal everyday scene on a warm summer afternoon would find a bunch of old men seated on the benches in the historic Lexington town square. Using the excuse that they had to go to the post office just down the street, those old-timers met at the benches daily, weather permitting, to discuss the issues of the day. The memory of what they had witnessed over the years and yarns of the local history they knew were recalled. Unfortunately, most of those wonderful memories went to the grave with them.

Harry Smith bought one of the first color slide cameras and on a warm afternoon he photographed a group of these old-timers, his friends, at the park. At the time you had to mail the exposed film to Eastman Kodak in Rochester N.Y. for it to be developed. When the slides came back he dated the pictures, August 1947. These slides were rediscovered in 2006, at Medina, in the possession of his only daughter, Helen Smith Steiner.

Harry took a couple of pictures that day and then changed places with Fuller Temple who snapped the picture above. It's a classic photograph in the southeast square park. From left to right are William Hirth, Rolla Armstrong, Morris Graham, Harry Smith, Louie Dickson, Ed Treisch, Ralph Lindsey and a Mr. Hughinart.

Bill Hirth was at one time involved in the livestock auction barn on Plymouth Street. After the barn burned in 1939, he farmed a little and became a dealer in wool. He was an honest, hard working man. However, he was also a terrible driver.

One time Bill was driving in the middle of the road as he came over a hill on Route 97 west of Route 314. With his head turned 90 degrees to his direction of travel, Bill was staring at something off to his right. A teenage driver put his dad's pick up truck in the ditch, narrowly missing Mr. Hirth as he barreled over that hill. Your writer recalls looking in the rear view mirror to see if Bill had also crashed. He hadn't! In fact he was still in the middle of the road, head turned 90 degrees and totally unaware of his close call. When they finally took away his license and car, Bill continued to drive around town . . . on his tractor.

Armstrong, a retired farmer, was dressed like most of the group of retirees. A blue work shirt, suspenders, a hat, and cane marked their station in life. They were not bums, just retired and as one park bench member once commented, "I just came down to get away from the old lady."

Morris Graham, who lived in part of the old Frye house on the square, could tell a wealth of stories. He was particularly fond of one about the time an alleged member of the Jessie James gang had lived west of town on the Grahams' former farm. When asked about some past event or person, Graham usually started "Well sir, I'll tell you how that was." And the details were sure to follow.

Harry Smith was a genius who did more for this town and area than any other person. The son of a doctor, he was an inventor, teacher, industrialist and grand benefactor. He helped shape Lexington and make it what it is today. A chapter on the Smith family is included later in this book.

Louie Dickson lived on Frederick Street and was a rural mail carrier for many years after rural delivery started in 1901. Ed Treisch had lived on a small farm west of town, but lost it when they built the Clear Fork dam.

Ralph Lindsey was another longtime rural mail carrier. He was the son of Seymore Lindsey and had an unusual "haw, haw, haw" laugh that could be heard all over the park. When Lindsey laughed, everybody within earshot laughed with him, even if they didn't know why. The last gentleman in the photograph wasn't one of the old-timer regulars. His name was Hughinart or something like that. He worked out of the B&O Railroad station, possibly on the section gang, and just happened to be in the park the day of the picture.

When the writer was a kid, these men were a curious bunch to observe. Friendly arguments about the actions of people and what they should have said or done were common. Talking a little loud to be heard above the traffic, their language could be a little salty at times, except when a woman walked by. Then a quiet respectful manner prevailed.

Dimmy-crats and Repub-lickins

One time an energetic argument examining the deeds of some "Dimmy-crat" named "Rosie-felt" and merits of "danged Repub-lickins" waxed hot and vocal. Seated

Photograph courtesy of Harry Smith Collection

In 1947, the park on the southeast corner of the town square park was the best place to find the afternoon shade and escape the summer sun. The old tavern building is in the background. Bob Wade's barbershop was in the one story addition to the tavern building.

near the center was one old codger who took no part in the debate. That soon came to the attention of the others. A sudden quiet prevailed as all eyes turned on him. It was time for him to strike his colors as the big question came; "What are you, a Democrat or a Republican?"

"Neither" he said as he leaned back. "I'm a vegetarian", to which the whole group erupted in a head jerking, belly wiggling, and cane waving round of laughter.

The writer laughed too, but at that age was too darned young to know what a vegetarian was. I figured it had something to do with vegetables, of which I was not particularly fond. At that point, one of them turned and spit warm tobacco juice on my bare leg. It was a signal to leave. They didn't want some damned kid hanging around.

The Unlikely Delinquents

Tales of Misspent Youth

One evening, three former delinquents sat around the kitchen table telling tales of some of the ornery things they had done in their youth. They laughed and pointed at one another as they recalled the mischief they had made.

When they were kids, "outhouse tipping" was one of the best-loved teenage pranks. So naturally, when the topic of Halloween came up, they recalled the time they had gotten word that an old man was hiding in his outhouse, ready to catch any mischievous rascals that would try to tip over his toilet.

Several of their "gang" accepted this challenge and quietly crept up behind the watchman's privy, tipping it over onto the door. Amid much cussing, all the old man could do was yell for help through the hole where his back side was normally supposed to go.

And then they remembered the time a friend of theirs, a country kid, came along and managed to fall in the nasty hole left after a "little house" had gone over. What a stinking mess he was! He couldn't go home that way! So they took him down and put him in the Clear Fork to clean up while one of the others went home and got some dry clothes to loan him. Laughing heartily, one of the men commented, "He was a really nice kid…but he hadn't been to town much."

Next, the oldest member of this trio recalled another of their classic pranks. From the indiscretions of his youth, it seems he learned first-hand how to put a buggy on a barn roof. He explained with a grin: "first you take off the wheels, then pull it up to the roof in pieces, and finally put the buggy back together." (You can imagine the buggy-owner's reaction, when he came outside with plans to go somewhere.)

Then one of the most devilish stories spilled out across the kitchen table. They remembered the time they had upset the outhouse of an old woman who lived way up on Delaware Street. She was a short, heavy, and very shy person who was too embarrassed to ask neighbors if she could use their privy.

The woman was so afflicted that she only took small "baby" steps, one foot barely in front of the other. The poor woman kind of shuffled along, ever so slowly, like a penguin.

One night the three upset this poor woman's outhouse. Unfortunately, the only public facility in town was at the railroad station and the need arose.

And so off she started, creeping all the way down Delaware and West Main, through the square (where everybody could see her), and on down the East Main hill to the B&O station. Mission completed, she crept back up the hill on East Main, thru the square (where everybody could see her again), up West Main to Delaware and slowly up the hill to home.

The poor woman must have had some internal disorder that day, because she no more than reached home, when it was time to head back to the railroad station! She spent the whole day going back and forth to the B&O privy.

Delinquents Unmasked

Claude Gore graduated with the Lexington Class of 1927. As a small youngster he and a cousin, Lowell McIntire, were playing with matches in the attic of the Gore family home. It burned to the ground.

Claude Gore who, with his cousin Lowell McIntire, as a youngster burned down the Gore family home. Both men later served as Mayor of Lexington.

Luckily, both escaped the fire. And later Claude went on to earn a freshman numeral in football at Purdue

University. He eventually worked as a conductor and engineer on the Penn Central Railroad for 33 years.

A ready volunteer, Claude belonged to several area fraternal organizations and he loved to fish.

Claude grew up to be a two-term mayor of Lexington, served two more full terms on the village council, and finished a third unexpired council term. He also served two terms on the Lexington School Board and was once elected board president. In addition, Claude was one of the chief organizers of Lexington's Little League Program. He was also a life-long and active member of the Presbyterian Church.

Beside Claude sat his older brother, Richard Gore, of the Lexington Class of 1922. During his life Richard worked for several Mansfield businesses, including 27 years at Mansfield Tire as a scheduler.

Photo courtesy of Mary Kay Leedy
Richard Gore

Like his brother, Richard was active in civic affairs. He served two terms as the mayor of Lexington, as well as two terms on the village council. He also served on the zoning board and was a charter member of the Richland Transit Board.

In addition, Richard was an elder, deacon, Sunday school teacher, and longtime choir director in the Presbyterian Church. He also belonged to Masonic Lodge 376 and played the saxophone in Gfrer's and several other local bands.

The third devilish character at the table that night was Ralph Lutz, of the Lexington Class of 1916. The year after graduation from high school, Ralph taught in a one room school at Fairview on Bell Road. He later took over the operation of the Lutz Lumber Co. with his brother Floyd and ran the company for nearly 50 years.

Photo courtesy of Richland Foundation
Ruth and Ralph Lutz

After his father died in a tractor accident, in 1933, Ralph took over the care of his brother Clarence "Spike" Lutz for many years. "Spike" was tall, thin, and mentally very slow from the effects of having scarlet fever as a youngster, thus the nick name.

Ralph served as the town marshal, and was elected mayor in 1934. He also served two terms in the Ohio State Legislature from 1935 to 1941. In addition, he served on the first Board of Public Affairs, was a charter member and the first president of the Men's Service Club, as well as a charter member and first president of the Kiwanis Club. Ralph was also the president of the Lexington Chamber of Commerce and served on the board of directors for both the Richland Bank and First National Bank.

Ralph's first wife died in childbirth. He later married his secretary Ruth Derrenberger in 1950. The two of them were members of the Presbyterian Church, where he served as elder and Sunday school superintendent. Ruth taught piano and played organ.

When they died, the Lutzs left $2.3 million dollars to the Richland Foundation, the largest amount that charitable organization had ever received at the time. Ruth also left funds to several musical causes.

Back to the Table

And there the three of them sat, laughing hilariously around Richard Gore's kitchen table, recalling the devilish pranks of three darned ornery kids. The three former "juvenile offenders" laughed so hard that one of them, Claude, had tears in his eyes.

Lexington is a much, much better town because of these three unlikely delinquents.

Our Man Watson

Amariah Watson, founder of Lexington

Pre-Lexington

In 1805, Amariah Watson Jr. emigrated from Pennsylvania to the forest of Knox County, where Mt. Vernon would soon develop. He was a skilled and industrious millwright who had mastered his trade at an early age and was employed at mills in Knox County that year. The following year, he bought land near Fredericktown, which he improved, and in April of 1811 Watson was granted a license to operate a tavern on that property.

This property was later sold when he pulled up stakes and moved north into what would become Richland County. The Clear Fork Valley was still wilderness relative to areas further south, but it presented numerous potential sites for water-powered mills. And the best of these sites was the narrow channel at what is now Lexington.

Founding a Community

So in early May of 1812, the rugged frontiersman moved his wife and young family from Fredericktown up along the Clear Fork River wilderness to settle into a log cabin that he had built along that stream. According to Amariah's grandson, this first hastily constructed home was on the east side of the stream at what is now the front lawn of the Lexington Cemetery. At the time, the only other settlers in what was to become Troy Township were William Gass and Calvin Culver, both of whom had arrived during the previous fall and winter.

The thirty-two-year-old Watson and his twenty-five-year-old wife Sallie had three children of ages four, three and two. Very shortly after arriving at their new cabin Sally gave birth to their fourth youngster. On May 12, 1812, Cynthia Watson became the first non-Indian child born in the township.

Watson was a shrewd, hard working businessman and, with an eye to the future, he bought a considerable amount of land. On January 7, 1812, in what would become Troy Township, he selected all of section 13 (640 acres), the northwest quarter of section 14, and the northwest quarter of section 24, a total of 960 acres.

In simple terms, he owned all the land from the present day Junior High School all the way north to Hanley Road. Three months later he bought the north-east quarter of section 24 and in 1815 added the north-west quarter of section 25 south of town, giving him a grand total of 1,280 acres!

Watson built a dam across the Clear Fork, north of the present day bridge on Main Street, and began to build a water-powered sawmill. The sawmill was necessary to provide the lumber required to build a more complicated gristmill. And the gristmill would be needed to attract more settlement into the Clear Fork valley. Evidence suggests that Amariah was assisted in this work by his two brothers, Samuel and Noah, who also settled here at a very early time. The Watsons were barely off to a good start when the War of 1812 broke out in June.

War of 1812

Watson, his family, and the few scattered neighbors were on the edge of what was then the western frontier. There were no white settlements west of Lexington. And the British, with their dreaded Indian allies, were bent on keeping the Americans out of the Ohio country. So the presence of Indian villages in what would later become Richland County led to a feeling of unease among the widely spread settlers.

There were three Indian villages in the eastern part of the county in 1812. Greentown, Jerome's Town and Helltown were primarily Delaware Indian villages. However, a few Mohawk, scattered members of other tribes, and some white captives, raised as Indians, were among them.

Greentown, located a few miles east of present-day Lucas, was the largest local Indian village. It was under the leadership of Delaware Chief Thomas Armstrong and his sub-chief, young Captain Pipe. One account states that there were 150 bark covered huts or small cabins and a 60-foot-long council house along with a cemetery and playground area in Greentown.

Jerome's Town derived its name from a French trader by the name of John Baptiste Jerome. It was located near present-day Jeromesville.

Helltown, smaller than the other two villages, was located north of present-day Butler. Its name was derived from a combination of the German word for clear (Hell, which was learned from Moravian missionaries) and the English word for village (town). In other words, Helltown literally means the village on the Clear (Fork) river.

All these Indians were peaceful for the most part and accepted their new white neighbors. Some were even Christians, having come under the teachings of Moravian Missionaries.

However, the memory of the Indians defeat of Col. Crawford's army in 1782 and of the torture and burning at the stake of the Colonel was unsettling. In fact, warriors from both Greentown and Jerome's Town had actually taken part in the 1782 battle with Crawford. And it was Delaware Chief (old) Capt. Pipe who painted Crawford's face black, the sign of torture and death.

This prior event and the possibility of hostile actions by the Delaware must have been on the minds of all who were living within the Mohican frontier in 1812. Watson, along with his family and friends, must have measured the risk if they stayed where they were and pondered pulling up stakes and going back south to more heavily settled areas such as Clinton, Mt. Vernon or Fredericktown.

That June, President Madison ordered Ohio Governor Meigs to raise an army of 1,200 troops, which were assembled at Dayton and placed under the command of aging Brigadier General William Hull. With that order came the authority to seize needed supplies, transportation, and order a draft.

Amariah wrote well, but his limited frontier schooling is evident. Sentences did not always end with a period or start with a capital letter: Still, in one of his letters, Watson wrote of his experiences during the War of 1812. That letter

In 1964, I interviewed Mrs. Georgia Fox of Mansfield. Her mother was Cynthia Watson, that first child born in Lexington back in 1812.

Over the years Grandmother Cynthia had save many letters written to her by her father, Amariah. These letters had been passed down to Georgia, who in turn, loaned them to me to copy. Sadly, Georgia died a few months after that interview.

What I didn't know in 1964 was tht I had only copied half of this great collection. Years earlier, the other half had been loaned to Harry Smith. However Harry died in 1961, leaving that portion of the letters unreturned.

Fortunately, in 1966, Harry's sister-in-law, LuDella Hainer, rediscovered that part of the collection among Harry's files. LuDella didn't know what to do with them. So knowing my interest in area history, she gave them to me.

I then had access to the entire rare and priceless collection of letters. What a find!

First page of a 4-page letter written by Amariah Watson in 1853

is as follows, with minor corrections made for readability.

Hard ship & frontier life of Amariah Watson & Calvin Culver during the last war with Great Britain and the Indians, during the years 1812 & 1813.

I moved my family into Richland Co. onto the ground where the town of Lexington now stands in May of 1812. Calvin Culver had moved his family some time before. We were now the outside settlers in the west part of the county. In June 1812 war was declared against Great Britain & now our troubles commence.

Capt. Newel had orders to draft 3 or 4 from his company which include but 20 or 30 militia in the whole county. Capt. Newel summons us to attend, we did attend, and it fell to the lot of Amariah Watson & Calvin Culver to be two of the persons chosen to go. We were to serve under Capt. Joseph Walker of Mt. Vernon. We wrote to Capt. Walker & requested him to come & see our exposed situation. He did come with Capt. Newel to my house & both said they did not blame us for refusing to go. They thought we would have trouble in guarding our own front and homes so they let us stay where we were & Capt. Walker sent us seven muskets & ammunition for our defense at home. Capt. Walker went with his company to Detroit & was there at Hull's surrender and left us in the woods with the Indians.

After Hull's surrender & the Indians had killed our neighbor Jones, we assisted in building a fort & blockhouse on the ground where the town of Bellville is under the command of Major Samuel Watson. At the time when Jones was killed the whole county fled in confusion to the settlements south. We moved our wives, children & cattle to the settlement south.

From the time of the murder of Jones, to the victory of Capt. Perry on Lake Erie, we were continually on the scout or on guard or in fort or on the alert some way from the summer of 1812 until September of 1813, the whole of this time which was more than 12 months. We were harassed by Indians killing our neighbors, Seymores family four in number were killed, next, Copus was killed and several other men at his house. Now we had to move our wives & children again and bury our effects in the ground.

General Crooks comes on to the ground where Mansfield now stands, with a large army & remains until winter then presses all the teams in the county to move him & his army St Dusky (Sandusky). I was pressed with two teams, one ox & one horse. The following names were with me on that trip; Jacob Cook, Samuel Watson, Brubaker Blann, Richard Roberts, Wm. Farquhar & others, - all dead perhaps.

We had a hard time of it while on this duty for Uncle Sam, froze our feet & we considered our selves in the employ of the United States from the time of our standing the draft under Capt. Newel to (the) Perry victory on the Lake Erie which was more than a year. Captains Walker & Newel considered the same & sent us guns & munitions of war to the care of Samuel Watson at Watson's Mills where the town of Lexington now stands. We were some of the time stationed at Watson's Mill, some times at the fort at Bellville, some times on the scout & some times hauling with teams for the United States & the whole time both night & day we were exposed to a savage front for more than a year.

Now if there is any man living in Richland County at the time we were called together by Capt. Newel to stand a draft & at the time that Jones was killed & at the massacre of the Seymores family & Ruffner, & at the battle at Cobuses (Copus) house where Cobus & several other were killed, I say each and every man then living in Richland Co. is or ought to be entitled to a piece of land.

The fact that Calvin Culver & Amariah Watson were enrolled on Capt. Newel's roll book, & after, transferred to Capt. Walkers as two of the persons ordered from Newel to serve under Walker & Walkers consenting that we stay & guard the front of Richland Co. was only changing the place of our service which was more dangerous than it would have been to have went with Walker to Detroit. But we had the satisfaction of being some of the time with our families to guard them.

While we were forted at Bellville there were present the following persons & many others; James McClure, Samuel McClure, Samuel Watson, Jonathan Oldfield, Elisha Robins (Watson's brother in law), John & Peter Wirich, a number of Coonses, the Steltzes, Zents, Stoulses & so on.

Now I believe agreeable to the law granting land for services in time of war in the United States would entitle the following persons in Richland County Ohio & in Illinois to land; Calvin Culver, Noah Watson, John Culver & many others if living in Ohio & Amariah Watson of Illinois.

Many years later Cynthia Watson's son was to write:

When the settlers were force to go to the block house at Bellville my mother must have been an infant in her mother's arms. It is told that the Indians shot through the straw tick on which she was sleeping, the ball passing under her body, and she (Cynthia Watson Lewis) used to tell how her father would stand guard with his gun while her mother milked the cows.

Where or when this attack occurred is not recorded. At any rate, Perry's 1813 victory over the British in the battle on Lake Erie brought an end to the dangers on the Mohican frontier.

The First Mills

After the war, Watson had both his saw and grist mills running in short order. These mills were the first to be built on the Clear Fork River.

A gristmill was a pioneer necessity. As soon as a spot of forest land was cleared, crops were planted. Wheat and corn had to be turned into flour and cornmeal at a mill. So as a result of the mill operating, a flood of new arrivals soon moved into the Clear Fork Valley.

The capacity of this first grist mill was not great and may have had just two run of buhrs (mill stones) with a bolting system for the manufacture of flour. A small dam was up stream, near the present-day park, and there is evidence of a head race (the channel which brought water to the mill's water wheel). It is probable that this waterway was destroyed when the railroad was built in 1850. A new higher dam was built adjacent to the mill at that time.

A family story handed down through generations of Watsons relates that Indians would visit during the construction and early operation of the grist mill. There were several hunting camps in the area. (One was at the spring next to the fire station on West Main Street and several more were along the Clear Fork, just north of town and along Isaac's Run, the small stream that goes north towards Alta.) So the mill was not far out of the Indian's way and was a marvel for them to behold.

In 1872 a contemporary account was written by an individual who knew Amariah Jr. and his two brothers Samuel and Noah. The three brothers worked closely together:

By much labor, difficulties and privation they succeeded in erecting a saw-mill and getting it in operation in the fall of 1812, on the north branch of the Clear Fork. They still persevered in the line of machinery until they got the grist mill started in 1814. These were the first mills in that section of the county and were incalculable benefit to the settlement. About this time Mr. Watson laid out the village of Lexington.

Roads

On April 10, 1812, a petition had been presented to the Knox County Commissioners "for a road beginning at the house of James McClure (the future site of Bellville) and run the nearest way to a mill seat belonging to Amoriah Watson." This road was surveyed and granted. We now know this road as State Route 97.

On December 6, 1814, the newly-elected Richland County Commissioners granted the survey of another road "beginning at Watson's Mill and running in a northwesterly direction to intersect the road on which the army marched to Upper Sandusky." This is now the Lexington-Ontario Road. In short order, roads fanned out in all directions from the new mill.

Building a Town

rent cemetery drive. His second house is the center section of the house pictured here. The two-story addition and porch were added by a later owner.

Shortly after his mills were operational, Watson built a second larger home on the west side of the Clear Fork on the south side of East Main Street, next to the present-day B&O Bike Trail. He then set about laying out a town.

Records indicate this town was to be called "New Lexington." However, when the town plat was filed, it was simply named "Lexington" after Lexington, Massachusetts. (Watson's father, Amariah Watson Sr., was twenty-three when the battle of Lexington and Concord opened the Revolutionary War. Watson Sr., a Patriot, quickly volunteered for the Connecticut militia. So our town was named in honor of that first battle for American independence.)

On December 14, 1815, Watson filed his plat establishing Lexington. This makes Lexington older than Bellville, whose plat was not recorded until a week later.

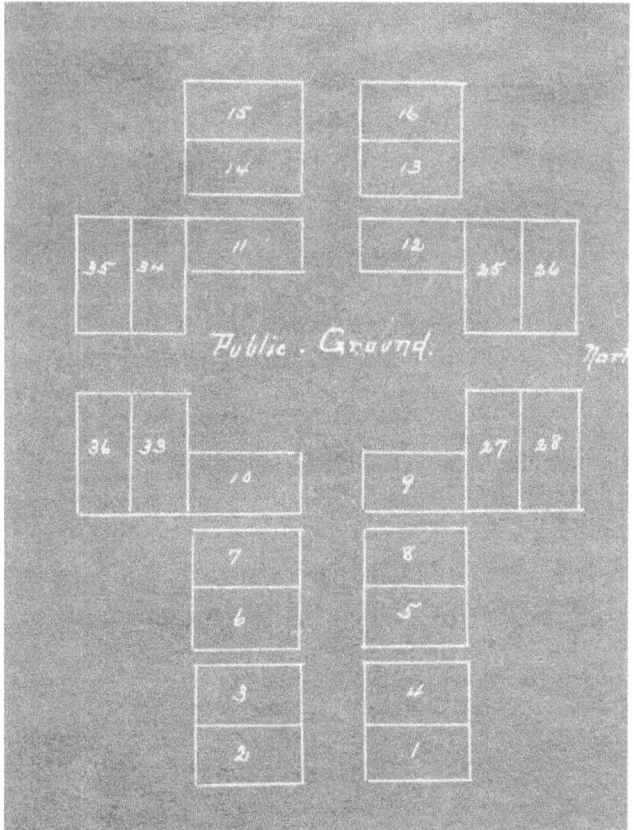

Plat of the town of Lexington, recorded December 4, 1815

The attraction of Watson's Mill (the first in the Clear Fork Valley) would draw many new settlers and encourage the establishment of other businesses in the new town and area.

On July 30, 1813, David Williams was appointed the first postmaster of Lexington. By 1819 a number of Watson's lots had been sold and with lumber from the saw mill, buildings were going up regularly.

Jacob Cook owned lots numbered 1 and 4 where he opened the town's first tavern in 1816, near Watson's mill. Cook and Watson had been neighbors in Knox County and a tavern would do a good business with patrons waiting their turn at the mill. Some people came from as far away as the Galion and Bucyrus areas for just that purpose.

Ephraim Clark bought lots 3 and 5; John Halderman, 9 and 10; Arthur McLean, 6 and 7; Lathrop Sutliff, number 2. No exact record exists, but evidence suggests that on each lot the trees were cut down and perhaps a small building or log cabin was erected to indicate that the tenants were engaged in a trade of some type. Lots numbers 8, 11, 12 and 13 were sold but apparently not improved during this period.

Strange as it may seem, Amariah Watson never lived in Lexington proper. His home and mills were just outside the town limits. However, he was to play a pivotal roll in the development of the new village.

Watson's mills were a necessity for everyone in the area and payment for his services came in the form of land clearing, furnishing goods and help putting up business buildings (which may have been sold on credit to new shop keepers until they became established).

In lieu of cash payment, a miller was allowed by law to extract one sixth of the wheat or one fifth of the corn he processed for his services. However, Watson also extended credit, loaned money and in effect the new town revolved around its founder. In a way, he was the town banker. The town soon prospered and at one time even rivaled Mansfield.

The Family Fortune

Amariah later built three or four more mills north of town. An oil mill (a mill that extracts oil from grain or vegetables) and a distillery, operated and later owned by his son-in-law, Sterling Graves, was located just north of the bridge over the Clear Fork on the east side of Lexington-Springmill Road.

In addition, Watson constructed another gristmill and sawmill set on the west side of the road, 425 feet south of Cockley Road. Tax records indicate a son, Ashel Watson, also ran a fulling and carding mill (for processing wool) near that location. Just northwest of the junction of Hanley and Lexington-Springmill Roads was another sawmill which son Michael Watson ran. That mill was in operation for many years and traces of the head race are still visible.

These early mills weathered and the vibration from their own operation could shake them to pieces over time. Friction fires were another hazard. So, these mills had to be rebuilt routinely and sometimes were changed to a different use. Unfortunately, exact records no longer exist.

At any rate, Watson's mills and land holdings made him the wealthiest man in the Lexington area. He had built a frame house across the road from where the present railroad station Senior Center is located. A great granddaughter, Georgia Fox, was told that George Coleman, who was from the south, added the two story southern style porch when he owned the house. She said Coleman called it the "gallery."

The ultimate expression of Amariah's prosperity was the new two-story, brick house he built across the street from his frame house in 1824. This home was located where the Depot – Senior Center is now situated. It was the first brick building in a township where most folks still lived in log cabins. In fact, there were only six wood frame houses at that time and the other nearly one hundred and some homes in the township were made from logs. It must be remembered that Troy Township was six miles square encompassing both of what are now both Troy-Richland and Troy-Morrow townships.

Photo courtesy of Chalfant Family Collection

Watson built the first brick house in Troy Township in 1828. The Shepard family was living there when this picture was taken. The house was torn down and the railroad station / Senior Center is on that location now.

The Family Tree

In 1805 Watson met and married Sally Leonard in Knox County and as previously mentioned they had three children when they moved to Lexington. Cynthia was born almost upon arrival and five more children would follow. There were three girls and six boys in all.

The family presence would continue to grow as Amariah's younger brothers Samuel, (who had five children), Noah (who had six children) and older sister Elizabeth Robbins (with her five children) and her husband Elisha all arrived with him in 1812 or shortly thereafter. Later Amariah's children Michael, Hugh and their sisters Eleanor, Hanna and Chole married and settled in Lexington or the surrounding area.

So the new settlement would be well propulated with the descendents of old Amariah Watson Sr. In fact, anyone from the Lexington area with the names Patterson, Wright, Taylor, Baldwin, Lockhart, Woods, Constance, Lewis, Sowers, Mount, Dailey, or Maxwell (and so on) can usually trace their ancestry back to the Revolutionary War soldier, Amariah Watson Sr.

Watson Jr.'s wife Sallie died on November 14, 1827, leaving him with children at home ranging in age from 4 to 18. A short time later he remarried a widow, Phoebeann Wolf, who according to family tradition put much of the housework on 13 year-old Cynthia.

This was not a happy union and was further complicated when Watson's mother died back in Pennsylvania, causing his 80-year-old father to move to Lexington to be near his children. Amariah Sr. died five years later on November 21, 1836, and was buried in the Lexington Cemetery. For many years most believed that it was Amariah, Jr. interred there.

Further West

By 1832-33 Amariah Jr. was ready for a change. His younger children were pretty well grown, Cynthia would soon be married to William Lewis, and the Wild West was beckoning with opportunity and cheap land. As the story was handed down, Watson moved his chair back from the kitchen table one morning and announced he was ready to go west. He asked if anyone wanted to go with him? Of course, neither Phoebe nor the younger ones were packed or ready. So he got on his horse and left. He and Phoebe apparently were later divorced and he would never again return to Ohio.

His son, Michael, evidently went with him. The journey took them to Bureau County, Illinois where Amariah had bought tracts of land (540 acres) by 1835. Some of this land would be suitable mill sites on the Bureau River, near a village called Indiantown (a name later changed to Tiskilwa).

Another early settler in Lexington was a young man by the name of Cyrus Langworthy. He and Watson were well acquainted and had served together as Troy Township Trustees in 1817. Cyrus had settled near

Indiantown by 1832 and may have influenced Watson to locate there or they may have gone together. The truth of the timing of their moves is not really known.

Within a couple of years Amariah's sons Riley, Theory, Asahal, daughter Clarisa Graves (with husband Sterling), and Watson's sister, Elizabeth Robbins (with her son) all moved west to be near him. Watson and sons built at least three more mills and may have been involved in others there in Illinois.

In 1836, 56-year-old Amariah met and married Rachel Drake, a young woman of twenty-one or twenty-two, by whom he had two more children. He had known her father back in Ohio and may have first seen his future wife when she was but a child. In the early 1840's Amariah and Rachel moved to nearby LaSalle where he would spend the rest of his days.

Amariah continued to be a wise, wealthy land speculator and business man. He encouraged and assisted his children and sister Elizabeth in locating near him in LaSalle or Tiskilwa. So one by one the entire Watson family moved west, until only William and Cynthia Lewis remained in Lexington.

Lewis had a dry goods business in town and was the Post Master at one time. Amariah located good property for them in Illinois and offered them his military pension land, but for some reason they were reluctant to go west.

The Late Years

When the gold rush started in 1849-50, Watson's sons all went west to Pikes Peak, the Rocky Mountains and California. They eventually settled in the west with their families and the old man missed them. He also greatly missed his daughter back in Lexington. His letters to her almost begged that she come to Illinois.

Cynthia and her young son did go visit her father shortly before he died. In 1921 the son wrote what he remembered of that visit:

When I was a child probably three or four years of age in about 1857 or 1858 my mother took me on a trip to LaSalle to see her father. I think it was made on account of seeing her father who was sick. I believe it was grandfather's last sickness though mother and I returned home before he died. The only recollection I have of this trip is that grandfather was sick in a bed in a room off the parlor. I don't think I ever saw him standing up or out of bed.

Amariah Watson, frontiersman, soldier, millwright, inventor and the founder of Lexington, died in LaSalle, Illinois, on May 10, 1862. He was 82.

He is buried in lot 304, Oakwood Rockwell Cemetery. Sadly, the top of his tombstone is broken and missing, leaving only the date of is death.

William and Cynthia Watson Lewis set up housekeeping in this brick home. It was a short walk to the Graves, Watson, Lewis gristmill and distillery. It was located across the road and a little south of the current Garden Gate Farm Market.

The Fate of the Old Bell

The 1850 School House once had an ornate bell tower. The building, on Church Street, is now home to the Richland County Museum.

The old 1850 Lexington schoolhouse, now the county historical museum, once had a large bell tower atop its roof. The Columbian Grange #1393 bought the building when the new red brick school was opened. (The "new red brick school" is the old, rear portion of the current Junior High). For some reason the Grange trustees decided the bell tower had to go. An interesting November 1899 newspaper account recorded the deed:

The cupola on the old school house has been removed and the space it occupied roofed over. To many people fond memories of the vague and distant past cluster about the quaint cupola and its destruction seem like a vandal act. Carved and written on the lattice work and frame are names of a score of people who went to school in the building in juvenile days nearly 50 years ago. Some subscribed their names to lines of original poetry that was expansive of their aspirations to attain distinction in life. But nearly all are dead of those who, so long ago, wrote their names thereon and this fact is a sad commentary on the brevity of life and the fallacy of aspiring to climb the heights of fame.

The old bell was sold to the highest bidder in December of 1899. Grange member T. E. Dunshee paid $4.80 for it. Whatever became of the bell is unknown.

This photograph was taken on school picture day, during the 1880s. The bottom of the bell tower can be seen. The student to teacher ratio is unknown, but it must have been high. Class crowding was evidently less of an issue then.

Back Down the Road

Township road crews were made up of local residents who were either hired or worked off their road tax assessments by laboring on the road. This photograph was taken near Johnsville.

Taxes

Both taxes and roads can either be a pain or an asset, depending on your point of view. It seems you can't have one without the other. It's always been that way.

The Troy Township Trustees enacted the first road tax in April of 1816. The trustees met at Jacob Cook's tavern, at what is now the corner of East Main and Walnut Streets. Their tax order read: "Ordered that a Road Tax be laid equal to the County Tax for the year 1816, which is thirty cents for horse creatures and ten cents for horned cattle each."

For those who were unable to pay their taxes, the thoughtful trustees passed the following rule in August of 1819:

Ordered that any person owing Road Tax on lands have the privilege to work out the same at the rate of 75 cents per day under the direction of the supervisor of their district and producing a receipt to the trustees.

Crossing Over

The early roads were laid out following the easiest path. Sometimes this was an old Indian trail. And when a creek or stream had to be crossed, travelers found a shallow spot and just went on in. So bridges quickly became a real necessity.

The first bridge on record in Lexington was built by three men in 1820 for a total cost of $5.56. It was built across the Clear Fork near the present-day Bicentennial

Park on the Lexington-Ontario Road. In 1820, this was known as "the road from Lexington to Garrison's Mill." Amariah Watson no doubt saw to it the Clear Fork was bridged at his mill in town at an earlier date. However, no record exists.

In town, a new covered bridge was built across the Clear Fork in September of 1858 by a Mr. Marshall for $599. (This was on Main Street near the current Senior Center.) Workmen building this bridge were reported to have had trouble finding a firm foundation.

While this new bridge's roof protected the timber structure from the weather, at night it also provided shelter for wandering livestock. Old-timers recalled their parents telling of young men coming home on a dark night, after courting their girl, only to stumble over a hog or run into the rear end of a cow. Passage of this bridge at night became an unwelcome adventure.

Apparently, too many folks let the family milk cow run loose and pigs were hard to contain with a rail fence. And the covered bridge was the stock's natural gathering place.

So in 1858 Lexington citizens petitioned the village council to pass an ordinance "prohibiting so many swine from running at large." A few years later a law was passed that required hogs, horses and cows to be tied up at night. Evidently they could roam free in the daytime, but the owners were still responsible for any damage done.

The covered bridge went down or was badly damaged sometime in 1877, when a heavy steam engine broke through it. This forced travelers to again begin fording the stream just below the mill dam, a real hardship compared to the bridge.

Since the Delaware Road (now US 42) had become a main highway, replacing that bridge fell to the County Commissioners. Unfortunately, they were slow to react and construction on a replacement did not begin until October of 1878.

Faced with another winter in the water, the Lexington council ordered that a temporary bridge, and a foot bridge, be built. Village officials also ordered that lanterns be placed at both ends at night. They also thoughtfully barricaded the old bridge's abutments so that no one would drive off them.

These temporary bridges were no doubt simply logs laid over the embankments with planks placed across

The ill-fated iron bridge across the Clear Fork. It had stone abutments set on and back-filled with gravel, which led to its collapse in 1913. (This picture was taken looking southeast.)

them. One footbridge floated away during high water and had to be replaced.

The County Commissioners had decided to build a new iron bridge by the Smith Bridge Company from Toledo. However, the job of replacing the old abutments dragged on through the winter and it seems the abutments were built on, and backfilled with, gravel from the pit next to the cemetery. This would lead to an uncertain future for the whole structure.

The completed new 130-foot span was not finished until the late summer of 1879 and the village had to pay $255 to have a 3-foot-wide walkway added to the south side. By December of that same year, the side wall fill had started to cave in and village council met to look into the situation.

In June of 1883 the new bridge was closed. And once more a temporary one of logs was placed across the stream until repairs could be made. Again in August of 1887, the bad design appeared when questions surfaced about the condition of the bridge and its abutments, one of which appeared to be settling. The County Commissioners were again requested to examine it and makeshift repairs were made.

Not much was done to improve the bridge after that. And during the flood of 1913, it simply rolled over and went down.

Dusty Streets and Wrong Turns

When Lexington was incorporated on February 16, 1839, the Troy Township Trustees were relieved of responsibility for maintaining streets. That task fell to the new village council and the lot owners who were, by ordinance, compelled to work two days a year on the streets and to keep them clean.

> **Classic American poem on the state of roads**
>
> *This road is impassible,*
> *Not even jackassable,*
> *If this road you must travel,*
> *Just bring your own gravel.*
> *Anonymous*

Lexington didn't pave streets with gravel until the late 1800s with the advent of the automobile. Main Street was "graveled" from the railroad to Beverstocks on the square in 1876. However, gravel streets presented their own problems, namely a lot of dust.

The Lutz Bros. steam engine was used to pull a road grader on Plymouth Street sometime around 1910. Photographer Harry Linton lived in the second house from the left.

In the early days, folks headed south for Mt. Gilead or Delaware often somehow managed to wind up in Blooming Grove or Galion. So, in the 1870s, "Finger boards" (direction signs) were put up at the junction of West Main and Delaware streets to guide travelers.

Then in the summer of 1903, Dr. Henry H. Smith laid 1000 feet of water lines in four directions from the square. Water was pumped by an electric motor in the power plant to sprinkle the dusty streets. The expense was defrayed by the property owners affected.

By 1914, it was necessary to put oil on the roads in summer to keep the dust down. Seymore Lindsey was also hired to paint speed limit signs that year.

In 1919, Main Street was repaved with brick from the railroad (Bike Trail) to Short Street. That brick street was 28 feet wide with stone curbs and the project cost $8,800. At the time, it was a big improvement project for such a small town.

Outside of town, the Township had to be content with simply grading the roads and maintaining culverts. There was simply a lack of funds to do anything else for many, many years. However, in 1859 a new covered bridge was built over the Clear Fork north of town. It was made with timber and planks from Samuel Carter's water powered saw mill, which was located a few hundred feet north of it.

Getting to that bridge was a challenge at times. In 1903 one observer commented, *The amount of money expended on roads tributary to Lexington for years might as well have been tossed to the winds. The mud this spring has been deeper and the roads present more the*

Ray Ogg, who worked at the Smith Power Company. He had a little trouble with the mud and water on Plymouth Street, near the present Lexington Park, around 1910. (This photo was taken looking northeast, across the fields of present day Garden Gate Greenhouse and Farm Market.)

appearance of mortar beds than highways of travel. On the road leading north of town mud scows and canoes trimmed with sails could be more advantageously used than wagons in getting through the stream of mud. This condition should cause people to give thought to a good road movement which is a more important cause than others which absorb the public mind.

In late March 1907, J. A. Rutherford tried to get his horse through a muddy sink hole on the road west of town (now present-day Route 97), near Clover Hill School. His horse became so helplessly mired that he had to wade or crawl out and go get a team of horses and a long rope to pull the poor animal out. It wasn't just township roads that were a problem. The state routes were a challenge too. In March, 1920, a newspaper column reported that trucks and cars, headed north from Johnsville towards old Lex, were forced to turn back due to the deep mud.

Route 42 was eventually paved with concrete in 1923. However, there were many miles of township roads, following hilly terrain, which would have to wait for the age of the automobile before they would see pavement.

A Place to Walk

Crossing the Clear Fork was one thing, but walking across town was another. The darned farmers always fed their horses before they came to town. So the streets were dirty and filled with mud and manure. What a mess.

Spring and wet weather compounded problems for foot travel, especially for women in long dresses. So in 1851, the village fathers passed an ordinance requiring lot owners to build sidewalks across their lots. The specifications were as follows:

According to the grade established by Council, lay down a plank walk in the center of grade, three feet wide, the plank to be of oak, chestnut or walnut, two inches thick, laid down on cross ties four by six inches, of good durable timber, and the plank well secured on the cross ties. The top of the plank to be four inches above the surface of the grade, cross ties not more than six feet apart.

At that time, the school and three churches were at the west end of Church Street. So that sidewalk, between Delaware and Frederick streets, was built on the south side only and was six feet wide. Wooden walks didn't hold up very long and had to be constantly maintained. It was the law! So eventually the sidewalks changed from wood to stone. One of the first flag stone walks in town was laid in front of the Park Hotel in the summer of 1900.

The Square

The town square had been a parking lot of sorts for horses since an early time. Shade trees had been planted, but were marred and killed when animals were tied to them. Wagons and buggies also broke down the sidewalks. So the parks on the square must have resembled a barn yard in those days. Then in 1861 the trees were boxed with wood, which helped some. And in 1877, out of necessity, the parks were fenced. As a newspaper reporter described it:

The public square is now enclosed with a handsome fence and arrayed in a beautiful verdure is in marked contrast to its former unsightly appearance.

By 1900 the square park had been "swept", and grass and flowers planted. The appearance was so enhanced that an occasional church service was held there in summer. Lexington was rather quiet in those days.

A view of the public square, as seen from the southwest looking northeast, sometime shortly after 1900.

Taverns and Hotels

To operate a tavern, you had to have a license that could only be granted by the County Courts or Commissioners. Several citizens had to testify that the applicant was of good honest character and that the proposed tavern met state requirements for operation. By law, the tavern keeper had to have the following: *"A good house containing at least four rooms and three fireplaces, and furnished with least four beds, and that he is moreover provided with a good stable, divide into at least six stalls."*

The intent of the law was to prevent houses that pretended to be taverns, but were really only saloons, from getting a tavern license. This was important because, by law, only licensed taverns were permitted to sell liquor by quantities less than one quart. (Stores could not sell quantities of less than a gallon.) This was an effort to suppress liquor sales, especially to Indians. The law specified "that no rioting, reveling, gambling or drunkenness be allowed in the house or on the premises." (It was also against the law for judges to hold court in a tavern, which seems a good precaution.)

Political office seekers occasionally made speeches at taverns, where, depending on the crowd, they were either cheered or had to beat a hasty retreat. All-in-all, the local tavern was the center of social activity in most towns.

The Cook Tavern

As mentioned earlier, Jacob Cook built the first tavern in Lexington. Cook had known Amariah Watson when they were neighbors in Knox County. So it was only natural the two should remain close when they moved to the new frontier forest along the Clear Fork.

The successful completion of Watson's mills would almost necessitate the locating of a tavern in the vicinity. Mill customers might face a day long travel just to get there and then have to wait quite awhile for their turn at the mill.

So in 1815 Cook bought lots number 1 and 4, which overlooked the mill in the valley of the new town. No doubt with the assistance of Watson and his sawmill, Cook built a substantial two-story wood frame tavern building on lot one. This was located directly across the street from the present-day Home Savings Bank building on East Main Street. There was a stable barn located behind the tavern. A good business was guaranteed, as at the time it was the only tavern in Troy Township and was located next to the only mill.

Jacob Cook met all legal requirements of a tavern keeper and was granted his license in 1816. He undoubtedly enjoyed a brisk business providing, by law, entertainment, shelter, food and drink for both man and beast.

The Ohio Register, an early newspaper published in the village of Clinton in Knox County, carried this notice on March 26, 1817:

The Elegant Full Bred Horse RAVEN

Will stand to cover mares in the ensuing season, from the first day of April until the first day of July, at the following stands; viz, the first three days of the week at the stable of Jacob Cooks, Innkeeper, in Lexington; the ensuing three days at James McClure's Tavern in Mansfield.

Ephriam Clark

Cook's Tavern was "the" gathering place in the infant village. The early Troy Township Trustees meetings were held there, as were political and social discussions. It was the place a weary traveler found food, drink and a place to rest. These folks were eager to exchange news from where they came and gather advice and directions for their destinations.

Cook only ran the tavern for three years or so and then moved on to other interests. He bought a quarter section of land (160 acres) a mile or so southwest of town (near Lindsey Road and US Route 42) and built a small frame house. A family history says that he liked to roam the wild forests and streams and the confines of a tavern operation did not agree with him.

Evidence indicates Amariah Watson bought the tavern property back from Cook and in 1822 sold it to John Halderman, who in turn resold the lots and building to Adnah Coleman by 1824. Coleman must have continued the tavern operation and he also opened a tannery on the south side of Main Street along the Clear Fork.

Sometime around 1843–44 the old tavern on lot number one became the property of the new partnership of Coleman & Alexander, with Coleman building a new house next door on lot four. The next owner was Samuel

Caldwell and in the late 1850's Jacob Baughman bought the tavern and operated it as a hotel and saloon until the Temperance folks were able to vote the town dry on several occasions. A writer once referred to the place as "that aperture to hell at the foot of Main Street." The elections of 1855 and 1856 were held at the "Mohican House" which may have been the name Baughman used. What a place to vote!

The next business effort by subsequent owners was a restaurant and pool room. Town records are a little sketchy when it comes to business names. They didn't advertise but the old Cook Tavern as previously mentioned was evidently known as the "Mohican House" while Baughman owned it although an 1856 map identifies it as the "Baughman Hotel." Previous owners could also have attached other names.

The last years of the old tavern—hotel were rather colorful. The temperance movement was in full swing in Lexington and Baughman's saloon was a popular place to eat—and drink. The farmers, laborers, mill and railroad workers were regulars. There were fights and drunkenness along with what was termed "rioting." One old timer the writer interviewed in the 1960's recalled that "the place was dirty, but Mrs. Baughman made good soup."

In 1883, one of the several times when the town was voted "dry," Baughman stopped selling liquor and refitted it as a restaurant and pool room. He later sold the aged building.

The old tavern burned to the ground along with the house next door in January, 1899. A newspaper account gives these details:

A blaze was discovered in the building owned by Miss Jane Smaltz on Main Street. The building contained six rooms and was occupied by the family of Harvey Eller. There was a pool room in the half story building alongside where the fire was believed to have started....There is no fire apparatus in the village and although a bucket brigade turned out and went to work the building was burned. Nearly all the household goods belonging to Eller were burned, but the two pool tables were saved.

The former Cook Tavern must have been in a deteriorating condition. The estimated total fire loss for the tavern and the house next door both described as "old frame buildings," was estimated at only $800 and contents at $50. Thank God they saved the pool tables! What would the town have done without them?

It was a popular place for the men to hang out prior to the fire, but the wives and mothers hated the place. The fatal fire may have been accidental or someone with the temperance group could have helped it along. The law defined such acts as arson. Others called it abating a nuisance. No one knows.

The Hotel on the Square

The old building on the southeast corner of the public square IS NOT the Cook Tavern and WAS NOT built in 1812. The writers of "Grahams 1880 History of Richland County" erred when they printed the chapter on Lexington by not researching more carefully and leading some writers, including this one, to stumble along and believe the old hotel on the square was the Cook tavern. However, that was wrong, wrong, wrong.

In 1880 the old "Cook Tavern" was still standing on East Main Street down near the railroad station. The persons who gathered information for Graham's History simply wrote down what the old-timers told them and figured everyone would know the location. A century later others, like this writer, didn't check the facts either and didn't know it had burned down. Wrong building identified.

The desirable lot number 10 on the future town square was still vacant until April of 1822, when Watson sold it to John Halderman, who in turn sold it to George Coleman for $50.00. In March of 1827, Eliab Lindley bought that same lot for $70 and it was he who built the tavern – hotel building with construction starting that year.

The trees were cleared and the main tavern building was finished and in operation in 1828. The extension to the rear may have been added later. In 1839 it was the most valuable property in Lexington and its real estate taxes were $7.99 a year. At this writing it is the oldest known building in Lexington.

In its earliest days, several stagecoach routes diverged from Lexington and the tavern was the starting point for coaches. Early elections were also held there and Justices of the Peace often heard petty lawsuits argued by local lawyers in the place.

These lawyers are said to have used the roar of their voice, and wild dramatic gestures, to cover their lack of legal knowledge or logic and common sense. G. M. Fry, Lexington's only lawyer for over fifty years, was often challenged by Harvey Baldwin who was of

Hotel on the Square – At different times it was known as the Lindley Tavern, Farmers Hotel, Custer House, Park Hotel and Joslin Hotel. It is the oldest building in Lexington and currently home to J.E. Slaybaugh & Assoc. accountants. (Note the electric lines that were installed by Harry Smith in the 1900s.)

somewhat the same caliber. Mansfield's John Sherman argued here too, as did Samuel J. Kirkwood who later became the Governor of Iowa.

Eliab (nicknamed "Gabe") Lindley ran a good tavern with the help of his wife Elizabeth, who no doubt oversaw the meal preparation and comfort of the guests. It was a busy place and keeping the rooms, bar, and stable clean, along with getting wood for the fire would have required considerable organization. The stables and barn yard always created a problem and the "pungent aroma" was a constant source of annoyance to villagers, as well as a disposal problem for the stable boy. Drovers needed enclosures for the cattle and hogs they were driving to market and these provisions were difficult to maintain in small towns and villages. Rural taverns were better equipped to handle larger groups of livestock.

Eliab Lindley lost his life in a steamboat disaster on the Ohio River in 1839 and Elizabeth Lindley may have attempted to continue, but it would have been a burden. It also may not have been socially acceptable for a widow to operate a tavern. It would have given the local wags something to cluck about. How or who managed to keep the place going is not recorded. And even though Widow Elizabeth maintained ownership of the property until 1857, at some point in time the tavern must have closed.

An advertisement in a Mansfield weekly newspaper carried the only information that the writer could find covering the period after Eliab Lindley died. A notice in the 1844 edition *Richland Bugle & Independent Press* contained the following information:

LEXINGTON HOTEL

This established and well known stand is again opened under management of Mr. O. Saunders. The best accommodations will be furnished to the traveling community that care and attention can secure. His table shall be the best that the country affords. He tenders his services to Travelers, Pleasure Parties, & c.

Lexington, June 1844

How long Saunders held the tavern keepers post or whether he was hired or just rented the place is unknown. One record suggests the name was changed to the "Farmers Hotel."

Mr. I. A. L. Spaulding was the new owner in 1857. Not much is known of him or the name he may have attached to the inn. Sometime in the 1860's Spaulding sold the east half of lot number ten (which may have been a stock pen) to Harriet Delamater. A building was then erected, part of which became the post office for many years. The two buildings were attached. In 1872, Spaulding sold the old tavern property to Civil War veteran George W. Custer, who was reportedly nephew of General George Armstrong Custer (of western Indian War miscalculation fame).

The name was changed to the "Custer House" and it was written that *"he has repaired the old hotel to a great extent where now can be obtained ample accommodations for man and beast."* An 1883 newspaper correspondent commented, *The office of the Custer House has been remodeled in a very ornate manner and now presents a metropolitan appearance.*

It was "the" place for dances and parties of the time, especially for the younger folks. And some events with laughter and local music lasted into the wee hours of the morning. As a rather windy reporter once observed; *The leading feature of Lexington is the Terpsichorean Club which executed some rare artistic evolutions at the Custer House Friday evening.* The club sponsored dances which were a regular form of village entertainment.

It was the social center of the village and its location next to the town square placed it in the center of the growing business district. Step like benches along the front of the Custer House were often a popular hangout for guests and the public alike. The Post Office next door provided an excuse for folks to "sit a spell" during warm weather. In winter kids could ride sleds down Main Street from there as well.

This is the oldest known photograph of the Lindley Tavern. It may have been taken in the late 1860s or early 1870s. The attached building to the left housed the Post Office and stores. Note the grass growing in the intersection of Main Street. The building on the far left was a saloon.

One humorous incident was reported in January of 1877: *A few days since a mettle steed attached to a firm and jaunty cutter, occupied by two young ladies, came down Main Street at a lively rate and when opposite the Custer House, the cutter collided violently with a nondescript concern on runners on which were seated two young men, completely wrecking it, fragments of the frail structure and the young men being scattered in inextricable confusion over the snow. The cutter however, was uninjured, and the ladies in a hilarious mood at the ridiculous plight and elongated countenances of the young men, sped rapidly on.*

This is the earliest known account of women drivers in Lexington.

In April of 1888, Custer, like a surprising number of other Lexington area folks, was bitten with a case of western fever and decided to move in that direction. A Lexington item in the *Bellville Star* noted: *Our hotel keeper George Custer has sold his property to George Maxwell. Mr. Custer is out of the hotel business and is preparing to move to Colorado Springs, Colorado, the first of next week.*" Custer had paid $2,700 for the hotel in 1872 and sold the aging building for $1,200. George Maxwell was a local businessman who had a dry goods business. So there may have been other considerations paid, but not mentioned in the deed.

Village records refer to the "Hotel Maxwell" although Maxwell evidently didn't operate the old place. A newspaper story in 1893 stated, *Chalmer McClure is acting as Boniface of the old Custer house while Ed Walters, the lessee, is doing time in the workhouse for buying the swag of the Bellville Burglars.* In the spring of 1895 the property was leased to a Mr. A. Alspach who changed the name to the "Park Hotel."

At the turn of the century Charles "Pappy" Mitchell ran a popular barber shop in the rear of the building and his family lived on the second floor. In 1908 he moved down the street to the empty tile pool room building and the following year moved to Willard and went to work for the B&O Railroad.

After George Maxwell died, his heirs sold the property to Charles Joslin in 1908 and the old-timers always referred to the place as the "Joslin Hotel."

The big livery barn behind the hotel had been leased to Samuel, William and Charles Logan in 1907 and in later years William Dickson ran it.

At this time the old tavern had become a second-class hotel or boarding house. How long it remained in operation is unknown. In 1897 B. F. Minnear had built a large new brick hotel just down the street which took away any business prospects. After a time it was converted to rental apartments and owner Robert Wade had his barber shop in the rear section for many years in the 1940s and 50s.

The exterior has undergone several changes over time. In the 1950's the ancient wood siding was covered with a stone like stucco material which was popular for a while. Fortunately this was removed in 1980 by Greg Freiheit who had bought the building from the Wade family and installed new redwood siding similar to the original design. Several apartments are in the renovated building which, as stated earlier, is the oldest building in Lexington.

Even today the historic Lindley Tavern building, circa 1828, is still the grand old lady on the Lexington town square.

The Minnear Hotel

B. F. "Benny" Minnear was a Civil War veteran who witnessed Lee's surrender at Appomattox. He came to Lexington in 1896 and bought a fine brick house with a brick store in front on the south side of Main Street which he remodeled and enlarged into a twenty-two room hotel. The large extension was to the front or street side of the building and the family lived in the rear house section. Minnear came from Johnstown where he had been in the grocery business since 1885. What prompted him to come to Lexington and change careers is unknown, but he had the means to establish a very good small town hotel.

The hotel had a pool room in the west end of it and a barbershop in the basement. In later years a bar room was opened in the basement with the stone walls painted with rural pastoral scenes, possibly the work of local artist-painter Seymore Lindsey.

That basement room had a special old world ambience to it. Among the clutter of liquor, beer, cigar and cigarette advertising were numerous antique fixtures and relics collected by Paul Minnear.

The Minnear Hotel at the beginning of the 1900s. Belle and Benny Minnear are in the doorway. On the steps are Paul, Beulah, Waynon and Mabel Minnear. The hotel was located where the present day Home Savings and Loan bank building stands.

The lobby of the Minnear Hotel as it appeared shortly after 1900. Mrs. Belle Minnear and one of her children stand behind the counter. Old-timers recall that you had to be 18 to enter the pool room, but Belle generally ignored this rule for anyone with 5¢.

One of the larger pieces of that collection was a Conestoga wagon box, which rested on a pile of rocks between two large maple trees along Mill Street. The wagon had once belonged to Daniel Miller, one of the early settlers in Troy Township. (Miller lived a mile or so south of town.) School teachers sometimes walked their class down to see it as a history lesson. What became of that wagon box is unknown, but hopefully it was salvaged after being exposed to the weather for many years.

Historian A. J. Baughman was to describe the Minnear as follows: *The hotel . . .is an index of the character and advantages of Lexington, for the hostelry will rank favorably with those of a much larger place, and its genial proprietor neglects nothing that can add to the comfort of his guests.*

The bar and lunch room, named the "Rathskaller," had a character of its own and many of the regulars were the local characters who sometimes referred to it as the "Rat Cellar." Old-timers could usually find a good card game, good company, laughter and tall tales to share at the cellar. And the place was packed on Friday and Saturday nights.

Benny Minnear and wife Belle were well liked and ran a good hotel. It was a family operation with Belle doing most of the cooking. When Benny died in 1922 at age 76, son Paul and daughter Beulah took over the place. But times were changing and the age of the automobile found it more convenient for travelers to stay in Mansfield, a city with more modern facilities.

The pool room was converted into an apartment and the barbershop which had been moved to the lobby area closed in 1943. Only a few long-term tenants remained into the 1950s and some of them only due to the kind hearted generosity of Beulah Minnear after her brother died. The Rathskaller, then run by nephew Denny Dillon, was their chief source of income.

Beulah Minnear died in 1959 and the property and family antiques were sold at auction, which drew a large crowd. The building brought a mere $13,544 and was torn down the following year to make way for the bank building there now.

Another Main Street landmark was gone.

Photo courtesy of Mrs. Beverly Bowers

Beulah Minnear as a young woman. In later years this kind-hearted woman would give a person a place to stay or a meal to eat if they needed it. As one of her aged beneficiaries once said, "Beulah ain't much to look at, but she has a heart as big as a mule."

A 1924 news story carried this photo of the old Bell Tavern.

The Bell Tavern

Robert Bell settled in Washington Township sometime around 1821, on land purchased from Amariah Watson. Bell had been one of the earliest settlers in the Bellville area before moving to what would become a busy highway for stages, teamsters and travelers. His log cabin was a home and possibly could have been used as a tavern if it met State requirements, but the date of construction is unknown.

A new frame tavern building was built in 1840-41 on the site of the old cabin and at this writing it is still standing. This building is the main two-story portion of Wayne's Country Market near the corner of Route 42 and Hanley Road.

The 1840-41 Bell Tavern now houses part of Wayne's Country Market. Several additions have been made, but the building still serves the public.

A stable, barn and feed sheds were built, as was a distillery along the stream in the valley behind the tavern. A small "corn cracker" mill was also on that stream. However, it is unclear whether Bell or his neighbor Noah Watson owned the mill, which would have been needed for whiskey production at the distillery.

A Bell descendent once recalled that one charge was made for "the man's lodging, for horse keep and a drink of whiskey." Also recorded was a time when as many as twenty wagons were corralled around the old tavern. Meanwhile the hungry drivers and teamsters along with four or six horse teams were inside refreshing themselves.

Four generations of Bells owned and lived in the old tavern well into the 1920's. A writer once described the place as "staunch and strongly built, its nine big, low ceiling rooms are as spacious and redolent of hospitality as ever, and it is good for another 25 years more, of happy and useful memories." That was written in 1924.

How long the Bell family ran a tavern is unknown but the coming of the railroads in the early 1850's put most of the teamsters out of business. Business at the tavern would have greatly dwindled by the end of the Civil War.

The handsome building was a residence for the Jacob Auer family at one time and in later years remodeled by Ray Bush for a furniture business. At this writing the old tavern, with additions, is the heart of Wayne's Country Market. It should be good for another century.

The Watson Tavern

Noah Watson was a half brother to Amariah Watson Jr. and came to Lexington with him in the spring of 1812. He helped build the first mills and in 1858 made this statement.

Noah Watson (1790-1863), came to Lexington in 1812. He built his tavern in 1842-43. It stood straight and strong until the day it was demolished in 2000.

I, Noah Watson, certify that I helped to build the first two cabins in the vicinity of Lexington, and also did a job of clearing on Amariah Watson's first field, commencing on about the 8th of March, 1812. I also entered the southeast quarter of Section 7, range 18, township 20, in which I now live, and commenced clearing in 1813.

I was born December 21, 1790, in Plymouth, Luzerne Co., Pa., and am in my 68th year.

Noah Watson

For being one of the very early settlers in Washington Township he was presented with a special ax. Noah Watson owned the land which is now occupied by part of the Gorman Nature Center and he built his cabin just across the road from the center's current entrance. He had volunteered during the War of 1812 and was a respected pioneer.

It is unknown exactly when Noah went into the tavern business. In one sense any cabin in the forest would take in a traveler out of common courtesy. Whether his log cabin complied with the tavern law is open to speculation. Tax records do reveal that the two story 20 X 40 frame tavern building was built in 1842-43. A contemporary

This is the Watson Tavern shortly after the Mishey family bought the property. It was standing straight after over 60 years.

The Watson Tavern, pictured a couple years before its demise. It was still as straight and strong as when it was built in 1842. It's a shame it was torn down.

description of the Watson Tavern and family was written by Amariah Lewis of Galion in 1921. His grandfather was Amariah Watson and his mother was Cynthia Watson Lewis. He wrote of his visits to the Noah Watson home as a young boy:

Noah Watson lived on the left side of the road leading from Lexington to Mansfield in a large frame house with a park covered with trees lying between the house and a large barn standing on the same side of the road but about 25 rods to the north and on the same side of the road. My father and mother used to take me with them when they drove down from Lexington to visit Uncle Noah's. I do not recall that I very much enjoyed my visit to Uncle Noah's as the visits were usually made on Sunday and Uncle Noah's family were very religious and there was no play around there for children. I recall that an old colored lady, a servant in the family, was also a block against my happiness when visiting there. She was the first colored person probably which I ever saw. At the time I knew Uncle Noah's family his children were grown up and had moved away except for son Avery.

D. W. Garber in his *Tales of the Mohican Country* series which appeared in the *Mansfield News Journal* wrote of a practical joke played on the tavern keeper. Allen Beverstock, Tom Coleman, and a man named Adams were in the public room of the tavern and pretended to be having their fill of Watson's home distilled whiskey. As the evening wore on, one appeared to be passed out and the other two not far behind.

Enter an accomplice who soon mentioned that he heard that an officer was coming through from Delaware inspecting taverns. Horrified, Watson had three drunken friends on his hands and faced jail time and the loss of his license if they were found. Unable to arouse or get them to leave, he hitched up a horse and wagon to haul them away. Half carrying and half leading the first and loading him on the wagon, he went back for the second. As he brought the second out he met the first one crawling back in on his hands a knees. And so it went, one out, another back in, until exhausted he finally gave up, resigned to losing his license. At this, his friends took pity and suddenly regained their senses and the four enjoyed a good laugh on the bewildered inn keeper. At that point one could imagine drinks were on the house.

The public room and bar was in a 16 X 19 room on the south side. The Mishey family, which owned the old tavern building from 1906 to 1948, was told that Noah had a distillery somewhere behind the house. There was a large fireplace in the middle of the west side of the house and the foundations for two more at each end which apparently were never finished. The building had a full basement and perhaps Watson was ahead of the times by using an early furnace instead of the required three fireplaces.

Noah became Dr. Noah Watson at an early time, but what medical training he had, if any, is a mystery. He is listed and known as the first medical doctor in the Lexington area. A descendant recalled that he put wild cherries in whiskey as one his cures for colds. It's possible he treated horses too, as many early patent remedies were good for man and beast.

Watson died in May of 1863 and his passing no doubt ended the tavern operation.

The historic and beautifully designed building was bought by the Wappner Funeral Home family. It was torn down in May of 2000. It was a shame it wasn't saved and renovated for another century of use as were her sisters, the Bell and Lindley taverns.

The writer walked through the old place before it fell to the wreckers. It was as strong, straight and solid as when built with a full dry basement. The windows and interior needed redone and an ill designed addition had been tacked on the back by subsequent owners. However, the basic building was the classic design with an open center stair and hall with large rooms. Quality construction was evident and with some finely fit hand hewn timbers of oak and walnut. One hewn oak timber was a 12 X 12, forty feet long and perfectly straight.

All too often good and historic buildings are demolished by owners who lack the imagination to see their future use. In the case of the Watson Tavern, Richland County now has another field full of brush, trees and weeds.

What a pity.

The Buckhorn Tavern

The Buckhorn Tavern is the best remembered of the old inns in the area for just one reason - it's unusual name. None of the other local area taverns had special names or signs such as The Eagle, The American (there were a bunch of those), The Red Bull etc. However, the

"Buckhorn" was a name well remembered by the old-timers and tales of the tavern became almost legend.

Some of the tales tell of travelers who spent the night at the Buckhorn and were never heard from again. They were, as the story goes, murdered and their bodies buried in the basement. However, no facts have been uncovered to support these tales. In fact, research has cast new light on some of these legends.

The Buckhorn was located at the southeast corner of the intersection of State Routes 314 and 97 west of Lexington. In those days, 314 was known as the "Wheat Road" due to the heavy traffic of wheat wagons headed north towards Milan. (Milan was where grain was loaded on boats and shipped to eastern markets.) As many as 56 wagons were reported to have passed in a single day. What is now known as 97 was a busy east-west route for drovers and teamsters. So as you might expect, the Buckhorn did a thriving business.

The history of the valley around this intersection dates from 1820 when George Mitchell bought a section of land and built the first water powered sawmill in the valley and then started construction of a gristmill. He died in 1824. Francis McEwen and son John finished the mill and in 1832 opened a post office known as McEwen's Cross Roads in the mill. Evidence suggests that a small country store and a log school house were also located at the crossroads.

Photo courtesy of Arlow Stull Collection

The colorful Buckhorn Tavern was located on the southeast corner of what is now the junction of State Routes 97 and 314.

McEwen lost the mills at Sheriffs sale in 1833 to William Shauck, a miller from Johnsville. Then in 1839 McEwen sold the balance of the land to Doctor Samuel G. Miller, who built a new house one tenth of a mile west of the original crossroads. (The old Wheat road twisted its way across the valley. So when it was straightened, the intersection was moved to its present location.)

Dr. Miller had just settled in when his newly-built house burned to the ground. So in 1842 he built a second home and this was the building which later became the tavern.

For reasons unknown, Dr. Miller sold the place a year later to John and Florenda Pugh and they established the first tavern operation in addition to the post office, which had been moved there from the mill.

The Pugh's ran the place until 1845, when they sold the tavern and 30 acres of land for $2,700, three times more than they paid for it less than three years earlier. (Now that's what I call a good return on investment!)

The new owner was Levi Lewis from New York State. It was he who gave the tavern wide recognition by placing the horns of a buck (shot by a 12-year-old neighbor boy, Nathaniel Mitchell), in front of the building. From that totem the tavern was named the "Buckhorn."

The tavern was a popular hostelry and a contemporary account states that *"the Buckhorn was patronized by the best of people. The young people of the neighborhood held parties there, playing games that were popular in that day; I won't be home till morning, We will go another bout, and Rise and Choose your Lassie. There was a large room in the building where the young people danced the Honeymush, the Opera Reel, and the French Four."*

Lewis's Buckhorn Tavern became widely known and gained a fine reputation, but this was not to last. Construction of the Sandusky, Mansfield & Newark Railroad in the early 1850's (and other railroads to follow) resulted in its decline. The drovers and teamsters, with their multiple hitches of horses and oxen, ceased to travel the old roads. The water powered mill, which had also supplied some business, also closed in 1852. And the post office had already been moved away when Lewis bought the place.

As business at the tavern declined, so did its reputation. The January 11, 1860 edition of the *Mansfield Herald* reported that *"On the evening of a week before last, a party from this city, Shelby and Lexington had a ball at the Buckhorn Tavern, Morrow County, when a dispute arouse between the Mansfield and Shelby crowd. The matter was settled (or unsettled) by a free fight in which knives were freely used."*

The Lexington group was not exonerated, for the article continued, *"On the following Saturday a drunken row occurred in Lexington in which a number were engaged,"* and concluded that *"It is quite time that such disgraceful disturbances should be stopped."*

Upon another occasion a fight broke out during a dance held in a large room on the second floor and one of the participants was thrown out the window.

During the years that followed, the reputation of the old tavern sank even lower. In 1973, Lee Cully, who lived on the farm just south of the Buckhorn, told the writer that his father told him that "They had a wild woman down there and everybody in the county came there. She wore bloomers. They finally took her down to Lexington and buried her. Dad said you could hear the fiddling and goings on from here." Perhaps not so coincidentally, the Morrow County 1911 History says that Lewis had two daughters who wore bloomers, which were the style at that time.

With the tavern, Levi Lewis's fortunes also sank. Of the 130 acres he once owned, he was forced to sell off small parcels from time to time until he had only 14 acres left in 1867. Cully contends that Lewis "got into trouble with his old lady and had to keep selling off land to pay her off."

At any rate, Lewis died a short time later and his wife, Mary, sold the tavern in 1872. That may have ended the Buckhorn, but as late as 1894 a Bellville newspaper story indicated that there were still people of questionable character living there.

No record of a murder has been found even though old-timers claimed to have seen blood stains on the second floor. According to Lee Cully, the only robbery that occurred there happened one New Years Eve. The sledding was good and most people in the neighborhood had gathered at the tavern. A large turkey was roasted and a big feast prepared. While everyone was upstairs watching the dance, someone crept into the kitchen and cleaned out the whole works.

There was a brick courtyard next to the tavern and one Morrow County writer claimed that a large barn with stalls for 35 horses was across the road. Neither Lee Cully nor another old neighbor, Ray Baker, remembered their parents talking about it. In 1952 when the steep hill on 314 was improved, they both remembered bulldozers digging up cherry logs which were once part of a corduroy road next to the tavern site. The logs were in good shape, considering they had been buried for over 100 years.

Ray Baker tore the old tavern down in 1938. His father had bought the property years before and the building had been used as a farm tenant house for a few years. It was no longer occupied, in disrepair, and no longer worth maintaining.

No one knows what became of the buck horns that had once adorned the tavern. The only reminder of McEwen's Cross Roads is the old brick Buckhorn Schoolhouse on St. Rt. 97. It marks the original site of the crossroad and has been saved and expanded into a beautiful home.

The fact that the once proud hostelry spent its last days as a house of "ill fame" may account for its never receiving much recognition in the county histories.

Little Known Taverns

At the top of what is known as "Sandy Hill" on route 42, just before you get to the present day Cable TV Company, there was the Robert Beaty Tavern. It was built in 1841 and Styrl Mishey, who had grown up and lived in the Watson Tavern from 1906 until 1948, knew of its existence. The dilapidated building was torn down in the early 1950's.

Another mystery tavern was in the old home of John Vanderbilt, two miles south of Lexington, on what is now Route 546. In the early 1960's the writer was shown a number painted on an upstairs bedroom door frame. This indicates it may have been a tavern at an early time. However, the home had been remodeled at some point and the Vanderbilts knew little of its history. Land records do indicate that it may have been built by Jacob George and was later owned by the Dunshee family.

The Carter Tavern was on the southeast corner of the intersection of Lexington Springmill and Alta roads, north of Lexington. The tavern was built in 1842-43 and few details of its operation have been passed down by the family. This is upsetting since Robert Carter was the writer's great-great grandfather.

Carter came to Springfield Township in 1819 from Pennsylvania with his wife Rebecca. They had twelve children, ten boys and two girls. Then, in 1830, they took in two orphaned boys and had a bound girl to help with the spinning. So where they would have had room for travelers is a puzzle. However, it is remembered that they kept a good tavern and that dances were held there.

A large barn with an overhang that ran its full length was across the road to the north. Bill Finney, an old neighbor, said he was told the overhang was needed during bad weather when horses were changed for the stagecoach, which used that route for a year or two.

Robert Carter died in 1865 at age 79. The tavern was torn down around 1949 and no picture exists. Darn.

In the 1850s, Blooming Grove had the J. Lortchen Hotel and the John John's Hotel. Another tavern or hotel by William Howell was at the intersection of present-day State Route 288 and the Williamsport Blooming Grove Road.

In Johnsville, Asa Cover opened the town's first tavern in 1839 and ran it until 1860. Enoch Ogle opened Bellville's first tavern in the 1820's. Steam Corners also had an unnamed tavern mentioned in the *1880 History of Morrow County*.

There were perhaps other local taverns lost to the pages of history. Small town taverns and hotels often came and went.

Al Moore, Correspondent

In the early 1800's any news about Lexington or the area was quite naturally carried by word of mouth. Some was gossip, some was truth and sometimes the latest news was stretched and embellished a bit to make it more interesting to the listener. That's how many of the inaccurate stories got into the history books.

Without a newspaper of its own, Lexington readers had to rely on the Mansfield papers for anything missed from next door. However, the early Mansfield papers were heavily political in nature and carried mostly Ohio, national, and war news. So any local community items, often confined to only part of one page, were sent in by correspondents who were paid by the inches of space their contribution used.

Perhaps the greatest of the Lexington reporters was a young man by the name of Al Moore. He began writing for the *Mansfield Herald* in the 1870's and later continued as Lexington's correspondent for the *Mansfield News* until 1905.

Little is known of Moore's personal life. He was evidently a small, likeable man who was raised and went to school in Lexington. Apparently, Al also once taught a dance class organized by young women. However, he never married.

His father was H.S. Moore, who was described as a carpenter and joiner. H.S. came to Lexington in 1852, fought in the Civil War, and was a contractor and builder who worked in North Dakota for a while in late 1880s.

It is unknown whether Al worked with his father for any period, although a brother did. However, Al's writing alone would not have provided sufficient income for support.

Businesses in Lexington didn't advertise. So the names, types and locations of businesses are often hard to pinpoint. However, the Moore family evidently had a retail store of some type on Main Street in the 1860s and 70s. And at one time, H. S. Moore was paid by the village for "stamping bonds." This may indicate the business might have been a bookstore, possibly in connection with the Gailey Seminary, a private high school.

Al's colorful writing began in the *Mansfield Herald* in the late 1870s. He would sign many of his early articles with the initials A. H. M. Later he moved to the Mansfield Weekly News where the editors evidently condoned his vocabulary and wit.

During his career, Al recorded the visits, the fires, the fights, the progress, failures and politics of old Lexington. His observations ran the gamut from a new birth to the extremely detailed account of an autopsy performed by local doctors. He finally stopped writing about Lexington in February of 1905.

He had a way with words that delighted, or disgusted, some readers. And he no doubt baffled those who were poorly educated or possessed a limited vocabulary.

Fair and balanced he was not. Al favored the temperance movement and its supporters, and praised the Republicans (the Weekly News was a Republican paper after all). At the same time, he condemned Democrats, who were often referred to as the "Rock Ribbed Bourbons."

His personal opinions were crafted into his columns, which painted a word picture of life in small town Lexington. His weekly columns were a wonderful legacy for future generations. (His columns can still be found on microfilm at the library.) Paid by the inch, his words stretched each report to the very limit. Just a few of his memorable writings are shared here.

January, 1877:

Burglaries and nocturnal depredations of various kinds of late, have been rife in Lexington and vicinity. But a few nights ago burglars gained entrance to the H. P. Maxwell grocery, by wrenching the door from its fastenings and abstracted two dollars from the till and otherwise raided the establishment to the extent of five dollars. The same night an unsuccessful attempt was made to burglarize the drug store of Wilson Bros., the burglars being foiled by Wallace Wilson who was sleeping in the store. More recently, two attempts were made in one night to burglarize the residence of Rev. Proctor, during the absence of Rev. and Mrs. Proctor. The members of the family discovered the burglars and the sharp report of a pistol in the hands of John Proctor Jr., which rang out on the night air, caused them to vacate the premises. They had the temerity, however, to return in about three hours and make a more audacious attempt. Mr. Proctor, who was upstairs, peered out into the darkness and decried two men beneath him, and fired, the ball passing in near proximity to their craniums, which thoroughly intimidated them, and caused them to rapidly recede from the spot.

In February of 1877, sled riding Bloomer Sowers was kicked in the face by a horse:

Mr. B. Sowers who recently, while engaged in the congenial and exhilarating pastime of coasting, received a severe kick from a horse, is again pursuing his usual avocation, his physiognomy presenting a variegated appearance.

He detailed what was one tough woman:

Mrs. Winters, the female Sullivan, whose exit from here we announced last week, went to Independence (Butler) and for attempting to indulge in the pugilistic art a warrant was issued for her arrest, but she eluded the officers and again disgraced Lexington by her presence. The Marshal of Independence got on the trail of the depraved female who again eluded his grasp, and her sinister eyes and massive frame are still a terror to our village.

Springtime romance on Delaware Street in 1881:

A few days ago a young man arrayed in faultless attire and a young lady apparently in the first blush of womanhood, handsome and also attired a la mode, seated in a jaunty little phaeton which was drawn by two nettled steeds, put in an appearance in Lexington and lingered briefly on Delaware street. The young man's arm encircled the graceful form of the young girl, and he sipped the nectar from her rose colored lips, gazed deeply into her lustrous love-lit eyes and dallied with her luxuriant tresses, which hung like molten gold over shoulders of immaculate whiteness and faultless symmetry. The young girl was not a bit coy, but seemed to be in a happy listless languor. The scene exceeded in interest any act of Sarah Beruhardt, the queen of the histrionic art, and was witnessed by a small but appreciative audience.

And then in the summer of 1883 there was a dance in "Sower's Grove," which is now the front lawn of the cemetery. A dance in the cemetery? Well, then it was a sugar camp dotted with large beautiful maple trees and was the place to go.

Last Thursday evening the spacious platform in the grove was brilliantly illuminated for the entertainment of the Gilt Edge Terpsichorean Club. The courtly grace of the young men, the harmonious blending of the beautiful in the costumes of the young ladies and their radiant beauty and artistic evolutions of all to the electrifying music of Kyner Bros. orchestra, conspired to make the scene one of weird enchantment.

There were fast horses in Lexington:

Those blooded coursers, A. Shortess' Electric Light, record 2:38; Messrs. S. Lindsey and H. Williams' Cyclone, record 2:37 ½, and Mr. John Williams time annihilator, Meteor, record 2:42, are being groomed for a race to take place soon.

In May of 1883 Lexington was a little rough:

Nicholi Jarvi one day last week imbibed to excess of whisky and menaced with death all who would question his knowledge of the abstruse sciences, and without provocation he dealt an inoffensive citizen a blow above the right optic, for which diversion he was confined to the village Bastille. After his incarceration, strange hallucinations entered his brain and he discharged the contents of his revolver at objects which were fantasies of his imagination, the missiles passing in dangerous proximity of the craniums of bystanders.

The number of inhabitants in Lexington was the subject of another column, also in 1883:

The population of Lexington a little exceeds 500: it contains no less than 38 widows, 20 females of uncertain age who are not reluctant to embrace connubial joy, 14 of more tender years of marriageable age, and to extricate this large coterie from the calamity of celibacy there are but 21 men, and between the ages of 70 and 80 there are 19 persons, and 3 between 80 and 90, and one whose silvered head is the weight of 94 years, the revered Mrs. C. McCune, whose tenure of life is apparent will soon expire.

And then someone fell off the train (or was it the wagon?):

Mr. John Cook, who returned to the Infirmary for additional repairs to his frame, having last summer sustained a broken leg, a broken arm, a contused cranium and a badly lacerated muscle of one ankle, when attempting some ground and lofty tumbling from a passenger train while wrestling with booze, is slowly but surely being restored to his normal condition.

The town put up "tramps" at the Custer Hotel in 1885 for twenty-five cents a night. It became so popular that

Moore reported on a new method the village used in July, 1900:

Deputy Marshall Blair arrested a weary tourist if the genius hobo type and lodged him in the gloomy confines of the town Bastille. The hobo persisted in his determination not to work for his provender. He was very defiant and said in substance hell would become an ice pond twice over before he would sweat his brow and grime his hands with toil. The officer put him on bread and water and in three days released him from the torrid heat of his cell. The hobo sniffed the air of freedom with great joy and uttering sulfurous expletives he left town.

There was music in the air in 1897:

Bob Prosser's whoop'em up band is a prominent feature of Lexington. It is an aggregation of lusty lunged vocalists, fog horn artists, banjoist, etc., and the music is of the comic and pathetic, and lulls the fiercest breast. Bob has fine qualities as a musical director and his "orchesty" is in great demand for wedding functions.

On July 10, 1900, this was filed:

A horseless carriage or automobile passed through Lexington Wednesday night, coming from the south on the Delaware road. It was in charge of two men and the light of two lamps gleamed from the front. It sped rapidly by and is a wonderful innovation on the old ox cart method of conveyance in pioneer days and the villagers viewed the machine with as much awe as Pacific island pagans would with the advent of a steam engine among them.

Not everyone liked what Al wrote. In 1884 he commented:

Some of the rib-breaking, nose atomizing, skull contusing fraternity who we struck in the raw in the columns of "The Herald" have sent us an anonymous letter in which they threaten not to leave enough of our frame to fill a sardine box if we persist....We append a copy of this blood chilling communication:

You dam little devil you think you are mighty smart riting about people in that lousy Mansfield herald you better take a little advise if you don't you will get lick sure as hell is hot, you are a meddlesome little devel and you will be lick like hell this is the last time you will be warn.

Al Moore was also a long time member of the "Bachelors Club," which was composed of young men of marriageable age who resisted matrimonial entanglements. (There was the possibility no woman would have wanted some of them anyway.) Taking this position as a group caused a stir locally, since another group of the local eligible men had already gone west.

You couldn't play pool on Sunday in the early 1900s. Still, the remnants of the "Bachelors Club" could hang around smoking cigars. It seems rather odd, but now exactly the opposite is true.

For a brief period, the young women of the town formed a "Women's Bachelors Club" as well. The women's club failed after several months. However, Moore's regular reports of the men's meetings are rather amusing. Always looking for something to write, he came up with the following samples:

December, 1896: *There are over forty ancient maidens here and their hearts are warm as sun beams and a tint of rose yet suffices their cheeks. Eight more years must be marked on the calendar before another leap year and then the winter of life will have blighted their tendrils of love in the bachelor's hearts.*

Several years later the Bachelors club was still intact:

The meeting was held in the loft of the chop shop which is black with dust of years and festooned with cob webs. The stifling air of the gruesome place was made more mendacious by the smoke of cigars which President A. G. Englehart furnished....The proceeding began with the election of John Oberlin since treasurer Ed Garret resigned. Brother Garret turned over forty cents to the new custodian of the clubs shekels and the bachelors were much elated by the clubs good financial condition. Oris Pollock was admitted as a member and took an iron clad hair raising oath to remain celibate for at least five years.

By March of 1899 progress was reported:

It is noteworthy that the bachelors are displaying aesthetic and cultured tastes that it was thought they did not possess. They are not degenerates as is shown by the improvements in their manners and in their gruesome quarters, the loft of the chop mill, which has been swept and garnished, matting covers the floor and bright cuspidors take place of the oyster cans and any old thing. The walls are adorned with lithographs of famous stage beauties, pugilists, flaming circus bills and other pictures of more artistic merit and refining influence, and the whole has a subduing effect on the dark grimy place. The President now has a wicker chair and a neat table instead of a beer keg and store box and there are other improvements which show that the members have a love for the beautiful above that of the average coterie of bachelor vagrants.

Moore reported a near disaster to the club in September 1903:

President Grubb's now cold and stony heart was once warm and mellow with love for pumpkin-faced mildewed old maid from Steam Corners. But when he thought he was fondly enshrined in her heart she suddenly turned him down for a yellow-haired, knock-kneed "rube" from Bungtown and her cruel perfidy to him stung like a vipers fangs and the most witching woman could not again set aglow the spark of love so dead in his heart.

The young ladies of town apparently had their own opinion of Moore's writings on the subject of love and marriage. As Moore reported November 1903:

The unsophisticated correspondent was the victim Halloween night of the cunning pranks of a coterie of Lexington's charming feminine buds. Surely he was done up by these smart and rapturously beautiful buds by a scheme which in cunning could have been conceived in none but their fertile brains. The correspondent will smother the emotions of sorrow and humiliation that sting burning pain in his heart and will tell the brief tale that the News readers may know that he has never dwelt in to glowing terms on the wit and sagacity of these sparkling maiden buds. He found at the door of his bachelor den at the first peep of the rosy dawn Sunday a little mushy cabbage head to which was tied with silken cord a note which was yet fragrant with the sweet odors of the breath of the celestial maidens. Attached to the note was a ringlet of golden hair clipped from one of the maiden's silken trusses.

But the note is breezy and unique. It is this: This is to represent the HEAD which originates the so called brilliant (?) eloquence of our Lexington correspondent. Compliments of the rosy cheeked, pearly teeth, swam like neck, alabaster brow, violet eyed, golden hair hanging down their back maidens.

There is one puzzling period however starting in December of 1877 when Moore stopped writing for a few months. Did he quit? Was he fired? Or was he a genius that was not quite understood?

The answer may found in a Lexington item published in a February 1878 edition of the Bellville newspaper:

Albert H. Moore, a medical student of Lexington, was taken by Sheriff Ritchie to the Central Lunatic Asylum at Columbus last Friday.

The Lunatic Asylum! Do all writers wind up there?

Lexington Newspapers

Early Attempts

The town's first newspaper of its own, of sorts, was a seasonal publication called the *Lexington Pictorial* published in 1875. It contained news, engraved illustrations and advertising. The paper's motto was "Stern Fate Will Smile on Enterprise and Prosper Those Who Advertise." It did not long endure.

The second paper in town was the *Lexington Times*. It was a weekly, published by the Times Publishing Company of Butler, which also published the *Butler Times*. The first Lexington edition was printed in July of 1904. It also did not last long. There simply was not enough advertising or subscriptions to support it.

Another attempt, this time to publish a bi-weekly paper, was made in 1906 by Rev. A. E. Proctor. The town was growing by that time. However, the Reverend's paper was a financial failure like its predecessors, lasting only a few months. No copy has ever been found.

In the fall of 1930 *The Minute Man* was published by the journalism class in Lexington's brand new high school. It was a well done and professionally printed four page paper carrying only school news with local business advertising support. A February 1931 edition recommends "Save your copies of the Minute Man as they will be valuable memories of your school days." Free to students it was delivered to homes of non-students for a small subscription fee. Of nine scattered copies found, the last was dated February of 1942, which gave students instructions on what to do in case of an air raid.

A December 23, 1931 copy of The Minute Man, published by the high school journalism class. Note that haircuts only cost 25¢ back then and Junior Class was selling candy. Some things change and some stay the same I guess.

A fifth paper was the *Lexington Advertiser*, published in 1940 by longtime Lexington Postmaster Frank Griebling. It was printed in Mansfield and distributed to all of Lexington's rural and post office box holders. It was discontinued after Pearl Harbor.

Lexington Shopper News – The News of Lexington

It was not until 1955 that the next local publication appeared. Its history was printed in the paper's final edition in 1960:

*On August 31, 1955, the first issue of the **Lexington Shoppers News** was distributed. Robert Snyder, local funeral director, set up his printing shop six years prior to this date to print funeral memorials. Local orders for other printing needs increased until finally demand grew for a local newspaper.* **The Shoppers News** *had a free distribution until Oct. 24, 1956, when it became a subscription paper and was published weekly.*

On December of that same year application was made and granted for a change of the name of the newspaper....Now after five years of publication, **The News of Lexington** *will stop the presses with this Dec. 22 issue. For five years this newspaper has ably served the community as a voice, a friend and an advertising medium. It will now take its place in the newspaper history of the Lexington area. Someday, perhaps, the need for area*

Lexington SHOPPER NEWS

BULK MAILING
U. S. POSTAGE PAID
Lexington, Ohio
Permit No. 7

POSTOFFICE or RURAL ROUTE

BOX HOLDER, Local

VOL. I No. 1   Published in Lexington, Ohio   Wednesday, August 31, 1955

About Your Publisher

BUY or SELL

RATE   25 cents per line per issue, with a minimum charge of $.50. Cash with order, except when under contract.

---

16 ACRES with modern Home & other buildings -Johnsville area - $9750.00

12 ACRES - Modern buildings - very neat, $9000.00

3 ACRES with new Modern Home near Lexington at $14200.00

Several 70 to 100 Acre farms, Johnsville area.

BUILDING SITES - Mill Run Rd. $500.00 and up   U.S. 42 South West - $800.00 and up.

SEVERAL LARGE LOTS IN LEXINGTON Corporation with utilities $1100.00 and up.

SEE US for farms, we have many to offer from 50 to 600 acres.

CRING REALTY
Lexington 3631

FOR SALE
HIT AND MISS RUGS
Cotton and Wool
Hand Woven
27" width - any length
Mrs. B. M. Owens
Lexington, O. Rt. 1   Owens Rd.

WANTED TO BUY

Antiques, Furniture, Glass, Missc. Also have some Antiques for sale.
Lexington Rt. 1 Owens Rd.
B. M. Owens

Six years ago your publisher started in business with an Antiquated hand feed printing press and four fonts of type, which was adequate for printing funeral home Memorials. Then local churches and stationery orders required a second "Hand feeder", and more type. At this point your hand setter could not match the efficienty of the hand feeders. This was remedied by installing a Linotype that casts type automatically.

Recently Snyder Printing further modernized it's procedure by purchasing two automatic presses, electric metal saw, folding machine, paper drill and stitcher. Snyder Printing now has a complete line of equipment necessary to handle all the printing requirements of this community.

Your publisher wishes to express his sincere thanks to the many people who have encouraged the publication of the first issue of the Shopper News, and the many more who have expressed their desire for the success of the publishing of Lexington's second community paper. The first paper was published by Frank Griebling about 1940 and was discontinued with the onset of Pearl Harbor.

Not forgotten for their advice, guidance and help, are the various Publishers in the community. To the Bellville Star, Loudonville Shopper, Fredericktown Citizen, and the Morrow Co., Registarer. The Shopper News extends Thanks.

NOTICE

At this late hour, your publisher is informed from good authority, that their was another paper published in Lexington around 1904.

BACK TO SCHOOL for over 800

School will open on Tuesday Sept. 6 for a half day session. An increase in enrollment is anticipated. The number of pupils enrolled at the close of school last year was 776 with an expected increase of $25 to 850 this year. Bus routes and schedules will be the same as last year although some changes may be necessary after school opens. The school cafeteria will be open on Wednesday Sept. 7th.

The Board of Education has approved one extra teacher in the Elementary School and three extra teachers in the High School. New teachers are as follows.
Mrs. Mary Terry - Kent, Ohio - Fourth Grade; Mrs. Sylvia Healea - Johnsville, Ohio - Fifth Grade; Mrs. Norma Stanfield - Mansfield, Ohio - Biology & Gen. Sci.; Mr. James R. Davis - New Paris, Ind. - History & Soc. Sci.; Miss Carmela Morales - Galion, Ohio - Junior High English; Mrs. Jean Broeske who taught fourth grade last year will be teaching Math in the High School. Mr. John Hill, St.Claireville, O. Science and Math..

Faculty meeting for Elementary teachers will be held in the New Elementary Building at 1:00 P.M. on Tuesday August 30th.

Faculty meeting for High School teachers will be held in the High School Building at 9:00 A.M. on Monday September 5th.

Driver training will be offered for the first time this fall. Mr. Knapp, Mansfield, Ohio who just completed the Driver Training Course at Bowling Green State University, will be the instructor.

The 'Guiding Step Club' of the Ohio Child Conservation League, will meet Thursday, Sept. 15th at the home of Helen Herman with

NOTICE TO STUDENTS

Through the efforts of numerous business executives, your community of Lexington is now affiliated with the Junior Achievements of Mansfield, Inc. This program, now in its fourth year is centered around a company of students forming a corporation, manufacturing and selling some product. They sell stock in their company and etc. The officers are: J. R. Kelly, Westinghouse, J. D. Bolesky, President of Thermodisk; D. J. Jones, Pres. Humphreys; B. L. Blair, Barns; and R. H. Phillips of Stevens manufacturing here in Lexington.
Further information will follow in the next edition of the Shopper News.

Starting with the next edition of the Shopper News, a column will appear for and from the employees of the Stevens Manufacturing Co. It has been noted at this writing, that all of the original group of ladies that started with the company two years ago in Newcomers garage are still with the company.

OLD SCHOOL REUNION

The annual Old School Reunion was held Aug. 20, 1955 at the Congregational Church. Forty-six members attended with three from out of state, Rev. and Mrs. G. M. Sauder - Penn., Fred Beverstock - Kansas, and Mr. and Mrs. Virgil Myers, Detroit, Michigan.

The class of 1902 was honored with three of that class attending: Edna Cambell Whiteleather, Ada Patterson Taylor, and George Maxwell.

The class of 1904 and 1905 will be honored next year.

communication will prompt the publication of another paper, since the connecting link in life in this suburban community will vanish when the presses roll for the last time on this final issue of **The News of Lexington.**

Robert Snyder, who, along with wife Dorothy, published a very good local newspaper in Lexington from 1955 to 1960.

This paper filled a gap the Mansfield News Journal was reluctant to print. What Snyder carried were articles covering everything from the Cub Scouts, PTA meetings, a full page or more of school news by Ann Ackerman's journalism class, weddings, funerals and varied news items from local neighborhood correspondents. Council, school board and township meetings were covered. Snyder's editorials were a balanced, common sense approach to local problems.

The local merchants bought advertising space, some full page. It was a darn good newspaper with the articles written by a wide assortment of local contributors, making it very interesting to read.

However, the opening of the Johnny Appleseed Shopping Center in the summer of 1957, and the others that soon followed, hurt some local business ventures. In September of 1960, Interstate 71 opened from Columbus as far as Medina and the Highway Patrol noted traffic on Route 42 dropped 70%. In Lexington, Marshall Wayne Weirick estimated the decrease to be at least 50%. As a result of the local businesses suffering, advertising revenue for the paper decreased until it was no longer financially possible to continue. The paper, which recorded and promoted progress in the Lexington area, died. It was a victim of that same progress.

Robert and Dorothy Snyder were remarkable people. They ran Snyder's Funeral Home, where they lived on the second floor. For 30 years (1938 until 1968) the Snyder family furnished ambulance service for the community. And after World War II, all phone calls to the Fire Department were answered at the funeral home. The fire siren on the old town hall (used to summon the volunteer firemen) had to be started from Snyder's. This meant that someone had to be at their house 24 hours a day. It was a burden the Snyders cheerfully carried for years, at little cost to the taxpayers.

In addition, Bob was involved in community organizations and the schools. Through his business, he had contact with nearly every family in the area, at some time or other, and everybody knew and respected him. He always had a warm greeting for everyone.

In 1970 the family moved to Colorado and the village was saddened by their departure. The Fire Department had a going away party for the Snyders and had the siren button chromed, mounted on wood, engraved and presented to them as a memento.

The writer has the only known file of *Shoppers News* and *The News of Lexington*. A copy is on microfilm at the Mansfield Public Library. Strange as it may seem, the Snyders never kept one for themselves.

Richland Reporter

In October of 1964 the *Richland Reporter* became the next newspaper devoted to Lexington. Published by Herbert T. Cobey with Thayer Waldo as editor, it was a very professional-looking publication. Waldo had a twenty-five year career in the news business. He had even covered the Kennedy assassination and was only 15 feet away when Lee Harvey Oswald was killed.

The first issue carried some local news items as well as columns by published syndicated writers. Most prominent among them was Drew Pearson, who Waldo had worked for at one time. Pearson wrote a special column for the new *Richland Reporter* under this dateline: *"Washington; As originator of "Drew Pearson's Best*

Manure – All Cow, No Bull, I am delighted to write this column welcoming my manure partner, Herbert Cobey, into the newspaper business.

Pearson recalled visiting here one time with the Venezuelan Ambassador and none other than Dear Abby. (Now that was a combination.) And in fact, for a while, Pearson owned a farm on Route 97 just west of 314.

The headquarters for the "manure business" was in the old Pennsylvania Railroad roundhouse in Crestline. There was a large paid staff. This was a serious attempt to compete with the *Mansfield News Journal*.

Evidently the manure business pooped out, the paper was not profitable, and Cobey lost a great deal of money in the venture.

Editor Waldo, who had served as a correspondent in 14 countries, was not destined to find much in the way of international news in dull old Lexington. It was a noble effort, a well-written paper, but short lived, ending in 1966.

Ledger

The next attempt at a local newspaper was the *Lexington Ledger*, published by Phil Wiseman. Started in March of 1967, it only lasted a few months. Lack of local news, subscriptions and advertising led to its early demise.

The Lexington Times

It was not until March of 1983 that the next paper would appear. *The Lexington Times* was published by Terry Wolf, a professional newsboy, and his wife, Carole. They put a great deal of effort into the project, as he was a one-man band of sorts. He wrote some very good, in-depth stories and the photography was excellent.

During Bob Snyder's days, in the late 1950s, most folks knew nearly everyone around town. However, by the 1980s Lexington had changed. It was now a bedroom community, with folks working and shopping in Mansfield or other towns.

The Snyder print shop, located in a crowded garage behind the funeral home. Some of this equipment later served the Tribune-Courier.

By 1970, the village was somewhat divided in a friendly fashion. There was "old" Lexington, slow to change and "new" Lexington, where the young people with a station wagon full of kids lived in the rapidly growing developments. More women had entered the working world by this time and the faster pace of life left little interest in what was going on in Steam Corners or Orchard Park.

Something had been lost along the way. In addition, by this time, many people had bought subscriptions for other local newspapers in the past…only to see those papers go out of business. And advertising alone could not support the paper. It needed community support too. So, unfortunately for Lexington, Wolf's paper ceased operations in the summer of 1983.

Tribune-Courier

Frank and Betty Stumbo had the encouragement and help of Bob Snyder in starting a weekly paper for the developing community of Ontario. Thus the *Ontario Tribune* was created.

The Stumbos bought some of Snyder's printing equipment and his linotype machine. When Snyder offered to give them his type, Betty went into a back room to look it over and found, to her horror, that it was all neatly stacked in an old casket!

John Kirschenheiter was looking for a temporary job while he was going to school and was hired by the Stumbos as one of their first employees. That was 47 years ago. He's still there and he's now the editor.

In 1962, Stumbo began printing some Lexington items that were refused by the Lexington papers or which had missed imposed deadlines. After the Lexington Ledger went out of business, Stumbo began publishing two papers, the *Ontario Tribune* and the Lexington Courier. The first edition of the *Lexington Courier* appeared in June of 1968.

Both papers enjoyed good advertising support from Lexington, Ontario, Galion, Shelby and Mansfield. However, disaster struck in the summer of 1969, when the Richland Mall opened.

Editor Stumbo recalled that his advertising "dropped like you wouldn't believe" and he was forced to combine the two papers. *The Tribune Courier* still serves both communities along with Madison Township. It has been a long-standing asset to the area, covering what the *News Journal* does not.

John Kirschenheiter (right), Betty Stumbo (center) and Frank Stumbo (left) of the Tribune-Courier. Kirschenheiter took a "temporary" job with the paper…47 years ago! He hopes to find a more permanent job someday soon.

Law and Order

Lexington was incorporated February 16, 1839. This signaled the election of the town's first public officers and the end of rule by the Troy Township Trustees. One has to wonder if the trustees felt a degree of relief. If only they could have known what Lexington would face during the rest of the century, a period of jollification would have ensued.

James M. Pennel may have been the first mayor or at least he was in 1841. Early records are missing but in an effort to get serious about their responsibilities, the mayor and council passed an ordinance which stated; "No mayor, clerk or member of council shall not be absent at a meeting without a satisfactory excuse or pay a twenty-five cent fine."

It appears doubtful that there were many votes cast in that first election. Women couldn't vote and a good guess would be that less than 50 men were eligible.

A Town Hall

In those early days, the elected officers had no permanent quarters and were forced to rent meeting space or a room in various stores, the school, taverns and Odd Fellows Hall. The village officials didn't have a town hall or meeting place of their own until June of 1884 when they bought an ancient one and a half story brick house from Daniel Miller. It stood on the lot where the present village hall stands. The Lexington government had a home at last.

The village paid $1,100 for the house and attached shed, issuing bonds payable over five years. However, the building must have been poorly maintained and was in disrepair when they bought it. It was condemned in 1909 and B. F. Ritchie was paid $81.82 to tear it down the following year.

The old town hall (1914-1988) was a classic design, which seemed to say what it was. No sign was necessary.

At that time, a 12 X 18 addition was added to the remaining shed for a jail and council chambers. The town "band boys," a local concert band, were allowed to practice in the council chamber "unless there was sickness nearby."

In 1911, architect Harlen Jones was hired to design a new and larger Town Hall. The new building was estimated to cost $8,000 but bids for construction came in much higher. So to cut cost, it was decided that the basement would be left unfinished. After some delay, additional bonds were issued and a construction contract for $12,882.77 was awarded to Albert Hancock in April of 1913. Completed a year later, it was a good strong building that would last until the 1980s.

It's interesting to note that after the new high school gym was finished, in 1932, the new town hall building saw little use. It was in such disrepair, that there was talk of tearing it down in the late 1940s.

The 1932 high school gym had a large meeting hall with a stage and portable seating for 308. A room for the Mayor's office and another for council meetings were located on the first floor. And there was a jail room in the basement, complete with an iron cage, for law breakers, drunks and tramps. The town's fire equipment was also housed in a basement garage.

The gym also had a movie projection booth and screen. This enabled Frank Beverstock to rent the town hall, for $5.00 a night, to show silent movies. Plays and musical programs were also held in the gym and, with the seating removed, all local high school basketball games were played there until the next new school gym was finished in 1932. The town was proud of this new symbol of progress.

Law of the Land

To govern the new town in its infancy laws and regulations would have to be enacted for the good of all. Looking back, one can get a mental picture of what the life style and conduct of citizens were expected to be. Over the years the Mayor and members of Council passed ordinances that would never fly in today's culture. There were the usual peace and quiet rules but they were to go well beyond those standards.

In 1850 it was against the law to pitch quoits, horseshoes, play ball or any game of any kind. No squibs (whatever they were), firecrackers or fireworks of any kind were allowed. In addition:

No person shall ride, drive or lead any horse, mule or ox, or draw any wagon or vehicle upon any of the side walks (except as necessary for passing.)" Figure that one out.

No person or persons shall ride or drive any horse attached to or not attached to any carriage or vehicle of any kind through or across any streets of the village at a speed greater than eight miles an hour.

In 1858 a petition from a group of citizens requested a law prohibiting so many swine from running at large. There must have been too many pigs in the park! The petition was "laid on the table for further action."

In 1860 it was ordered that no person shall weigh out or sell any (gun) powder during the night season. Only legally constituted military companies could fire any gun, pistol, revolver, firecrackers or powder. That never worked, especially on the Fourth of July or political rallies. Johnsville people would occasionally be invited to arrive with one small cannon.

No theatrical performance, circus, menagerie, puppet or other show, rope dancing, tumbling or slight of hand was permitted without first obtaining a license from the Mayor. Musical concerts or lectures on religious, scientific, literary or moral subjects were exempt. In 1865 they even considered building a jail on the town square for offenders of this rule.

That same ordinance made it illegal to disturb any meeting or to destroy, disfigure any sign or house, upset or injure any outhouse, or houses. (That could have taken the fun out of Halloween, although old-timers recall that it was a tough one to enforce.)

In 1870 the ever thoughtful officials amended the 1850 law against having fun, by making it illegal to roll balls on any nine or ten pin alley. No playing croquet on the public square or throwing or pitching balls along or across any public streets. At one time even playing baseball was not permitted on Sunday.

They also later passed a rule that only cows were permitted to run loose in the daytime. This might indicate a shortage of lawn mowers. (Horses and hogs were still to be kept tied or fenced.)

Four years later they passed this dandy: *No person or persons shall enter into the waters of the Clear Fork of Mohican creek within the limits of the corporation of Lexington in a nude state for the purpose of bathing*

The town swimming hole was at the mill dam. Kids could also make a little money washing buggies. This picture was taken from the bridge, near the current cemetery entrance, looking toward the northwest.

or swimming in the daytime . . . . Persons may bath or swim in the Mohican creek after night fall in places where he or they may not be exposed to view. The shortage of bathing suits and the fact that the mill pond was the swimming hole (which could easily be seen from the bridge) must have prompted complaints, probably from the women.

There is one law that should never have been repealed. In January of 1875 the village fathers decided that after a snowfall of 2 inches or more, all sidewalks were to be cleaned off by ten o'clock in the morning or the town Marshal was to clean them and collect twenty-five cents from the lot owner. If the law is still on the books, it would give the police something else to do and lot owners would be delighted to see them coming.

In 1881 things got real serious. One would suppose the local ministers and church people were pushing this ordinance:

Be it ordained by the council of the village of Lexington that no person or persons shall either in person or by agent, on the first day of the week commonly called Sunday, engage in or transact business within the village of Lexington by bartering, trading, selling or giving away or offering or exhibiting for sale any wine, cider, beer, ale or porter, or other liquors or any groceries, cigars, tobacco, goods, wares or merchandise of any description whatever.

There were a few exceptions. Works of necessity or charity were permitted, the hotels could stay open and drug stores could sell medicines as could physicians. The drug stores were a gray area in the law. Most patent medicines had rather high alcohol content and the druggist could also sell whiskey or other liquor to cure a customers alleged bad cold, toothache, snake bite, or whatever. When the saloons closed, the drug store was the place to go. One druggist was arrested for selling liquor to a person who was in the habit of getting intoxicated. That too, was against the law.

Temperance Movement

By far the most divisive and controversial ordinances ever passed in Lexington dealt with the subject of liquor and the temperance movement. The battle started at Lexington in 1847, with the formation of the Mohican Division, Number 212, of the Sons of Temperance. That year the group printed the first book published in Lexington. It was a temperance manual which stated its purpose was *to shield us from the evils of intemperance, afford mutual assistance in case of sickness, and elevate our characters as men.*

Men who joined the group took this pledge: *No brother shall make, buy, sell or use as a beverage, any Spirituous or Malt Liquors, Wine or Cider.*

```
            CONSTITUTION
                 AND
              BY-LAWS
                 OF
       MOHEGAN DIVISION, No. 212
               OF THE
         SONS OF TEMPERANCE,
               OF THE
       TOWN OF LEXINGTON, OHIO
         (Instituted April 30th, 1847.)

              MANSFIELD
         J. C. GILKISON AND SON, PR'S
                1847.
```

The first book printed in Lexington was a temperance manual. In 1830, the national per capita consumption of whiskey was 10 gallons per year for every person over age 15. Evidence suggests that Lexington was above average in this respect.

The first meeting of the Sons of Temperance was held at the Presbyterian Church. (Other churches and meeting halls were used at later meetings.) The group expressed their gratitude to the "Ladies of Lexington" for their presentation of Holy Scriptures to the organization, but the women noted that for some strange reason they were barred from membership. It was a "men only" group.

The organization's purpose was not widely accepted at first. Over in neighboring Washington Township an Anti-Temperance club was formed and the members met regularly to drink and party. To this day there are numerous elbow benders in that township. Many still consume alcoholic beverages, but today they lack the organization.

In July of 1858 a writer for the *Mansfield Herald* penned these words: *For the last few months, an increase in the use of intoxicating liquor has been visible in this village. Large numbers are seen in a state of intoxication, among whom are many young men. Now this state of affairs should not exist in as moral a community as this is. Steps should be taken for the suppression of this traffic immediately.*

The Village Council was pulled into the movement in 1866 when they passed an ordinance making it illegal to sell intoxicating drink of any kind to a minor (no age specified) without permission of the parents. Also, no one could sell to a person in the habit of getting drunk. Violation carried a five dollar fine or one to five days in jail.

The town went "dry" closing the saloons in August of 1870 and remained that way until 1875. Then the seesaw circus began. The town was voted dry in 1883, wet in 1884, dry in 1886, but booze was OK again by 1890 with some unbelievable restrictions.

In 1890, saloons and places where liquor or beer were sold had to close by 9:00pm and on Sunday, everyone had to enter and leave by the front door and the owner was not allowed to put up, keep or maintain any shades, screens, painted or frosted glass, partitions, curtains or any kind of obstruction between the door and the bar. Also no shades or screens over the doors or windows or transoms were allowed. No boisterous, noisy or disorderly altercation, conversation, outcry or behavior was allowed including card games or gambling. Minors were not permitted to remain inside for more than five minutes. No musical, theatrical or other entertainments were permitted, nor any singing, dancing, revelry or turbulent noises. Evidently, patrons were expected to simply keep quiet and drink their beer.

The intent of the ordinances was simple. No one could sneak into a local bar or tavern through the back door and have a short snort without the temperance people noticing them. They were watching, and although those who would imbibe might be indifferent to the stares from outside, drinkers who were seen may also have had to go home and face piercing stares from across the kitchen table. There were no doubt a few of the tavern crowd who pondered the real meaning of the word "hell" from time to time.

Life was not always easy for elected officials either. In August of 1883 the Village Council and Mayor Hamilton received a petition signed by 73 voters (men) and 148 ladies asking for a vote on the question of prohibition. The ladies attended the meeting en masse and through their spokesman, Professor Jasper Wilson, they asked for the privilege of voting at the same time and place as the men (women didn't have the right to vote yet) in a separate ballot box so as to get a full expression of the ladies on the liquor question.

There must have been a heated discussion that night, for it is recorded that during the meeting Deputy Marshal Follen became "disorderly" and was brought before the Mayor and a fine of $5.00 was imposed. Then he was fired! The request was granted (what else could they do) and a month later the nonbinding vote was taken. The result was as one might guess.

At the next Council meeting it can be imagined that with a bunch of women staring down their noses at them, a resolution was offered for a Council vote on the liquor issue. They split, three in favor, three against. Mayor Hamilton had to cast the deciding ballot. With everyone watching, and at risk of losing friends (whichever way he went), he voted the town dry. Unknown is whether Mrs. Hamilton was present.

A newspaper account of the contest follows:

Of the ladies of Richland, none hate more the blighting contamination of intemperance and are more active in the effort to dethrone the hideous monster, King Alcohol, than the invincible brigade of Mrs. Col. Brown, who on election day arrayed her forces at the polls where by their logic and arts and wiles, they converted many of the sterner sex in behalf of the prohibitory amendment.

The daughter of Rev. Richard Gailey, Mrs. Mary Brown was a much respected former teacher in the Gailey Seminary. She was also a force to be reckoned with. Her husband Col. R. C. Brown, a decorated Civil War officer, receiving a $16 a month disability pension for varicose veins, may have elected to watch that battle from a safe distance.

The efforts to continue halting the sale of alcohol lasted until national prohibition set in. The last attempt to vote the town dry was in 1956. It was organized by Lexington's three churches and the Ohio Temperance League. It failed.

His Honor, The Mayor

Public service can be both rewarding and tormenting. In a small town where everybody knows everyone else, the duties of the mayor can be especially difficult. Law breakers, sometimes friends or neighbors, wind up in Mayor's Court where justice must be meted out in impartial fashion. His desk was where all the complaints, the drunks, fights, disorderly conduct, infractions of laws and rioting, as it was called, landed. He had to hear these cases and decide fines and punishment.

The position of Mayor was not always a coveted post. In 1862, William George was elected Mayor. He refused to take office or serve. How or who put his name on the ballot is unknown but his failure to take office was against the law. He was hauled into Mayor's Court and fined $2.00 by the man he was supposed to replace. In retrospect, it may have been the best $2.00 he ever spent.

Two years later in 1864 he was elected again with the same result. He refused to serve! Finally, forty-five years later in 1909, he agreed to finish the unexpired term of Mayor F. L. Williams. The reason Williams left office is not remembered, possibly work, moved, illness, verbal abuse or whatever.

In 1881 James Blair was also elected and he likewise refused to take the oath of office. He would later serve as Deputy Marshal, but that was as far as he wanted to go.

Perhaps it was a wise choice. In a twenty-year period beginning in 1884, there were 109 cases in Mayors Court. Thirty were charged with drunkenness or drunk and disorderly. Others were arrested for fighting, assault and battery, stealing, speeding with horses, and urinating on the town square. (The tavern was next to the park and Spoolman's saloon was just down the street.) And then there were the 12 tramps, rounded up by an armed posse, who went to court in one bunch.

There were also some odd cases. A barber and druggist were fined for being open on Sunday and a young man was arrested for disturbing the Negro-camp meeting near the cemetery and two more fined for stealing chickens. A B&O railroad conductor was arrested for allowing his train to block the crossing. One man was arrested for "wanton and furious driving" with horses, possibly making him the first hotrodder in old Lex.

As late as 1884 another news item reported this story:

There is a good deal of skirmishing about town in both parties for a candidate for the Mayor-ship, but up to this date none have been found that will accept that have been asked to run. Only one individual is known to want it and neither party wants him.

Fortunately for the village there were good, honest, dedicated men who served ably and willingly. Two of those men, William Earhart and Ralph Lutz, went on to serve terms in the Ohio Legislature. Dr. W. H. Wiles, lawyer George M. Fry, and quite a number of business and shop owners all willingly served their terms with distinction.

Council

Councilmen wrestled with establishing good streets and sidewalks, care and expansion of the cemetery, improving the village square and maintaining a fire department. In 1928 plans for the water works were underway followed in the 1950s with a sewer system. Seventeen acres on Plymouth St. were donated by Katherine J. Cockley. With village supervision and a good deal of donated labor a cow pasture was turned into the first village park.

In November of 1955 under the headline, "Is Lexington Expanding," Bob Snyder, editor of the *Shoppers News*, commented that 5 new homes had been completed that year and 10 acres of land owned by Rollin Cockley, Wright Armstrong and George Texter had been annexed into Lexington along Steam Corners Road. Seven new houses had been completed earlier. Snyder had no idea of what was ahead. By 1957, there were no less than 14 housing developments underway within a half mile of old Lexington.

All this took a good deal of time, effort, planning and cooperation within the Council chamber over the years by some good people.

Marshal

The post of Town Marshal wasn't always confined to keeping the peace. In the early days, they were directed to perform various duties. Town records reveal that they carried out some interesting functions.

Horses, mules, cows and hogs were rounded up by the Marshall and placed in the town impound lot on Short Street. (At times, owners had to pay to get them back.) Cows for some odd reason could roam in the day time but were supposed to be home by dark. However, hogs wandering the streets or in people's yard or garden, were an irritation and time to notify the law, day or night. It made the town look uncivilized, backward.

The Marshall was paid to bury dead dogs, oversee street and sidewalk construction and maintenance of crosswalks, which were gravel. Any problems were to be reported to Council. One summer he was ordered to notify the owner of an outhouse, which was "in a foul condition," to move it.

After the town square was fenced, inevitably somebody would leave the gate open. The result being that hungry cattle appeared to be fenced in, not out. It made the town look bad and the cows ruined the grass. So naturally, it fell to the Marshal to run the cattle off and close the gate.

The first officer of the law in town was Calvin Culver. He was elected Troy Township Constable in October of 1814. He evidently had nothing to do, as he was not paid for the twelve months he held the post. Only three of the Trustees were paid. They received only seventy-five cents each.

When Lexington was incorporated, the Marshall and deputies were appointed by the Mayor and Council. It wasn't a desirable job and could be a bit dangerous trying to break up a fight or corral a drunk. It was a low paying, part-time job but somebody had to do it.

A Tough Little Lawman

One of the toughest and best remembered early officers was Charles "Runt" Pollock. As the nickname would suggest, he was a small man. But he was tough.

In the summer of 1897 Sherm Garver and "Cub" Perry came from Galion, got drunk, raised a ruckus and were in a fighting mood. As they attempted to escape arrest reporter Al Moore filed this account:

They defied and ridiculed Marshal Charles Pollock because of his very short stature. But there is no sawdust in that valiant little officer's backbone and he attempted to take the braggarts from their buggy. They slashed the officer with their whip and got out and Perry struck

Despite his size, Charles "Runt" Pollock was one tough lawman. He is pictured here, in the Mansfield Square, 50 years after he rounded up the notorious "Lake Shore Gang."

at the officer, who in turn dealt his assailant a terrific blow on the head with his club and crawled up his long spinal column with the agility of a wild cat. He quelled the burly fellow and lodged him in the Bastille. Garver fled to the jungles when the melee with Perry began and escaped, but friends came from Galion Tuesday and paid $8.60 for his diversion from the ways of rectitude. Perry was also fined $8.60 Monday night and was released.

Three years later in the spring of 1900 the "Lake Shore Gang" hit Lexington. They stole four pair of shoes from the H. P. Maxwell Store, broke into the hardware store and Thuma's Meat Market. They also lifted other provisions from the railroad, including a half ton of coal, two coats and other items from a caboose on train #26. The gang was believed to have robbed a boxcar in Plymouth before coming to Lexington. Evidently they underestimated the town's small officer of the law.

It was time for action. Marshal "Runt" Pollock rounded up a posse consisting of Charles O'Doud, Charles Logan, William Cunningham, Charles Rusk, Nelson Castor, Melvin Blair, Charles Werrick, Albert "Poose" McNaul, B&O Detective Brooks, Deputy Sheriff Tom Bell, and a few others including young Vic Sowers. All were well armed with guns except Sowers, whom they felt wasn't "quite right." So they let him go along anyway, but only carrying an axe.

Seven members of the gang were found under the railroad bridge north of town and five more were rounded up elsewhere. There was no resistance. The coal and stolen items and provisions were recovered and all twelve were taken before Mayor Andrews.

Two of the gang were let go, on condition that they left the county and the other ten were stuffed into the town's tiny jail. They were later taken to the County Jail on the B&O, where five with previous records were sentenced to the Canton Workhouse. One "boy" was released and the rest were to leave the county.

That was a mistake as they later turned up in Willard and took a shot at Detective Brooks. He later advised anyone who saw them to "shoot first and ask questions later."

Infamous Murders

Despite what sometimes seems like an idyllic, small town atmosphere, there has been no shortage of horrific crime in the village. Two of the several murders committed here are still remembered.

In November of 1934, Jack Callender, 24, of Galion, killed his father-in-law, Claude E. West, at the intersection of Church and Frederick St. after a car chase of over 30 miles. The West car ran out of gas at that point and while arguing with Callender, West was shot with a shotgun. He died at the Mansfield Hospital. West, 41, was the father of eight children.

A young schoolgirl, Elsie Moore Simon, was an eye witness to the murder, as was Ira "Mike" Sowash and his wife. At the trial, Sheriff E. P. Long and Deputy Charlie Markley along with village Marshal Frank Linton, were also called to testify. Callender received one to twenty years in prison.

Another sad case stunned the village in June of 1959 when H. B. Penelton shot and killed Chester Chalfant. The sixty-seven-year-old Chalfant operated a Gulf Oil station at the top of the hill on Delaware Street. Penelton had just been released on parole from the Ohio State Reformatory three weeks earlier after serving a three-year term for armed robbery and burglary. He stole a car, found a gun in the glove compartment and shot Chalfant at least twice in the head after an argument over a bet on a ballgame they were watching on TV. He fled the scene and there were no eyewitnesses.

Penelton was the thirteenth child of a Mississippi tenant farmer and quit a failed school system in the fourth grade at age 11. His father died when he was 4. He married at 17, abandoned his wife and child, and eventually came to Mansfield. He had few friends and got into trouble. Penelton had been paroled to his mistress who soon deserted him. He was arrested in Mansfield driving another stolen car and still had the gun he used.

Chalfant was found by Wade Gerhart who lived on Delaware St. and police and an ambulance was summoned. He was taken to Mansfield General Hospital where he remained in critical condition and unable to speak. Lexington Marshal Calvin Fillings, Deputy Wayne Weirick and Special Deputy Emory Smith kept a 24 hour vigil at his bedside in case he regained consciousness. It was more than a week before he could communicate and then only by blinking his eyes or slightly moving his head.

Weirick recalled that when Chester was shown a photograph of Penelton and the gun he became very excited. Faced with the evidence, Penelton confessed to the murder the same day Chalfant died, exactly two weeks after the shooting.

Governor Michael V. DiSalle visited Penelton on death row. The Governor could find no reason to grant clemency, but did put some blame on the failed Ohio Parole and Rehabilitation system. Penelton died in the electric chair on March 17, 1961, the last person so executed in Ohio.

Chester Chalfant was well liked and his service station was a popular stopping point on busy Route 42. After years of fixing cars and pumping gas he was planning retirement and wanted to move to Florida. His dreadful death put the whole town on edge for a while. Wade Gerhart, the man who found Chalfant, died from a heart attack a week after the shooting.

The ordeal at the hospital was a terrible strain on the Chalfant family. But for his widow Ruth, no mere words can express the heartbreak, sorrow and the years of loneliness that followed. She lived in the big ancient red brick house on East Main Street, which she shared with son Charles' family.

She was surrounded by loving children and grandchildren. But she must have missed the love of her life, Chester, terribly. She was to be seen walking down Main Street, across the bridge and into the cemetery to stand at his grave marker on an almost daily basis. Cemetery workers would sometimes see her make the trip two or three times a day, just to stand there seemingly talking to Chester or perhaps offering a prayer. Weather permitting, Ruth Chalfant made these daily trips for nearly thirty years. She finally joined Chester in February of 1992. She was 97.

Photo courtesy of Robert Snyder Collection

The entire Lexington Police Department posed for a picture in the mid 1950s. Left to right are Marshal Ira Sowash, Deputies Carroll Lehman and Lloyd Whitney. All worked part time.

Traffic, Speeding and Road Hazards

Route 42 through town was a heavily congested highway jammed with truck traffic before the days of the interstate highway system. Heavily loaded semi trucks groaned noisily as they crawled their way up Main and Delaware streets. Coming down was a different story as brakes squealed and cars sped through the town square in all directions. It was the age of the more powerful V8 engines, the hot rods and, boy, was it fun.

However, the village fathers didn't think so. In the summer of 1956 the village bought a "speed meter" and in just two afternoons in July, 41 people were arrested for going at least 10 miles an hour over the speed limit. To that end they lowered the speed limit to 15 miles an hour on eleven side streets and all alleys. That kept Mike Sowash, the town policeman, busy with the radar unit.

The heavy traffic on 42 was a curse and a blessing, depending on whether or not you were an elected official. Many citizens thought the town a "speed trap." Council members up for reelection in 1956 published this explanation in the local paper:

Few thinking people would deny that Rt. 42 is a dangerous and constant menace to our children. Now what has been done with the money from our traffic convictions:

  Streets have been paved or revamped,
  Storm sewers have been installed.
  Street lights have been extended.
  A village dump established.
  A new village garage is being built.

Most of this money has been derived from our traffic court, for Lexington is one of the few villages around that has no operating levy. This is money saved for the local tax payers.

And so the cycle began. Between January 1952 and November of 1957 there were 2,060 court cases, which netted the village $18,081 (in addition to what was paid to the county and state) during Mayor Lowell McIntire's time in office. He stated this was equal to a 1½ mill tax levy.

The railroad crossing at the foot of Main St. was a big surprise for speeders. The main line had been raised but not the side track. And this resulted in a ski jump effect going down and an axle breaker for trucks going up. Bumper marks in the pavement and flying hub caps were a common sight.

In 1956 petitions were circulated requesting that suitable action be taken to "provide supplementary highway facilities to relieve the dangerous and steadily increasing traffic congestion on US 42." A few years would pass before Interstate 71 would be built and the heavy traffic would leave.

Dark Period

However, the village police couldn't part with the radar

equipment and by the 1970s and 80s they turned the town into a qualified speed trap. The mayor and council seemingly had their heads in the sand and it appeared to many persons that the Lexington Police Department was running the town.

A staff of underpaid, poorly trained officers had little to do except drive around town and run the radar. So they kept the Mayor's Court full. West Main seemed to be their favorite haunt, until some unknown hero went to the State Department of Highways and lodged a complaint. The result was the raising of the speed limit and the speed trap was partially shut down.

During this period, a number of officers and chiefs were either fired or forced to resign because of misconduct or breaking the law themselves. The department managed to be as much an embarrassment as an asset to the community. It was a dark period.

One clear exception to this sentiment was Officer Raymond Kinton. Ray suffered from a slight speech impediment, but did an excellent job. As a lifelong resident of Lexington, he knew just about everybody in town. Ray was judged by the writer to have the most common sense of any officer of his day. He was the exception and served with distinction for over 15 years. In the department's turbulent years he had the respect of those who knew him. It was something not always attainable by his fellow officers.

Back to the 50s

Mike Sowash was one of the well remembered town policemen in the 1950s. He was only part time, used his own Chevy as a cruiser and also had a trash collection business. Unfortunately he was abused and tormented by the village teenagers for a number of years. His property was vandalized on occasion.

Finally, one night around Halloween Sowash caught a vandal in the act. He shot sixteen year old Micheal Smaltz in the back end with a shotgun. The village was sued for $75,000. Sowash lost his job over the incident. (The truth is there were others who deserved a shot in the rear, including the writer.)

Sowash gone, the next officer hired was Calvin Fillings, a no-nonsense trained policeman from a New England city. He had excellent qualifications and impressed everyone, even the teenagers, with his approach to the job. He was paid $135 a month and used his own car until 1958, when the village finally bought its first cruiser, a four-year-old used Ford. By that time Fillings had a paid deputy, Wayne Weirick, and was making $400 a month.

After that, police officers came and went mostly due to poor wages or better opportunities elsewhere. Some were better than others. As mentioned earlier, a few should never have been hired.

The Girl Scouts march on Memorial Day. The town's first police cruiser, a used 1954 Ford, is seen on the left. It may have been checking their speed with radar.

The Dollar Kodak

That's about all the camera cost shortly before 1900, just a dollar or so. The film was extra. It was a black rectangular box with a viewer and lenses in the end. It was a simple thing, easy to operate.

Sid Earhart had one. He grew up in Lexington and knew just about everybody. Sid ran a pool room at one time, while the town was dry, and took a few pictures once in awhile.

In December of 1964 the writer interviewed Sid and his wife Myrtle at their home in Mansfield, at which time he loaned me a number of old photographs to be copied. He provided a wealth of information on Lexington and the people and events in the area shortly after the turn of the century. The pictures were a treasure.

Some weeks later I returned the loaned material and we talked about the pictures and finally discussed the camera he used. While I was there he excused himself for a few moments and when he returned he was carrying what he called his "dollar Kodak." It was a delight to see the camera that made those great old photographs, and as it was examined I noticed that it still had film in it, set for exposure number seven. I commented on the fact and was surprised he still used the old Kodak.

Then Sid told the story.

His son had been drafted into the army in 1943 during World War II. Before he left for service Sid put a new roll of film in the old Kodak and pictures were taken of the son and family. One can imagine that the same thought ran through mind of both the photographer and the subject. There were those who never came back from that terrible war and others who came back but somehow were never the same. The camera would record that unhappy occasion in their lives. Just in case he didn't come back.

But the Earharts' were lucky. After the war their son did return home. He was alright. And Sid, in a somewhat quiet voice, commented that someday he was going to finish that 1943 roll of film and get it developed. "We just don't take many pictures anymore," he quietly commented.

Sid and Myrtle are gone now. So is the son. I've always wondered what happened to the old Kodak. Could it be on some dusty shelf or closet somewhere still ready for exposure number seven?

Some of the scenes it recorded are in this book. They are to be found nowhere else.

Left to Right: Bill Castor, Sid Earhart and Ralph Lutz on Memorial Day 1971. Castor had four sons in World War II. Earhart owned the "Dollar Kodak" and knew a lot of our local characters and history. Lutz was always a strong community leader.

Fires, Floods, and Wrecks

Fires

The danger of fire and the destruction of life and property gained the attention of the village fathers at an early time. As the town grew, so did the possibility of serious conflagrations. The town was full of wooden buildings with wood shingle roofs. Ashes from stoves and fireplaces were often stored outside in wooden barrels. Defective chimneys were another peril. The whole town was a fire hazard.

In 1857, the village fathers appropriated $18 "for hooks and ladders for use of the corporation in case of fire." Not much was done, however, until the following year when Peter Englehart, a local store keeper, was appointed to find or furnish iron for making hooks. David Stough, the local blacksmith, was paid $11.00 for making chains, hooks and ironing ladders. Then in August of 1858, the village bought an old buggy for $10 and spent another $10 converting it into the town's first fire wagon. It was equipped with a number of buckets, two 16-foot-slide ladders, a 12-foot and a 16-foot standard ladder and one axe. The total expense was less than $100 and, there being no town hall, it was kept in a rented barn.

The fire equipment was presented to the newly formed "Hook and Ladder Company Number One of Lexington" in the summer of 1858. The new organization was to meet and drill on a regular basis under supervision of council. The plan looked good on paper – as long as the paper didn't burn.

Many fires were started by sparks falling on the wood shingle roofs in dry weather. Fires were difficult to fight with bucket brigades. So chains and hooks were used to simply tear burning shingles off the structure or sometimes tear structures down to prevent fire from spreading to adjacent buildings.

Things went along pretty well for a while, but over the years interest waned. One might guess the fire drills were held around a beer keg with more conversation than practice. And there were other problems. Some folks must have figured that since their tax money bought the equipment, it was alright to take a few buckets or borrow the ladders to fix their roof or whatever. The borrowed items were not always returned with any degree of promptness and the fire boys often had to hunt around town for their equipment.

In September of 1879 it was reported to the village officials that the Fire Department "had gone down" and the fire boys had SOLD the wagon, ladders and equipment! This news struck the village fathers like a bolt of lightning. Enraged, they planned legal action against the former firemen. However, a check of the town records revealed that the council and the mayor had given the equipment to the firemen. So it was their property to use or sell as they pleased. There must have been some tight jaws when the village officials left the meeting that night.

As for Mayor Abernathy, all he could do was growl and complain. The bridge over the Clear Fork had been out for two years, they had to fence the four sections of the town square to keep the blasted cows out, the temperance people wanted to dry up the saloons and now the fire department vanished. It must have seemed that the whole village of Lexington was going to hell. Abernathy decided one term as mayor was enough, thank you very much.

Another effort to reestablish the fire department was made, but it was reported in 1881 that "no organization or engine" existed. James Blair was elected mayor that year and refused to take office. Perhaps he saw the handwriting on the wall. Maybe it was politics. Or did he smell smoke? No reason is recorded.

Lawyer G. M. Fry was appointed to the post. As early as 1876 he had advocated passing a tax for buying an engine and building a station but nothing was ever done. With no serious fires, complacency had set in.

All that came home to roost on Sunday morning July 12, 1885. The Mansfield Herald carried this account:

The little village of Lexington was early Sunday morning visited by a conflagration, the largest ever seen there. At about half past one fire was discovered in the second story of the building occupied by Maxwell and Shauck, as a bakery and provision store. A general alarm was given and all the bells in the village were rung. The citizens all turned out and formed a bucket brigade and went to work to quell the flames. The fire spread very quickly and as the fire equipment of the little village was exceedingly limited, all efforts proved futile.

Every building on the south side of West Main Street burned in 1885. Only the brick Sowers building was left, although it was damaged as well.

A telegram was sent here (Mansfield) for our fire department and they responded very quickly, but as there was no locomotive here on the B&O that could be used, considerable time was consumed waiting on a north bound freight train, and after it reached here it started for the scene with one flat car and our fire department. They made the run of nine miles in eight minutes, which was indeed a remarkably fast time. When the department arrived there it was too late to be of much service, as the whole block had been destroyed. . . . Everything looked bad, as scarcely anything was gotten out of the burning buildings.

The entire block on the south side of West Main Street from the square west to present day "Deckers" was a total loss. The only building left standing was the brick building of George M. and Bloomer Sowers that today houses part of Kell Hardware and it was damaged from the heat and smoke. Sowers also lost another small brick building out back, as well as the baker's shop.

It was agreed that had the town owned a suitable fire engine or equipment the destruction could have ended at the hardware store. Two fire cisterns had been built a year earlier, one at the Congregational Church and another in the southwest corner of the public square. They were 12 feet in diameter, 12 to 16 feet deep and lined with brick.

The town did surprisingly little to improve its fire fighting capabilities after the Main Street disaster. They did appoint "fire wardens" to keep watch over designated areas of town. There were chimney and stove pipe inspections and ashes were to be stored away from buildings. However, little attention was paid to purchasing fire equipment even after the old Cook Tavern and the house next door burned in 1899, or when the Sowers grain warehouse at the foot of Church Street was lost in 1905.

In December of 1907, Fry's three story frame candy factory burned to the ground in another huge fire. A little candy, records and other office supplies were saved but lack of equipment left the firemen helpless. Two extinguishers and a bucket brigade could do little. Old-timers were to recall that most folks stood around and ate caramel candy while watching the destruction. Rats ran out "by the hundreds" and more than few people were sick the next day from eating so much. A news reporter called for fire fighting equipment. However, again nothing was done.

The village leaders did little to embrace the expansion of the town's fire fighting capabilities until 1914. On July 29, two young girls, Beva Craig and girl friend Barbara Logan were heating paraffin on a stove when it caught fire. The parents were away and the Craig girl had to run all the way down to the square to find anyone to summon help. By the time firemen arrived the house was in flames and it and the house next door burned to the ground and a third house owned by D. K. Andrews had its roof set on fire, but it was saved. For a while it appeared the new Church of Christ building next to the Craig home might also catch fire, but a bucket brigade was able to save it. A call to Mansfield for help brought only the fire chief and a minister by automobile. It would appear the town got the message. Get your own equipment!

The potential loss of their building must have scared the hell out of the members of the Church of Christ and a lot of other folks too. A citizen supported petition was presented to council at their next meeting requesting immediate steps be undertaken to provide the village with adequate fire fighting apparatus. To that end a committee of six was appointed to quickly investigate the request. And in August 1914, the town finally bought a hand pump fire wagon from the Howe Engine Co. of Indianapolis, Indiana, for $498.00. (Freight was another $6.37 when it was delivered a couple of months later.) The village had to issue $400 in bonds to pay for this equipment.

Harry Smith, C. E. Bliven, and William Wages were appointed to "look after the equipment and effect the organization of a fire department." Harvey Dial was named chief. The "bell system" was still to be used for alarms, probably from the Presbyterian or Congregational churches. At long last, the new firemen would have something to play with, something that would squirt water from the onboard tank (as there was no public water system).

A used hose cart from the City of Barberton was picked up for another $15.00. The equipment was stored in a one car garage in the basement of the new town hall. Even though more progressive communities were using steam or gasoline powered equipment at the time, at least (at long last), it was a step in the right direction.

In January of 1917, the Cockley Milling Company caught fire. The fire was discovered at 1:00 AM by employees of the Smith Gas Engine plant and men on the B&O Railroad. A newspaper account gives these details:

When first seen the flames were at the north end of the mill on the second floor and had gained considerable headway. Villagers with a hand engine proved unequal to the task of fighting the flames and with a hose that did not reach from the nearest water tap to the scene of the fire were powerless to save any portion of the building. The main building of the Cockley plant was of brick, four stories high and about 60 by 300 feet. A second building that almost adjoined was two stories high and 100 feet long by 60 feet wide.

The second building contained the cooper shop, barrel shop and some ware rooms. The main building was fitted with modern machinery some of which had just been installed and was not in complete operation.... Lost were 15 to 20 thousand bushels of wheat, one railcar load of clover seed, two car loads of timothy seed in addition to a large quantity of flour and feed.

The Howe Fire Wagon would have been pulled by hand down Main to Walnut Street to the mill site along the railroad. A stiff wind from the south fanned the flames and when two floors on the main building fell in the walls followed. People as far away as Mansfield could see the light from the fire in the night sky. The principal owner of the mill, A. B. Beverstock, was out of town at a health resort when the fire struck. The loss was estimated at $200,000 by H. H. Phelps, who was managing the plant at the time. The mill was partially covered by insurance.

The next major fire was on August 11, 1929. Once again complacency had set in and the village was ill equipped to handle the situation. Two young boys walking home saw smoke coming from Maxwell's garage on the north side of West Main Street.

Again, a newspaper account tells the story best:

Lack of water facilities accounted for the huge loss, Mansfield firemen, who were summoned to the nearby village, said Monday. With ample water pressure the blaze would have been confined to the garage where the devastating fire is believed to have started.

An August 1929 fire wiped out the north side of West Main Street. Among businesses lost was the Ford and Studebaker dealership. Before and after scenes are shown.

The heat from the fire broke windows across the street, damaged buildings and by 7:00am, Sunday morning nearly half of the town's business district was a smoldering mass.

This fire put greater emphasis on a village water system, which was finally finished with WPA labor sometime around 1934. It always seemed to take a major fire to move things along.

The hand pulled fire wagon looked a bit outdated and antique after the water system and fire hydrants were finished. So, sometime around 1936 or '37, the town bought a pickup truck chassis and added a homemade body of their own design. This proved to be their undoing as several engineering principles were ignored. When three or four good sized men got on the back, the front wheels would lift off the ground. Ted Welch, former fireman and mayor of Lexington, once recalled that many were the times they left the station with the front wheels in the air.

Low water pressure at the top of the hill on Delaware Street and other factors prompted the firemen to do a little horse trading with Ashland. They traded the wheels-in-the-air pickup for a real vintage fire truck with a pump As near as any of the old-timer firemen remembered, it was a 1917 Packard truck with right hand drive, open cab, a big search light, brass radiator, solid rubber wheels, chain drive and an 'impulse" starter. Perhaps the folks at Ashland smiled as it left town for the last time.

The starter was the weak point. Responding to an alarm with the Packard was often a three pronged effort. First, they tried the impulse starter and if the engine didn't come to life on the first try, the second effort involved hand cranking the huge engine. If that failed after a few turns, then go to the fire without the darn thing.

The writer was an eyewitness to one of these failures and watched with wide-eyed amazement as Irwin "Butch" Castor drove his 1928 Reo sedan up to the station door and several men threw rolls of hose, nozzles, hydrant wrench and an axe in the back seat, jumped on the running boards and away they went with "Butch" to the fire. If there was enough manpower available, someone stayed behind to coax the Packard back to life. "Butch" Castor and Harry Linton were reportedly the only two firemen that had any kind of luck starting the old girl. Mechanical expertise or knowing the right cuss words may have been their secret.

In 1939, the large livestock auction barn on Plymouth Street burned. At the time it was run by three men. Raymond Mentzer hauled livestock, Bill Hirth handled

Lawrence Kunkle (left) and John Welch are shown (in 1963) with Lexington's first fire engine and the newest of that day, a 1957 Ford Seagrave pumper. Unfortunately, both pieces of equipment were lost when the Fire Fighter's Club couldn't raise the funds to buy them for use as parade units. In 1963, Welch was the longest-serving charter member of the Fire Department.

the business end, and a Mr. France was the auctioneer. The barn had been built in the 1880s by a cooperative that later went broke.

Not all fires were big, most were just a single house or barn. However, a few are memorable. On a below zero New Year's night in 1941, the big garage behind Snyder's Funeral Home caught fire. The old Packard had an impulse to start that night (maybe "Butch" or Harry got to it first) and it came thundering up Delaware Street. However, when they arrived on the scene the fire hydrant was frozen.

Firewood and hot coals were pulled from Glen Myers' furnace, across the street, to try to thaw the hydrant. Fearing the funeral home might catch fire, neighbors Paul Schindler and Jess McIntire, along with young Bob Snyder, started emptying the contents of the second floor. Finally, the hydrant opened, the water flowed, the Packard roared into action and, although by then garage was a total loss, the funeral home was saved. Dawn on the first day of the New Year brought an unusual sight. Next door to the smoldering ruins was Paul Schindler's backyard full of caskets.

The Lexington Soy Products (oil process) fire.

The struggle with the antiquated Packard lasted until shortly after World War II when Ralph Lutz, the local lumber dealer, was instrumental in securing a 1942 Air Force surplus fire truck. The cost was $2,576 and the money was raised by public subscription, donations, collecting sales tax stamps and bake sales. The *Mansfield News Journal* reported at the time, "There's something admirable about the way Lexington handled the matter of getting themselves a new fire truck, and the way a group of volunteers is willing to fight fire at any time."

The truck was pretty well beat up and painted olive drab when it arrived. Maurice "Boots" Garverick, who ran a local welding shop, volunteered to do the body work on it with George Clever and Bob Snyder doing the painting in Snyder's rebuilt garage. It's remembered the paint fumes got so heavy they both felt a little drunk. The town council bought the paint. Chief Joe Maple and the rest of the volunteers worked hard and must have been proud of the community support and confidence placed in them.

Another notable event took place in March of 1956. The old stone house north of town on the Lexington-Springmill Road caught fire. Built in 1843 by James R. Gass, it had been the home of George Clever from 1890 until his son Lloyd bought it in 1927. In 1950, Dr. Ritchie of Mansfield bought the place and remodeled it.

No one was home when the fire started. So when one passerby noticed the smoke, another dashed to town to start the fire siren on the old town hall. The Lexington department responded and a short time later a fire truck all the way from Springfield Township arrived. The house was badly damaged but saved well enough to permit rebuilding.

There was kind of a stink over this at the next village council meeting. Some Councilmen complained that the Lexington Fire Department should only serve Lexington, and not Troy Township, since the township did not provide financial support. The fact that the town was unprotected while the firemen were outside the village was also raised. There was also a small degree of embarrassment as it was realized that Springfield Township, with a tiny crossroads called Ontario, had a department (this was before GM and the Richland Mall) and so did Washington Township, with no village at all. Once again it took a fire to move things along.

After a protracted debate over where to build the new fire station, a new truck arrived in 1957. The result grew into the present-day Troy Township Lexington

The 1942 Air Force Surplus Fire truck was in semi-retirement when the kids took over at the firemen's picnic in 1965.

Fire Dept., which ably serves the area with fire, rescue, and ambulance service from a well-equipped station. Joe Maple and Ed Wilson were early chiefs. Richard M. Carter served as chief for 40 years, retiring in 2002. And willing volunteers, too numerous to mention, also have many long years of dedicated service. We owe them a lot.

Floods

The worst flood to hit the area was the fabled flood of 1913. A heavy rain on frozen ground in March sent the Clear Fork into a raging torrent with homes and farms being inundated as water reached record levels.

Lexington was on high enough ground and suffered little damage, except for the bridge on East Main Street. The structure had a troubled past and apparently one support abutment had settled slightly. The heavy stone abutments had been laid on a vein of gravel that runs through the Clear Fork valley and may have simply collapsed when the swift water undercut them.

The March 13, 1913 flood was photographed by Harry Linton. The small building in the front is the railroad privy. In the background is the station.

In 1913, John Satterfield's duck hunting boat was brought by train from Alta and used as a temporary ferry after the bridge washed out. In this photo, Engineer Jack Cline is on his way to work on the west side of the river. Cline worked on the helper locomotive.

Photo courtesy of Harry Linton Collection

A temporary log bridge was built March 29, 1913. Several similar temporary bridges washed away over the years.

Onetime Lexington Marshal Ira "Mike" Sowash recalled that as a kid he and another boy were playing on the bridge when someone in a crowd yelled for them to get off. They no more than reached the ground when "the bridge just rolled over and went down." The last man over the structure was carrying a sack of flour. As he reached the east side, he set it down to rest and heard a rumbling behind him. He had just made it across!

When the water receded a few days later, John Satterfield, who had been the telegraph operator for the B&O station at Alta, brought his duck hunting boat to town. It was brought down by train and a rope was rigged across the Clear Fork to enable Jack Cline, an engineer on the helper locomotive, to get to work. Cline lived in the brick house on the corner of Castor Road and his job was across the river. Others needed help crossing the river too.

On March 29, a group of folks drug heavy logs across the stream and built a temporary bridge. It was needed for two funerals that had been delayed with no way to get to the cemetery. The new route over the stream was down the town gravel pit drive next to the cemetery, cross the temporary bridge and back up the drive that led to the old grist mill. It was a fun crossing on a dark night.

The flood of 1959 and the blizzard of 1978 did little damage. To be sure folks complained, but the Lexington area people are a resilient lot. They just pick themselves up and go on with living and make the best of it. That's what Amariah Watson and our forefathers did.

Wrecks

The main road from Mansfield to Delaware and Columbus passed through Lexington and that was a good thing. Good for business and travel. The way it passed through was not. The nearly 45 degree turn at the bottom of the hill on Delaware Street has been the scene of countless accidents since the age of the automobile and trucks. It started in the 1920s and continues to this day. Remarkably, the writer is not aware of anyone losing their life. However, many were injured at that corner, some severely.

The granddaddy of all these occurred on November 28, 1958, when a semi truckload of roofing materials came down the snow covered hill, went through the guard rail, narrowly missed two big trees, knocked the corner off the Lexian Restaurant, hit nine cars and went through the west wall of Fisher's Mobile station before it came to rest.

Jim McLaughlin, an employee of the station, saw the truck coming and shouted a warning while he managed to get out of the way. Paul Fisher, manager of the station and Harry LeClair were slightly injured as was the truck driver. By some miracle, no one was killed. Cars belonging to Loren Welch, Robert Scott, Robert Canterbury, Leland Bucklew, Alvin Rinehart, Ed Miller, and Lee McIntire were damaged, some heavily.

Fisher's new Ford Convertible was hit broadside and driven through a cement block wall. Harry LeClair's Ford was rammed against a raised lift rack inside and both cars were only about a foot or so wide in places. Later they were kidded about having the first compact Fords in town.

The Lexian lost the corner of its building and the station wall had to be rebuilt. After that folks were a little nervous about where to park in bad weather.

A number of other wrecks are detailed below. Sometimes pictures are better than words.

A Mayflower moving van missed the bridge in the 1920s. School was let out early so the kids could see the wreck.

Photo courtesy of Robert Synder Collection

The grand slam of all West Main and Delaware Street accidents occurred in 1959, when a semi went through the guard rail, between two trees, took the corner off the Lexian Restaurant, smashed several cars and buried itself in the Mobile station.

Francis Green, of Green's Hatchery on Castor Road, shows a Highway Patrolman the damage to his hatchery building. The car had jumped a four-foot embankment, skidded 200 feet across his lawn, hit a tree and then smashed into his building. Green was working 5 feet inside, at an incubator that held 2000 eggs. Quite a few were broken. 1958 Buicks were tough cars. Woman driver.

Mobilgas Special was 27 cents a gallon when this truck rolled into Whitney's service station in July 1951. The fire was put out quickly – as was the driver.

In 1956 a homemade peanut-popcorn truck managed to hit a car and power pole before it disintegrated in front of Hiser's Sandwich Bar. The driver was badly hurt.

Whiskey and Plenty of It

Flour, salt, and whiskey were three staples that were necessary on the frontier. The importance of the latter has usually been downplayed in the old county history books, which were written in the late 1800's during the temperance movement. However, the manufacture and sale of whiskey was considered an important part of the pioneer economy and it was a social requirement in nearly all frontier homes.

Whiskey was the refreshment, the pain reliever and key ingredient in most home remedies. Most churches had not taken a strong stand against its use. In fact, the first meetings of Troy Presbyterian Church (a mile or so west of Lexington) were held in the shed house of Ichabod Clark's distillery.

When the forest was cleared and crops planted, distilleries sprang up as soon as water powered grist mills began grinding the grain. It was easier to haul a barrel of whiskey to eastern markets than a load of corn and it could be readily sold or bartered. So making whiskey was the thing to do.

Richland County had its share of distilleries. The 1832 Auditors tax records shed some light on the subject and indicate there were 34 distilleries in operation that year.

It must be remembered that "Old Richland" was nearly thirty miles square and took in parts of what is now Ashland, Morrow and Crawford counties. However, it is also true that the tax records only list fulltime distilling operations. And numerous smaller, part-time stills (able to serve a limited clientele or family) were not taxed. The previously mentioned Watson and Bell Tavern distillery is an example of one such small operation. If those smaller operations were included, that would push the county's total number of stills much higher.

Troy Township had a least three. Sterling Graves, Amariah Watson's son-in-law, had a mill and distillery located a mile north of town along the Clear Fork near Cockley Road. The distillery of Christian Klink was two miles south of town on Mill Run Road. Ichabod Clark also had a water powered gristmill, sawmill, and a distillery (where the Presbyterians met) near the present-day corner of State Route 97 and Gass Road.

Washington Township, home of the alleged rowdy bunch, had four. Springfield and Perry townships each had one. And there was the fabled distillery at Jugs Corners in Troy Township, Morrow County, where customers often left their jugs to be filled at the end of a long muddy lane. It was on the southwest corner of Ross and Steam Corners roads.

Making good old corn liquor was a regular rural necessity until the Sandusky, Mansfield and Newark Railroad

Photograph courtesy of Sid Earhart Collection

In 1915, the Railroad's train #16 made regular deliveries of beer to a "dry" Lexington. Jack Cline (standing) and "Buzz" Galbraith pose with 35 cases of beer from Hulbner Brewing of Toledo. The town never was really dry.

was completed through Lexington in 1851. At that point large commercial distilleries, such as Henry Smith's at Newark and the Harkness 600 bushel a day distillery at Monroeville, shipped whiskey in by rail. During the 1850s, Henry Smith was shipping over 4,000 barrels a year north on the SM&N. This put small operators out of business.

During the same period, the large German population living in Sandusky developed several good sized breweries to satisfy the local thirst. Philip Dauch and Vincenz Fox each ran a brewery. The Phoenix Brewery advertised the best beer this side of Philadelphia. The net result was the railroad hauling beer south from Sandusky and Smith's whiskey north from Newark. All of this beer and whiskey didn't make the whole trip north or south. A good deal of it was unloaded here.

Records of the Englehart General Store in Lexington indicate that during one 13-month period, beginning in 1855, Peter Englehart bought the following for resale at his store on Main Street: 1,300 gallons of whiskey (32 barrels at 40½ gallons each), 48 barrels of Lager beer, 12 barrels regular beer, 14 barrels stock ale, 1,800 bottles of Sasafrila beer and a small quantity of Bourbon whiskey. A limited quantity of wine came from the Lake Erie Islands. It all arrived at the railroad station.

Whiskey, which retailed from 15 to 20 cents a gallon after the War of 1812, could still be purchased in quantity (by the barrel) by Englehart for 30 cents a gallon in 1855. At that time, bourbon cost 95 cents a gallon and beer was $5.00 to $8.00 per barrel (depending on type). Sasafrilia sold for 38 cents for a dozen bottles and there was a 50 cent charge for the 40 ½ gallon wooden barrels. All items were sold at a 25% mark up. Englehart ran a general store, not a saloon. He filled their jugs, buckets, or whatever and they lugged it home. He supplied the local taverns and bars as well.

This old tile building was built as a saloon by the Ferrow Bros. The town dry, it was used as a pool room, Hardware storage and later housed Mason's Refrigeration. Mason kept 2 live polar bears as a tourist attraction. Sadly the bears did not thrive in the basement display and had to be destroyed. The building was torn down around 1974.

What became of nearly 5,000 gallons of whiskey and beer in a town with a population of roughly 400 men, women and children? In the late 1960s the writer put that question to nearly 80-year-old former pool room operator Sid Earhart. He rubbed his chin, looked up to the ceiling and speculated that riff-raff from Bellville and Johnsville came in and drank it all. There was no evidence to support his theory.

The Englehart General Store sold vast amounts of whiskey and beer. The store was in the right side of this building, built in 1843. (Its located on the north side of East Main St.)

The last of the local distilleries was located in current Waterford, in northern Knox Cnty. Waterford was known as Leverings at that time. This ad is from the Nov. 4, 1886 edition of the Mt. Vernon Banner.

The last of the small rural distilleries was located near Waterford, south of Lexington just over the Knox County line. In 1886, that operation (Bigbee & VanBuskirk) advertised "Pure Copper Distilled Rye Whiskey." Some claimed the unadulterated small-still whiskey was better than the mass manufactured item. Either way, more than a few of Lexington's elbow benders made the buggy trip to rural Waterford (known as Leverings at one time).

In 1873 alone, the Ohio State Liquor and Brewers Assoc. estimated that Ohio had produced 900,000 barrels of beer and 20,000,000 gallons of whiskey. It ranked fourth in the nation in alcohol production.

It would appear that no one living in, or just visiting, the Lexington area ever went to bed thirsty. Even in the days of the Temperance Movement, when the town was "dry", folks simply ordered their favorite drink from out-of-town, picked it up at the rail station and took it home.

The drunkenness, misery, poverty, broken homes, and ruined careers caused by those who drank to excess took a heavy toll on the lives of many families. It often spilled over from one generation to the next. What was then called rioting (fights and property destruction) kept the village police busy.

A Lexington item in the July 13, 1859, edition of the *Mansfield Herald* commented: *The demon of intemperance is again at work in our midst and our village was witness to some of the most disgusting scenes in a civilized community. How long will these things last?*

The temperance people had their work cut out for them. It was an endless struggle. During prohibition when the whole country (including Lexington) was supposedly dry, a little bootlegging was going on.

Neighbors noticed quite a few cars stopping at John Satterfield's house on East Main. Orchard Park was another oddly popular stop. Roy Swigart also bottled some "stuff" in the back of his pool hall.

Some folks by the name of Tanley had a restaurant on West Main during this time. They also ran a "speak easy" out in the country near Steam Corners. The bar was kept quiet, until the day a driver tried to deliver a keg of beer to the restaurant by mistake.

There were no doubt a few other sources of alcohol in those "dry" days.

Photograph courtesy of Sid Earhart Collection

There wasn't much to smile about at "The Club" in 1913, while the town was dry. Pictured are (L to R): Walter Walker, Clarence Shingler, Jim Collins, Cliff Culp, Harold Boyce, Charles Markley, Morris Richie, William Lutz, Roy Swigart and Sid Earhart.

The Railroad

There was a serious financial problem facing the farmers of the Lexington area in the early 1800s. They cleared the land, planted crops and the surplus beyond their needs could be sold for additional family income. The problem was that no local market existed for these surplus crops. Nearly everyone had farm produce to sell, but the cash market was in eastern cities. And farmers needed cash to pay taxes and buy manufactured goods.

Solutions, But No Answers

There were several ways to solve this problem, none of them good. The most popular solution was usually four horse teams pulling wagons sixty miles north to Milan or Sandusky. There the grain, flour, pork, whiskey and so on could be shipped across Lake Erie to Buffalo and down the Erie Canal to New York or other eastern cities. No road as such existed between Lexington and Milan or Sandusky, and the wheel-breaking, rutted, mud-filled path generally limited teams to ten or twelve miles a day in good weather. It was tough going.

Then there was the option of going overland, east to Pittsburgh. It was hilly country and the trip could take nearly a month. The trip back could bring a load of iron or manufactured goods, but it was also a rugged trip.

The Ohio and Erie Canal had opened from Cleveland through Akron, New Philadelphia and on to Newark in the summer of 1830. This was a great asset to people in the eastern part of the state and those living in the vicinity of Newark. But for folks in Richland County and the Lexington area it was still sixty miles to either Newark or Lake Erie.

In the early 1830's a canal extension was proposed from Bolivar on the Tuscarawas to Lexington. This would have turned old Lex into a canal town. A survey was actually made by Col. Curtis of Mt. Vernon (a graduate of West Point Military College), but it was found that the area from Lexington to just below Perrysville was just too hilly and the project was abandoned.

Finally, An Answer

The answer was a railroad. The first rails south started at Sandusky and ended at Monroeville. The Sandusky & Monroeville Railroad opened in September of 1838. It was built almost entirely of wood with wooden rails that had a steel strap nailed to the top. The four wheeled open top cars with a tarp cover were pulled by tandem hitched horses. A primitive passenger car had also been fabricated and the 12.8-mile trip took 2½ hours. Freight cars took longer. A siding at the halfway point allowed for cars to pass and a change of horses.

However, the Sandusky & Monroeville line was a financial failure and only lasted 38 months. At the end, 24 of the horses could still pull cars, eight had been killed and the other six had been sold.

Investors in Richland County then hatched a plan for a railroad north to New Haven, a bustling business town at that time. The opportunity to connect the gap between this proposed line to New Haven and the existing Monroeville to Sandusky line could not be missed.

The State of Ohio agreed and sold the bankrupt Sandusky & Monroeville line to this proposed, but un-built, Mansfield & New Haven Railroad Company for the sum of $33,333.33 in stock. The new combined company was to be named the Mansfield and Sandusky City Railroad.

Stock sales for the new railroad went well and construction on the section between Monroeville and Mansfield began in 1844. However, a deep cut at Plymouth delayed completion. The old Sandusky to Monroeville section also had to be entirely rebuilt.

The First Steam Engine

As a result of those delays, the road's first locomotive, the "Mansfield," did not arrive in Mansfield until May 16, 1846. A large crowd was on hand for the arrival of this first steam engine and a few Lexington folks would have been there to view its arrival. Most had never seen a steam locomotive and when the engineer blew the whistle, it scared a good many people. Several women fainted as horses reared and dogs barked. A few men might have wet their pants.

The first engine was a simple nine-ton, single driver, open cab unit from Rogers, Ketchum & Grosvenor. It arrived at Sandusky Harbor by sailing ship. More would be needed for the new railroad. A story in the

The SM&N locomotive "Lexington" was one of seven Rogers engines bought in 1851. The "Independence" (pictured here) was very similar to the Lexington and each cost $15,384.

July 14, 1846, edition of the *Sandusky Clarion* relates the following:

Another new Locomotive from the manufactory of Rogers, Ketchum & Grovesnor, Patterson New Jersey, arrived on the brig Columbia, some days since, for the Mansfield and Sandusky City Rail-Road Company. It is about the same size as the "Mansfield" and is called the "Knox." The company now has four locomotives; the two mentioned above, the "Empire" and "Vigilance."

These engines had to be shipped on the Erie Canal to Buffalo and reloaded onto sailing ships for the trip across Lake Erie to Sandusky. There was no other way to get them there. Unloading them off the ship must have been interesting.

The prospects of a rapid business growth in Richland County spurred interest in Knox and Licking counties to the south, where plans for a railroad of their own were afoot. To the people in Newark, who already had a canal, came the realization that rail transportation was much faster and could operate year around. (Canals were shut down from December to April.) A bond issue was passed in Licking County and investors bought stock in the proposed "Columbus and Lake Erie Railroad." Construction of the new venture started at both ends, Mansfield and Newark in 1847.

The rails south reached Lexington in June of 1847, and what a sight that must have been. The tracks came alongside the grist and sawmill on the Clear Fork and right past the Sowers grain warehouse east of Mill Street. A small corner of the Sowers warehouse became the first railroad station.

A New Era of Prosperity

The prospect of taking a train from Lexington to Sandusky and arriving in five hours must have been astounding. Once there, one could take a lake-steamer or brig to Detroit, Cleveland, or Buffalo and points east. The business, freight, and passenger prospects in Lexington were enough to boggle the imagination.

MANSFIELD AND SANDUSKY CITY RAIL-ROAD.

NEW ARRANGEMENT.
THROUGH TO BELLVILLE.

FROM and after this date the Express train will leave Sandusky at 8 o'clock A. M., Mansfield at 12 M., arriving at Bellville at half past 12. Returning, leave Bellville at half past 2 o'clock P. M., Mansfield half past 3, and arrive at Sandusky at 7 o'clock P. M., connecting with the evening line of first class steamers for Buffalo.

Passengers going south by this route can take stages at Bellville on arrival of the cars, for Mt. Vernon, Newark, Lancaster, Zanesville and Columbus, arriving at these towns the same day, reaching Columbus early in the evening, forming the quickest and cheapest route to any of the above places. Fourteen miles of the road (from Mansfield to Bellville) is laid with T rail, and forms part of the Columbus & Lake Erie Rail Road. The company expect to complete this road to Newark by the 1st of October next, 60 miles from Mansfield, and 116 miles from Sandusky. Sixteen miles from Newark, north, is already completed and carrying passengers.

J. R. ROBINSON, Sup't.
Sandusky, Aug. 21, 1850.

Large quantities of wheat, corn, flour, pork, beef and wool went north from the area along with a wide variety of other farm products. It was a good time for business. The farmers now had money to spend in town and manufactured merchandise arrived at a lower cost by train for the storekeepers.

The Columbus and Lake Erie Railroad was not finished until January 6, 1851, when an engine and four cars arrived in Newark from Sandusky. There was one small detail that overshadowed the event. Although connected to the M&SC Railroad at Mansfield, the Columbus and Lake Erie didn't own a single engine or car.

Instead, the cost overruns on the 60-mile road, which had cost about $1,000,000 to build ($16,666 per mile, was big, big money in 1849), had forced the board of directors to lease the entire 60-mile railroad to the Mansfield and Sandusky City line. The M&SC was to pay one dollar plus 8% of the cost of the road construction per year in rent. The new combined line would be called the Sandusky, Mansfield & Newark Railroad.

The Calamity of '49

Prospects for profits looked great on paper, but a black cloud hung over the plan.

The wheat crop, the most profitable part of freight income, was down by one third in 1849. Wheat was the biggest cash crop for farmers and its transport to Sandusky, whether it was shipped as grain or flour, was a key source of railroad income.

A cholera epidemic also hit Sandusky that summer and the town, with a population of about 5,000, saw half (some accounts say two-thirds) of its population flee to other places. Most of these people were not welcomed at their destination and in some cases they were banned from entering.

Over 400 people died from this epidemic. Children became orphans and of the town's seven doctors, two died, two left town and the remaining three were worked to exhaustion. Seventy people were buried in one July weekend alone.

As a result, passenger and freight business ground to a halt at Sandusky, which was the main terminal of the line. The panic stricken public avoided the railroad and lake steamers. It is doubtful few in Lexington would risk unnecessary trips north.

Another problem was the deterioration of the tracks and bridges. The line south to Mansfield was built of native timber. It had timber crossties laid on earth supporting wooden rails topped by the previously mentioned iron strap. These timbers rotted, sank in the mud and the strap rail had the nasty habit of curling up, sometimes coming up through the bottom of cars.

The engineers had to carry a hammer and spikes and were forced to stop on occasion and nail the rail back down. From Mansfield south through Lexington to Newark, steel "T" rails shipped from England were used. However, the hastily built south end of the line needed leveling, additional side tracks, station houses and water towers.

The August 20, 1849 edition of the *Daily Sanduskian* offered this report:

We hear again the sound of the caulker's hammer and the sailor's cheerful voice, as they re-rig the vessels laid up during the prevalence of cholera. The rumbling of other wheels than the dead cart and other voices than those of lamentation, break upon our ears. Travel upon the railroads, has vastly increased the past few days, cars and steamers come and go, freighted with heavy loads of merchandise for the prosecution of an active fall trade, . . .

It was too little, too late. The railroad since its inception had never paid its stockholders a dividend and demands for buildings, new cars; locomotives and maintenance outstripped its income. The stockholders took a loss (several were from the Lexington area) as the road went broke and was reorganized under a new $730,000 mortgage arranged by investors in Ohio and New York.

The struggle for profitability would continue for years. From 1846 to 1869 only one dividend was ever paid to stockholders. By 1868 the railroads debt had grown to $2,307,314.50. The following year the road and rolling stock were leased to the Baltimore & Ohio Railroad.

Life (and Death) on the Rails

In the earliest days of the railroad there were occasional minor breakdowns and derailments. Male passengers were often expected to get off and help get the train back on the track or make repairs. If they were out in the middle of nowhere, what choice did they have?

The older "Camel Back" locomotives were used as helper engines until the early 1890s. The engineer rode on one side of the boiler, the brakeman on the other. The fireman worked in a stooped position under the tender roof.

The first major wreck on the Sandusky, Mansfield & Newark happened just north of Lexington where a small stream (Isaac's Run) crosses the present-day bike trail just north of the Hanley - Lexington Springmill Road intersection. The Sandusky paper reported the accident on May 10, 1853:

The freight train which left here at six-o'clock yesterday morning on the Sandusky, Mansfield and Newark Railroad was thrown from the track near Lexington by coming into contact with a cow. Being near a bridge which spans a small stream, the engine was precipitated into the water. We are pained to state that the Conductor, Mr. James Teegarden, of Mansfield, the Engineer, Mr. Joseph St. Peters, and the fireman, named McLear, were instantly killed. The two latter were horribly mutilated. Mr. Teegarden, it is said, was thrown into the water, and when the dispatch was sent, his body was still under the ruins. The Engineer resided at Newark and leaves a family. We have not learned of the probable amount of damage to the train.

A Little Help Please

Lexington was an interesting point on the 116-mile railroad. The Mansfield grade was a tough one for southbound engineers. From a standing start little speed could be gained before they entered the grade. Alta or Summit Siding as it was earlier called, had an elevation of 1287 above sea level and was the highest point between Newark (867) and Lake Erie (601). Lexington at 1180 feet and Mansfield at 1150 were at the base of rather steep inclines of a little over a mile in length.

Sometime in the early 1870s, after the B&O took over the SM&N, a "helper" engine was stationed at Lexington. This engine's job was to fall behind north bound trains and help push them up the Lexington grade to Alta and then return to wait for the next train. The crewmen had the advantage of living close to work but the 12-hour shifts seven days a week were demanding. Brad Tobin and Harley Hull were on the night shift, Albert Gore and Jack Cline were on days.

Between "through freights" the helper crews placed cars and pushed coal cars up the ramp to the coal chutes. On one of these return trips, the crew noticed a roof fire on Date Walter's house at the junction of Hanley Road. So the crew coupled the fire hose they carried (for railroad building protection) to the high pressure boiler's water injector pump and put out the fire.

Adam Hively had a blacksmith shop a short distance south of Alta. When the railroad, which was to maintain fences along the right of way, refused to pay for a cow it killed, he coated the rails with soap or grease one night. The next north-bound train stalled amid slipping wheels, thundering exhausts and a mad, cursing engine crew. Unable to restart, the train had to be broken into sections, taken to Alta or Mansfield and reassembled, causing serious delays. The railroad figured out what happened and had Hively arrested.

Bigger, Stronger Engines

Helper engines were positioned in Lexington until the onset of World War I. At that time, the B&O

Photograph courtesy of Harry Linton Family

Albert Gore (left) and Jack Cline pose with their helper engine #965, which was built in 1886.

bought 150 heavier and more powerful Baldwin Class Q1 locomotives. These were good 2-8-2 engines and 60 more were delivered the following year. These engines could usually make the grade without help. Long trains were double headed (pulled by two engines).

However, even with the bigger and more powerful engines these two grades, especially the Lexington grade, embarrassed engine crews when the double-headed trains snorted to a thundering halt. "It was hell to wait to build up more steam, take the slack out and try to restart the damned thing," according to one old railroader. Sometimes they had to split the train, take half to Alta or Mansfield and then reassemble the cars. This delayed schedules and drove the Trainmaster nuts. Even years later when #111, the first two unit diesel engine, was tested pulling a coal train, it reportedly stalled on the Lexington grade.

In 1918 another 100 improved Class Q3 Light Mikado 2-8-2 locomotives were added to the B&O roster. These 292,000lb. engines, carrying 10,000 gallons of water and 16 tons of coal, were numbered 4500 thru 4599. Several were still in use through Lexington until the end of the steam era. On February 18, 1958, the last one, 4592 renumbered to 389, passed through Lexington. It was the last of the dirty, smoky, noisy, but somehow truly magnificent steam locomotives. It had been in service 40 years.

Lexington had two water towers and a big coal chute where engines could load up before attacking the hill. (The engineer that ran out of coal or water before reaching Mansfield was in deep doo doo.) Old Lex was near the halfway point between Newark and Sandusky and handy for the run to the yards at Willard. So Lexington was a frequently used refueling station for many years. However, the bigger #4500's could make the Newark to Willard run without taking fuel. So the old coal chutes were torn down in 1940. A concrete wall along the present bike trail marks the beginning of the incline for the chutes.

The Big Conversion

The Sandusky, Mansfield & Newark had built on a five-foot-four-inch gauge (distance between the rails) instead of the standard or "Ohio Gauge" of four-foot-nine-inches which meant their cars could not interchange with other railroads. Freight had to be unloaded by hand to cars of other lines.

This disadvantage was addressed in March of 1864 when, in ten days time, the entire 112 miles of tracks

The coal chutes were a sizeable landmark in 1915. One time a careless engineer pushed a coal car off the end. Fortunately, it landed on its end, just missing a small building where Delbert Sheppard was sleeping - on duty! He woke up!

Lexington's second station built in 1871. It replaced the small room and shelter that was part of Sowers' grain warehouse. The station was built over the creek bank, on poles, on the east side of the tracks. In its last days, the station would rock when a train came through.

plus all switches and side tracks were reset to the standard gauge. The start of this work was made at Newark and trains of the old and new gauge met as work progressed north through Lexington to Sandusky. The axles and wheels of every car and locomotive had to be narrowed and in the case of some engines, whole new boilers had to be fabricated due to clearance problems.

This was a well planned but very, very expensive operation. And at the end of this conversion, all unchanged engines and cars were at the railroad's extensive shops in Sandusky. There crews were working frantically to complete the transformation.

There was both a bright and dark side to this huge effort. First, trains from Chicago could now enter the SM&N tracks at Monroeville and come south through Lexington to Newark, where they could connect with lines east from the Baltimore & Ohio Railroad. This increased traffic was a plus. Unfortunately, by the end of the year the SM&N was faced with a severe shortage of cars as theirs moved off loaded to other lines. Even with four new Locomotives (at $15,384 each) the line had only eight engines and was the weak link in the B&O chain from Baltimore to Chicago. Three old engines, the "Plymouth," "Lexington" and "Sandusky," needed new boilers and were not yet finished.

The Clear Fork provided water, which was pumped by steam engine to the tower tanks. Jack Cline (left) and Al Heskett pictured here in 1912.

Photograph courtesy of Sid Earhart Collection

In 1918, this nearly new B&O locomotive was detrailed when it hit Orva Day's runaway horse. The front wheels hit the siding switch at the south side of town, which wrecked the train.

B&O Takes Over

On February 13, 1869, the B&O leased the line and took over operations. It had the cars and engines the SM&N could never have been able to provide. In 1901 they bought the line outright.

How long the Sowers' warehouse was used as a station is unknown, but in 1871 the B&O built a new 18 X 33 passenger and telegraph depot station and reported that "the unsafe and unsightly projection over the warehouse tracks removed." This new station was set on poles over the embankment on the east side of the tracks and in its last years old-timers recalled how the building would rock when a train came past. Also remembered was the time a Railway Express wagon full of milk cans was left too close to the tracks on the station platform. A locomotive struck it with such force that it was nearly driven through the station.

In 1912 a new combination freight and passenger station was built and equipped at a cost of $10,575. Years later it was saved from demolition by the heroic efforts of the Lexington Kiwanis Club. Recently expanded, it is now Lexington's Senior Center. Most old stations were torn down. Bellville and Butler lost theirs by doing nothing.

Passengers loved the trains. They were safe, fast and much easier on the backside than a bouncing buggy on rutted, muddy roads. Earliest railroad records located indicate 2,542 arrived in town in 1858, 2,178 left. Oddly enough, Bellville greeted 3,196 but the record states only 3,159 ½ left. The other ½ must still be laying around town somewhere.

By comparison 3,629 folks boarded the trains at Lexington in 1864 during the Civil War. Some of these were soldiers going off to fight. Not all would return. The town was supplied with 223,913 pounds of merchandise and 26 barrels of whiskey and beer. Over 12,000 bushels of wheat and oats left town via boxcars along with 314 barrels of flour and 29,164 pounds of butter. Without the railroad Lexington would have died.

Railroad jobs were steady. Telegraph operators, stationmasters, track crews, manning the water towers and coal chutes, and including men on the early helper engines, these were all local people. However, the pay wasn't always the greatest.

John Satterfield was the telegraph operator at Alta in 1907. He worked 12 hours a day, seven days a week and was paid $57.00 a month. He worked 90 days and quit. The operator at Lexington got $62.00 because it was a busier station. By comparison Nellie Satterfield was paid $20.00 a month for teaching school at Vine Hill south of town.

The age of the automobile and the establishment of a bus service between Lexington and Mansfield in the late 1920's or early 1930's, ruined the passenger train service to Lexington. The last passenger train to stop was a special Baltimore & Ohio Cedar Point Excursion Special sometime around 1947.

News that enough tickets had to be sold in town before it would stop here was relayed to a few folks at Swigart's Cafe by Stationmaster Nelson Lewis and the word spread. A good crowd was on hand at the station to make the trip to the docks at Sandusky and board the coal burning side wheel steamboat "G. A. Boeckling," to cross the bay to Cedar Point. It was a memorable last trip. The writer was one of those lucky passengers.

Photograph courtesy of Richard Lewis Collection

Nelson Lewis became a B&O Railroad Policeman when he got out of the Navy. Years later he was the Lexington station agent.

Nelson Lewis was an interesting character. He was a telegrapher on the USS Wyoming in 1922, went to

Photograph courtesy of Robert Snyder Collection

Engine 389 made its farewell trip from Willard to Newark on Feb. 18, 1958. It was the last steam train out of the Willard yards. Written on the cylinder, in chalk, were the words "Last round up, we hope."

work for the B&O in 1928 as a railroad cop, worked for Union Pacific and Goodyear awhile during WWII, and came back to work for the B&O in Lexington in 1946. The railroad cars for the soy bean plant generated a lot of paperwork, which he hated. So he moved to the North Siding at the steel mill sometime in the1950s. For fun, train crews often irritated him. They'd ask him a dumb question when he was busy, just to hear him yell and swear.

The early 1900s saw large amounts of freight moving to and from the Cockley Milling Co., the Smith

Station master Nelson Lewis photographed the first diesel engine (#105) as it came through Lexington in the late 1940s.

Gas Producer plant, Lutz Lumber and the livestock yards. As late as 1948, and in some cases beyond, deliveries were still being made to Lutz Lumber, the Lexington Equity Exchange (Farm Bureau, coal and farm supplies), A.C. Kell Hardware (coal, lime & cement), Hickok Oil Co. (gasoline), United Implements and the Lexington Soy Products Company. The latter received a great many railcars loaded with soybeans and shipped many full of soy oil.

On April 1, 1987, the last regular train passed through Lexington. A short time later, crews started tearing up the tracks from Mansfield south towards Lexington and Bellville. The rails were removed in front of the Lexington Station on April 22, 1987.

There were more than a few spectators on hand that day to witness the end of an era as engineer J. W. McClain, brakeman C. J. Hall and conductor Donald Paxton pulled B&O engine 3745 away from the station, dragging a quarter mile of rails with them. It was the last locomotive to leave the old station.

Among the crowd that day was Claude Gore. His grandfather and father had worked as engineers and fireman on the B&O for many years. They both worked on the helper engine at Lexington and Claude, a retired engineer from the Pennsylvania Railroad, was seated in

This is the last train to leave Lexington in 1987.

front of the station on a flower planter made of cross ties. He sadly watched the rails slide aboard the specially designed cars. As a third generation railroader, what memories must have gone through his mind?

As he stared across the vacant roadbed from the station towards the cemetery, where his father was buried, there were tears in his eyes. It was a scene the writer will never forget.

Photograph courtesy of the Tribune-Courier

Third Generation railroader Claude Gore watched as workmen prepared to pull the rails fromt he old B&O-Chessie roadbed in April 1987.

Tales of the Graveyard

The Man Who Slept in the Cemetery

The Lexington Cemetery is a rather melancholy place. Full of memories of loved ones, their tears and laughter, this quiet island amid the growing sprawl of the village has a lovely serenity about it during the day. It's a peaceful place. At night, as one might expect, it is overtaken by the dark ghostly shadows, bringing forth thoughts of sinister spirits and death. It's enough to raise the hair on the back of a person's neck.

Charlie Trimble was one of the caretakers at the cemetery from the late 1940s through the 1960s. He also worked for Bill Templeton at United Implements, where he took care of the boiler and other jobs. At harvest time, he sometimes worked on Walter Shafer's potato farm.

Photograph courtesy of Donna Fuhrer Hoffner

Just as pictured here, Charlie Trimble was expected at meal time at the home of John and Mary Fuhrer…unless he decided to eat in town and spend the night in the cemetery

Charlie owned a small farm on East Hanley Road and lived alone in a house set back a ways from the road. His neighbors were John and Mary Fuhrer and family. Old Charlie always used to pitch in and help the Fuhrers with their farm work and, though not related, he was considered part of the family. He was expected at meal time and Mrs. Fuhrer did his laundry. Mary was a good, kind-hearted woman.

Charlie didn't drive a car, but had an old Allis Chalmers farm tractor. It was a fairly common sight to see him come slowly down Route 42 on his tractor and pull into the cemetery. Always dressed in bib overalls and wearing a farm cap, he was a friendly, good natured man who knew how to put in a good day's work. He dug graves and kept the grass neatly cut and trimmed in a day when little power equipment was available.

When possible, he would bum a ride to town rather than drive the old Allis. Quite often, after a lonely day among the deceased, he'd walk up to Swigart's Café to have some good food and wash it down with a couple of beers. Enjoying conversation and a little TV among the living was a pleasure after a whole day on his own. As a result, Charlie had a wide circle of friends.

But there were times when a ride home couldn't be found or when weather would have made the tractor trip uncomfortable. So back to the Sexton house in the cemetery he'd go.

Sexton house was a simple building. There was no electricity, but a kerosene lantern furnished light. An outside well pump supplied water and a quaint, white, but leaning outhouse was conveniently located behind. A small pot bellied stove along the wall could be used for heat.

Amid the clutter of tools, scythes and lawn mowers was a large wooden crate set on saw horses, complete with hinged lid. Actually it was a coffin crate, with handles on both sides, in which a very expensive coffin had been shipped half a century earlier. It looked like an oversized coffin.

Inside the coffin crate were neatly folded blankets of artificial grass, which were used to cover the ground and dirt pile around a grave during a funeral service. Into the crate Charlie would climb. And if it was chilly, a blanket of grass could be used to cover up for warmth. He must have slept well knowing he wouldn't be late for work the next morning. He'd be the first one there!

He was once asked by a member of the Cemetery Board if he wasn't afraid of sleeping there at night. Old Charlie replied, *The people down here won't bother you none, it's the ones walking around up town you have to keep an eye on.*

The old Sexton House in the cemetery was built in 1863 for tool and equipment storage…not for overnight guests.

His story came to a sad end one chilly night. After digging a grave, Charlie fell asleep in a chair, with his feet on, or too close to, the small stove. His pant leg caught fire and he wound up in the hospital with a severe burn. He never fully recovered.

Charlie died sometime later and now sleeps peacefully in the Ontario Cemetery. His ancestors and a brother, Lester, had lived west of there.

The Man Who Dug His Own Grave

John Williams was a talented man who lived at the east end of Castor Road. In 1882 he was hired as engineer, to tend the boiler and machinery, at the new Cockley Steam Mill. Previously he had worked as both a painter and stone mason.

Stone and cement was John's business. So as Lexington residents grew tired of repairing or replacing their wooden sidewalks, it was Williams who was usually hired to lay those big gray stone slabs. Some of those stone slabs are still in use today, after more than a century. The first ones laid were near the town square.

His skill with stone eventually took him to the cemetery. And in 1894, a newspaper obituary for aged John Logan noted that *his place of sepulture being a spacious vault, of which John B. Williams was the architect in the cemetery at Lexington.*

A few years later, folks noticed something strange and unsettling going on in the grave yard. Just up the small hill, past the Sexton house, old John Williams started digging a grave, even though no deaths had occurred.

It wasn't just an ordinary excavation either. It was more than twice the normal size, a double grave. Why so big? Was his health in danger? Was he plotting a murder suicide? His first wife had died in 1852. How were he and his wife Elizabeth getting along? It all looked suspicious.

Williams was a Civil War Veteran, serving with Company C, 15th Regiment, Ohio Volunteer Infantry from 1861 to 1864. His military duties took him from Tennessee to Mississippi and Alabama where he was often ordered to carry the wounded from the battle fields and work as a nurse in field hospitals. Later, one of these orders sent him to a smallpox hospital.

So John had witnessed human misery and death beyond imagination. Had this memory affected his mind? Serious unanswered questions were whispered among the townspeople Regular checks were made on the progress of Williams plot. The floor slabs went in and then the concrete walls. Great stone slabs would cover the top. Most puzzling was the day a stone wall was placed dividing the chamber into two sections. When asked about it, Williams reportedly replied, "That's so's me and the old woman won't get to fightin'."

To everyone's relief, Elizabeth was 80 when she died a natural death in 1915. John, a Charter Member of the Conger Post of the G. A. R. in Lexington, died five years later at age 92.

An honest, well-known citizen, John went to his eternal rest knowing that he was the only man in Lexington that ever dug his own grave. There must have great been satisfaction in that knowledge.

The Comfortable Coffin

The Snyder family has operated funeral homes in various area communities for decades. Starting in Johnsville, Ora Snyder was the first of that family to come to Lexington in 1926. His carefully run funeral service passed to son Robert after World War II. In 1970, Robert and Dorothy Snyder moved to Colorado and Paul Snyder took over. The present proprietor is Paul's son, Todd Snyder.

As the story was relayed to the writer, young Todd was a very active and carefree kid. One afternoon, after a busy day, he needed a short nap. Having grown up around the family business, he didn't see things the same way an outsider might. So he found a nice coffin in the back store room and climbed in for a little snooze. It was comfortable.

J. Todd Snyder, Manager of Snyder Funeral Home, seen with an 1883 horse-drawn hearse as he prepared to take part in Lexington's 175th birthday celebration during 1989. An adult now, Todd restricts his naps to his easy chair or bed.

Now that might seem to be a bit odd, or even upsetting, to some folks. But in his mind, at that tender age, it was a practical solution.

After all, no body else was using it.

Why There?

The location of the Lexington Cemetery has been a bit of a puzzle to some folks. A Mrs. Searls was the first interment there in 1816. At that time, the gentle rise in the forest land owned by Amariah Watson would have been a beautiful location overlooking the Clear Fork and the infant village.

A very early map reveals that the main road north from town followed what is now the main cemetery drive. It crossed a small stream and then connected to what is now Hanley Road (at the one-time sharp curve near the Lexington-Springmill Road). In that day, Plymouth Street went nowhere because of the swampland and wilderness along what is now the Lexington Park.

It was not until Watson located another mill north of the present-day park that the Plymouth Street and Lexington-Springmill Road we know were built. This happened in the early 1820s. The old road through Watson's forest was eventually abandoned, except for what went as far as the cemetery.

In June 1857 a request presented to the village council indicated that the burying ground is *without a fence and monuments are exposed to beasts of the field.* (It must have been those darned roving cows again.) It was then decided an additional acre of land was needed, which was paid for ($25) by public subscription. One hundred fifty fence posts and 900 feet of lumber cost another $56. And thus the cemetery was fenced.

In 1863, a sexton house was built with an agreement between the township trustees and the village. The magnificent row of maple trees were planted in 1889 and pine trees added along the west bank in the early 1900s.

Richard Worley was chief caretaker of the cemetery and records for most of 40 years with the help of wife Lottie and sons Jeff and Martin. Charlie Newman was employed in the 1930's and 40's. Walter Hendrickson was there for over 30 years and many more helped dig graves or keep the grass cut and trimmed in the summer.

Unfortunately the cemetery trustees have passed up several opportunities, in recent years, to purchase additional lands even though funds were available. At present, they have done little to plan for future years.

Photograph courtesy of Robert Synder Collection

Richard Worley oversaw the cemetery for 40 years.

Small Places - Strange Names

ALTA, north of Lexington, has no signs featuring its name, although the Alta Greenhouse does. The place where Marion Avenue crosses the B&O bike trail was originally called "Summit Siding" back in the early railroad days. There was a rail siding, which was the highest point above sea level on the railroad between Newark and Lake Erie, hence the name. There was a small station, and a "Y" track for turning cars and engines.

Even double-headed trains needed help climbing the Lexington-Alta grade in 1900.

At an early time, a post office and a general store were located there as well, which brought the rural community together. Sometime in the 1880's the name of the post office was changed to Alta. Who did this (and why) remains a mystery. The post office was closed in 1902.

The Alta store was run by someone named "Old Erb." Old-timers interviewed years ago couldn't remember his real name. It was C. F. Erb. The Griebling gristmill was located south of Marion Avenue at the junction of Griebling and Alta roads. Adam Hively had a blacksmith shop just across the valley.

A telegraph operator manned the B&O station with others being employed on the water tower. C. C. Joslin, John Satterfield, Lawrence Maher and a host of others took their turn at the telegraph key. Sam Thuma was the section master.

Alta station wasn't the most exciting place in the world. Excess railcars from Mansfield were stored on the siding.

In the 1940s, the Burkhart Lumber Co., Midwest Fabricating Co. and the W. P. Nutter Coal Co. were the main employers in Alta. After World War II, folks switched to gas for heating and Nutter closed. A disastrous fire in the early 1960's wiped out most of the lumber yard and John Morley moved Midwest Fabricating to Lexington about the same time. The Midwest office was in the little gray building still standing on the corner.

The hub of Alta must have been the B&O Station and the small store just down the road. Other businesses would follow.

The post office connected the area social life. In the 1890s, the Alta Rifle Club met monthly for a shooting match. Ladies of the Cottage Reading Circle often met for basket dinners and continued the tradition as late as 1922–23. They sometimes sold box lunches to raise money for the Grange Library. Sledding down Alta hill was a real thrill!

Old-timers remembered John Stone and his wife. They lived on the east side of the valley just past what is called the deer park, but has no deer. (Some idiot opened the gate and let them out.) Anyway, the Stones didn't get along well and one day old lady Stone threw John out of the house. He wound up living in a tent in the front yard. If this was an attempt to embarrass her and get back in the house, it didn't work. According to sources, he spent quite awhile out there. He worked as a fireman on the B&O between Newark and Willard and didn't get home often.

The original Alta Greenhouse, which was next to the railroad station, was built by Sam Clever in 1923. He and his wife ran it until 1938, at which time it was sold to Les Garber. Garber was a well-known character who cared for the plants and fired the boiler the next 36 years.

The Hartzlers bought the greenhouse operation in 1974. They greatly expanded and improved the business over the next few years. Most recently, in 1989, Jim and Mary Kay Leedy sold their interests to Roger Henry.

The greenhouse is the blossom of beauty in the picturesque Alta valley, especially in summer. The best place to take the bike trail is there. It's the high point of the old B&O and downhill either direction. However, the return trip from Lexington can be hard on the leg muscles.

JUGS CORNERS is a name more than a place. At the corner of Ross Road and Steam Corners Road, west of Lexington, stands a white frame building that was used as the home of the Jugs Grange. In the 1800s a distillery was located back along an often muddy lane southwest of the intersection. It was near a stream close to the corner of the Shuler farm.

In 1967, 87-year-old Carrie Shuler described the location and said four building foundation stones were still there. Empty jugs were sometimes left at the road near the corners to be filled and later picked up, hence the name. Other theories as to the origin of the name have been offered over the years. Carrie Shuler set the record straight.

A neat brick one-room school was built on the southwest corner of the intersection sometime before the Civil War. In 1868, young Adam Bectel was hired there for his first teaching job. After a few years, he went to Lexington School as superintendent and then later moved to Kansas.

Bectel kept up a correspondence with several of his former Jugs students for many years. In one of his letters, written in 1927, he told of meeting a youngster by the name of George while on his way to the school one day. The youngster had quit school to work on the family farm and Bectel asked why he didn't return to classes. "I'm too old," came back the reply. To this the teacher replied "You're never too old to learn." The teacher made an impression on the young farm boy and the following Monday he came to class rather than deliver a load of firewood to town.

George finished two terms under Bectel and went on to the Gailey Seminary, a private high school in Lexington. He attended the Iberia College and was hired to teach at a school north of Mt. Gilead. His name was George Harding, the father of President Warren J. Harding.

This 1869 class picture is the oldest known photograph taken at the Jugs Corners School.

A.E. Bectel (left) was the teacher. One of his students was George Harding, father of President Warren G. Harding.

Others pictured (L-R) are: Augusts Foltz, Leroy Hiskey, Wilbur Heatherington, Cassie Ruhl, Florence Heatherington, Arthur Eckert, Amannda Dimmermuth, Orlando Eckert, Hanna Meece, Albert Hiskey, Balinda Yeager, Agnes Ruhl, Jacob Meece. Kneeling are: Alice Hiskey, Emma Poland, Ermina Eckert. Reclining are: Wesley Texter, George Hiskey, Scott Poland.

When the Jugs School closed in 1930, the building was sold to the Cloverleaf Community Club, an active group of local folks. In March of 1940, the Jugs Grange #2680 was organized and they took over the school building.

By the 1950s, the Grange had over 300 members and had outgrown the tiny school building. So the old Mennonite Church from the Shauck Cemetery (at Johnsville) was moved to Jugs. Even this building had to be enlarged to accommodate the Grange group. In 1958 the old brick school was torn down.

The Grange was an active organization. It's interesting to note that folks in Troy Township, Morrow County have held on to their rural sense of community and common bond. However, Troy Twp. Richland became more urban as farms were cut up and developments gobbled up the landscape. That common bond was lost along the way. It was called progress by some. But was it?

BUNGTOWN was located west of Lexington. Just go out past Jugs Corners, west through Steam Corners and turn right on the first side road. After you go north a short bit, the road bends west and about quarter of a mile later you've passed Bungtown.

There are only a few houses on that road, but in the late 1800's there was a roadhouse or saloon somewhere along that country lane. The exact location has been lost to time. It gained a somewhat notorious reputation, especially during the temperance movement, and in 1967 87-year-old Carrie Shuler told the writer that it was sometimes known as the home of the "fighting Winbiglers" who were the principle owners. The liquor could often lead to problems.

Little industry existed in Bungtown. The principle business was a stone quarry, located in a ravine south of the road, which was owned at one time by Peter Treisch. A distillery was reportedly located somewhere along a small stream that meanders through the area. There was the bar room and, of course, farming. The temperance people, the lack of a railroad and the remote location doomed any chances of Bungtown surpassing its arch rivals Steam Corners or Blooming Grove.

STRINGTOWN was another almost forgotten small place in southern Troy Township, Morrow County. It is located two miles south of Steam Corners on present day State Route 314, at the intersection of the St. James – Bellville Road. Nothing much existed there, just a cluster (or string) of houses and barns on small parcels of land, which led to the name. The old Walters Schoolhouse was the main feature a hundred years ago.

STEAM CORNERS, with an odd name, is well known. The often repeated story of a steam powered sawmill that gave the crossroads its name back in the 1860's is memorable. No one ever thought they would live to see a traffic jam at the corners until the Mid Ohio Race Track landed the big races a century later. Time marches on.

By the late 1870s, the mill had attracted other interests to the locale. You could find Eggert & Weldon's general store, although it changed ownership several times, a post office, Dr. Watson McWilliams office, a fine two-story brick school, and Fortney Portner's blacksmith shop. By 1880 a shoe shop and carpenter shops made the Corners grow. A dozen or so houses could be counted, depending how far down the road you went. There were no set boundaries.

No church was at the corners until 1894 when a newly formed Methodist congregation built the main part of the present building. The active country church is the glue that holds the rural community together. In 1949 a parade and centennial celebration was held in which there were more than two dozen floats and the Steam Corners Band. All came rolling down the pike in a grand fashion. Former schoolteachers and graduates were part of a crowd of 1,500 in attendance, the largest group of people ever assembled at the Corners.

In the early 1900s Steam Corners was a place noted for music. In that era, the Lexington Conger Post of the G.A.R. hired the Steam Corners Band to play at the Memorial Day Parade in Lexington. (Lexington had no band at that time.) There was also the Steam Corners Octet, which was a group of young ladies led by John Rutherford. That group sang so beautifully at area social occasions, that they were to be remembered for decades after the women married and disbanded the group.

In 1965, George Ross along with wife Verna and son Clarence incorporated "Ross Field" as a flying field for planes. They built hangers for storage and offered pilot training. The Ross farm had long fairly level fields and offered an easy opportunity to establish a runway. Because of its rural location and modest facilities it was affectionately referred to as the "Steam Corners International Airport" by some folks. The relocation of the

Musically destitute Lexington occasionally had to hire the Steam Corners Band for Memorial Day parades

larger Galion Airport at about the same time (to a site between Galion and Ontario) limited the prospects for Ross Field.

Mary Eva Prosser was a resourceful woman. In the early 1950's she started a "farm vacation" service in her home south of the Corners to earn a little extra money. From feeding the guests wonderful home cooking, she was prompted by one to go into the catering business. An addition to the house provided room for feeding hungry groups, private parties and organizations. The Lexington Kiwanis Club sampled her cooking every Thursday night for 17 years. There were few thin members. Her husband "Spoke" and daughters Natalie and Bonnie helped with the meals. Later two granddaughters, Sherrilyn and Nancy would join to help Grandma feed the hungry. Mary Eva retired in the early 80's and her family-style dinning room is fondly remembered.

There had always been a country store at the corners since 1865, but when John Smith and wife closed up shop in 1985 it was the end of an era. Steam Corners is a quiet place now. Except, that is, on race weekends.

ORCHARD PARK was kind of born out of necessity in the eyes of some. It picked up its name when people were allowed to park their travel trailers in the orchard behind the store building. The original store building was located on the southeast corner of the intersection of State Routes 97 and 42.

Sid Earhart had a pool room called "The Club" in the old tile building next to the railroad station in Lexington. The building had been built as a saloon by the Ferrell brothers, but the temperance supporters kept voting the town dry and that ended that. A strictly regulated pool room in a rented building in a dry town couldn't have been very profitable. So Earhart moved out of town and Troy Township. He settled on a piece of land just inside the Washington Township line, just east of Lexington. He was then free of the village anti-everything laws and regulations. He could open and close when he wanted and sell whatever he pleased. Washington Township was wide open.

Sid built a small, rough, barn-like building with a low roof that held a limited line of groceries, beer, wine and tobacco and produce in season. The venture on the busy highway proved successful and sometime around 1930 John and Ida Leedy bought the place from Earhart.

Inside the Leedy Store, later known as Orchard Park. The girl behind the counter may be young Marie Hiser. The corner of a slot machine can be seen to the right.

The business prospered and Leedy hired Charlie Schroeder to help expand the original building. A small concession stand building was added to the east of the store. In the 1930s, yet another structure went up. It looked like an eight sided, upside down ice cream cone with doors that opened upward. The top was covered with tin and it proved to be a popular landmark for the busy intersection. Ice cream, pop, candy, snacks and beer were sold during warm weather. The main store remained open year round. It carried a line of groceries, milk, fresh produce, meat, beer, wine liquor and even had slot machines and punch boards. Gas pumps and motor oil made Orchard Park a one stop marketplace.

Leedy and his brother owned three pickup trucks and in season hauled fresh produce from Lake Erie keeping the shelves and bins well stocked. They operated a similar business near Huron.

Photograph courtesy of Jim Leedy Collection

The Orchard Park Market was run by John and Ida Leedy. The buildings were built by G.F. Schroeder in the early 1930s. The market carried a complete line of produce, canned goods, meat, baked goods, beer, liquor, punch boards and slot machines.

Jim Leedy, John's son, recalls the time Ida told her husband that one of John's employees was stealing from him. John couldn't believe any of them was a thief. Ida insisted there was, and if she could prove it, he would have to agree to take her to Florida. John consented and at that point Ida climbed up to a rafter that ran across the ceiling and came down with nearly a $1,000 in cash. She was the thief. They went to Florida.

Motion pictures were shown in summer on a large canvas screen stretched between two trees behind the store. Tarzan, The Lone Ranger, King of the Mounties and Hopalong Cassidy were a few remembered film characters. Patrons could sit on flat plank benches set on posts or in their cars. Some brought their own chairs. Popcorn and snacks and drinks were at the store and the free movies were extremely popular and well attended in that post depression era. It was good public relations and boosted business.

John Leedy was a hard working businessman, but a little more gambling than just slot machines and punch boards had been going on at his store. His luck ran out one night in 1939 during a high stakes card game. He lost Orchard Park to Jenner McBride, a neighbor who had a dairy farm just up the road. Leedy did the honorable thing. McBride took ownership and John and Ida moved to Huron. Unrecorded is the conversation when John broke the news to Ida.

McBride evidently had little interest in running the place. He farmed and had a milk route in town. Carl Dill, who had Dill's Café in Bellville, became the next manager. After a brief period, the business was sold to Eddis and Dorothy Kinton and the likeable couple ran Kinton's Orchard Park Market for more than 30 years.

In October of 1955, the old low roof frame building was replaced with a new modern brick store. It didn't have

Eddis and Dorothy Kinton took over the market in 1939. It was a popular stopping place. Movies were shown out back, on a screen strung between two trees, in the summer.

the atmosphere of the old place, but was a much more convenient market with the same friendly faces behind the counter. The Kintons retired in 1972 and the name "Orchard Park" could have vanished with them. But it remains burned into the memory of longtime residents.

Sadly, a sporting goods store that sold boats was a tenant. This was followed by a drug store, in which the police chief was shot when he walked in on a robbery. For awhile Polly Kunkle sold pies, including her famous "Grasshopper" pie, in the building.

"Polly" Kunkle, originator of the famous "Grasshopper Pie"

Polly was a remarkable woman. Starting with a home cake decorating business, in a short time she opened a restaurant in a farm house east of town.

From there she opened "The Atmosphere" in an old remodeled barn next door as her family business grew. However, in 1962 a fire leveled the place. Polly's eatery was then moved to Mansfield, but in 1963 she became manager and chief cook at Malabar Inn. For many years, on the Louis Bromfield Farm, she served guests from all over the world. Her warm personality, good home cooking and grasshopper pie are well remembered.

Most giant corporations don't particularly care what they do to a community, as long as they make money. The "Hardee" restaurant chain is a sad example. The poorly managed outlet, that stands where Kinton's market once stood, has at this writing become the village eyesore. An idiot employee contaminated a customer's drink, which was discovered and taken home to a deep freezer. As the story goes, the Hardee people offered a free meal and then a small cash settlement until they found out about the evidence in the freezer. That would cost them and they closed the place up. They left another similar building mess in Mansfield on Lexington Avenue.

THE CORNERS was across the road from Orchard Park and was a separate entity. The writer would suppose the name came from the sharper bend in Route 42 that existed years ago and the corner of Orchard Park road across the street. No one living really remembers.

In the early 1920s, Route 42 had been paved. With the increased traffic, Fred Meredith and his wife ran a gas station and restaurant on the bend in the highway. The "Linco Restaurant" and station were a popular stopping place for the locals, as well as travelers and truckers. There was good food, pop, ice cream and beer. Mrs. Meredith did most of the cooking, with son Paul helping out at times. They had a dance floor with music from a jukebox. However, often on Friday and Saturday nights a three or four piece orchestra would play and the place was usually packed.

The station sold gas, oil, and tires only. No repair garage was operated, but as an inducement for truckers to stop and buy gas an old interurban railcar was moved to the east of the gas station and equipped with bunks and a shower.

Mildred Suavely was a waitress at the Linco Restaurent in the late 1930s. The Linco was popular on weekends when a small bad played for the dancing public.

Photograph courtesy of Homer Wagner

In 1937, Lester Miller (pictured here) and Homer Wagner took care of the gas customers and flat tires at the Linco station.

Homer Wagner quit school in the 10th grade and went to work at the station in 1935 along with Lester Miller. They recall truckers paid little or nothing to stay in "The Truck Drivers Club" as it was called and there was no hot water in the shower. Quite a few truckers made it a regular stop. Wagner and Miller were young men who worked 12 hours a day, 7 days a week for $10. They got one free meal a day and a piece of Mrs. Meredith's pie for dessert. In a 2006 interview, they remembered that gas was only 16 cents a gallon back then.

In 2007, ninety-six-year-old Mona Schindler recalled how she and her ten year younger sister Helen had both worked at the Corners, although at different times. Fred Meredith would not serve African-American customers. Many truckers stopped there and one time a white driver came in for a meal and asked for a carry out dinner for his African-American partner waiting outside. Helen obliged, but Fred got mad and almost fired her for it.

Fred Meredith bought one of the old wooden temporary school buildings after the yellow brick high school was opened in 1932. He moved it to the point between Orchard Park Road and Rt. 42, across from the Linco station. It had a bar and a small dance floor and was run for a few years. It was a popular gathering place, especially on weekends. Folks watching the free Orchard Park movies could walk over and enjoy a short snort during intermission. Unfortunately, it was torn down shortly after World War II.

About that same time, Meredith sold the restaurant to Wilbur Wade and Dick Roberts. This popular duo may have changed the name to the "Corners." It operated under that name until the 1970's when it was torn down to allow the State Highway Department to round off the sharp curve on Route 42. At that time, Paul Cullen was the owner and had been running the bar and restaurant operation for a number of years.

The last night the old "Corners" was open deserves mention. Cullen had built a new place just around the corner on Route 97 and the move would be made the following day. The place was packed for that one last night. It was a somewhat sad farewell to the old building and the happy memories people had enjoyed there over the years.

During the course of the evening several patrons decided to help demolish the place. It started as a joke. A few more beers and the destruction increased, despite Cullen's efforts to settle down his longtime customers. Windows were knocked out, paneling and signs ripped off walls and ceilings. The mayhem continued to the point when an old beer cooler was thrown out through a window wall and the structural integrity of the building was coming into question.

The "Truck Drivers Club" was an old Interurban rail car where truckers could sleep for little or nothing. Even though it only had a cold shower, the bunks it offered were still popular with truck drivers. Pictured here are Ray Meredith (top) and William Farst showing off for the camera.

The Lexington police arrived a short time later and announced the immediate final closing time. A bunch of happy laughing people left the old "Corners" for the last time that night. It was the end of an era. They had been a witness to, and part of, that closure. It is doubtful that much effort was required by contractors to demolish what was left the next morning.

Part of Route 42 now passes over where a portion of the building once stood.

Paul "PJ" Cullen was the last owner of "The Corners" restaurant. He was a popular figure and his clientele followed him to his new establishment.

The old electric street car used as the "Drivers Club" burned down in the late 1930s.

The Doctors

If you're sick, fractured or broken and can't mend your own body, you need a doctor. It's either that or have the local undertaker stand by.

Harry Smith compiled a list of Lexington doctors years ago and his daughter Helen Smith Steiner was kind enough to lend a copy. Harry Smiths' father was Dr. Henry Howard Smith, a truly remarkable man, who practiced here from 1880 until his death in 1922, thus the family interest.

The list of doctors is provided here. Unfortunately, their medical training or length of time serving Lexington is not available.

Lexington Doctors
Dr. Noah Watson, (Died 1863)
Dr. Barnum
Dr. Anderson
Dr. A. Mann
Dr. L. B. Miles
Dr. Abernathy
Dr. McMillen
Dr. David Hahn
Dr. I. S. Samsell
Dr. George Carey
Dr. Cora Carey
Dr. Glen
Dr. Henry Howard Smith
Dr. John P. Stober
Dr. J. F. Sager
Dr. I. H. Lebarre
Dr. Otis Wiles
Dr. Milton Oakes
Dr. Ester Mast
Dr. Earl Mast
Dr. Riley England Frush
Dr. K. G. Wertz
Dr. Ludwig
Dr. Val Berzzarins
Dr. David Clymer

No information was provided with the Smith list. Only fragments of history have been gathered on a few of the early doctors.

Dr. Noah Watson ran a tavern between Lexington and Mansfield. His medical occupation followed in his later years and if he had any training, it possibly came from a book. Home remedies were a specialty. "Cherries soaked in whiskey" was one of his well remembered cures. Good for man or beast.

"Dr." Noah Watson was a soldier, farmer and tavern keeper. He was the first doctor in Lexington. As an early doctor, it is unknown whether he had any formal medical training or simply used home cures.

Dr. Abernathy's family owned an early store in town. He practiced over 30 years starting in 1836.

Dr. David Hahn was the son of Benjamin Hahn, who owned the water powered gristmill in town in the 1870s. Dr. Hahn died at age 64 in 1877 and he is buried in the Lexington Cemetery. The doctor was well respected and the Presbyterian Church was filled with those who came to pay their respects.

Dr. George Carey may have been the son of Mason Carey, who ran a jewelry store here in the 1850s. Dr. Cora Carey could have been his wife. No other information has been found.

Dr. Henry Smith was a well remembered citizen. He practiced from his office and home on the square from 1880-1922. A detailed history of the good doctor and his family is covered in another chapter.

Dr. John Stober is best remembered by the locals because he had three wives, though not all at the same time. When his first wife died, friends and patients expressed much sympathy. When his second wife passed away, some folks kind of raised one eyebrow when his name came up. He seemed to be a good practitioner, but a slight suspicion hung over the second loss. That ended, rather sadly, when wife number three outlived him. The good doctor started here in the 1930s and is buried in Lexington Cemetery next to two of his wives.

Dr. Otis Wiles was raised on a farm on Wiles Road. Both the road and part of the farm are now under the Clear Fork Reservoir. His office was in his home on Delaware Street and, in addition to being a good doctor, he was actively involved in church and village affairs. Dr. Wiles served on council and was mayor from 1912-1916. During his term in office a new town hall was built and the first fire fighting apparatus purchased.

It seems odd that although he treated countless patients and saved many lives, the one story that often surfaces, concerns Doc Wiles driving habits during his last years (in the 1940s). Old Doc had a Chevy sedan and an old Model "A" pickup truck. He would back out of his drive without looking either direction, in spite of the fact that heavy traffic and big trucks menaced Delaware Street. It scared the heck out of the neighbors. His family finally had to hide his ignition keys. Perhaps Wiles just figured God would look after old doctors and Presbyterians.

Doctors Oakes, Masts (both), Frush, and Wertz all practiced here for a few years and then moved on to Mansfield or elsewhere. It was more convenient for them to be nearer Mansfield General Hospital and the city's bigger clientele.

Dr. Frush came to Lexington in 1939. In 1942 he was drafted and became a flight surgeon during World War II. He was a train buff and had a big model train layout in the second floor room over the old bank and post office on East Main. It was the envy of any kid who ever saw it. He and friend John Newcomer went to Mansfield and rode the last regular B&O passenger train to Zanesville and back. Dr. Frush was 88 when he died in 1999.

Lexington had been without the services of a local physician for several years when the Men's Service Club took on the project of finding one who was willing to locate here. They sent out over 700 circulars over a period of time and contacted medical schools and institutions to no avail. The group even looked into establishing a hospital in town, but was advised by officials in Columbus that even a small facility would be very expensive to build and would lose money the first few years of operation.

An answer came after years of searching. Dr. Val Bezzarins located here in November of 1958. Born in Latavia, then a part of Russia, he graduated from Medical School in Germany and came to this country in 1951. Perhaps it was his stiff, entirely business attitude, his accent, or the fact that residents couldn't really warm up to anybody connected with either Russia or Germany. Regardless of the cause, his time here was a failure. He only stayed 12 months and saw few patients.

An answer to the dilemma came in 1963, with the arrival of Dr. David D. Clymer. Nobody found him. He found Lexington. Clymer and his wife Betty wanted to locate in a growing community with a good school system, halfway between his parents and his wife's parents home. Lexington was the place selected and Clymer fit right in. Raised on a farm in Hancock County, he spoke regular Ohio English and had served two years in the U. S. Army. The young couple quickly involved themselves in church and community activities.

In the next nearly forty years Dr. Clymer offered leadership in posts at the Church of The Cross and sang in the church choir (which Betty directed for forty years). He was also a longtime member of the Kiwanis Club, including a term as president, volunteered with Habitat for Humanity and served two terms on the Lexington Board of Education.

Doc Clymer was, almost without exception, to be found on the sidelines during Lexington football and basketball games. That was always a comfort to the parents of the players. And each fall, long lines were to be seen outside his West Main Street office, where student athletes awaited free physical exams. One year there were over 400 such physicals given.

Dr. Clymer retired in 1999. However, he remains active in the community at this writing. He has always been a good doctor and a good citizen to Lexington.

Old Soldiers

In every generation they were looked up to by those who would follow behind. They were (and are) the old soldiers, the men and women who have served their country in time of war. The great contribution of their lives…their service, sacrifice and dedication are what makes this country, and our community, the wonderful place it is. We owe them so much.

This chapter is an effort to mention just a very few of the hundreds of these remarkable local soldiers. There were those that served and thankfully came back home. Others left and never returned. And there were those who came back, but were somehow never quite the same.

There were so many. Here are a few, whose story caught the writer's attention over the years.

George T. Myers

Born and raised in Lexington, this colorful Civil War veteran was best remembered by old-timers as "Monkey" Myers. It was a nickname picked up as a small schoolboy, when class members were assigned to study and imitate an animal. Myers, who was rather short in stature, did an excellent rendition of an ape and classmates started calling him "Monkey." He hated the nickname. It angered him, every time he heard it. Unfortunately, that only made matters worse. The nickname would follow Myers the rest of his life.

In the 1960's several old-timers told the writer that Myers was a squirrel hunter, a term that referred to a paid draft substitute. In other words, a squirrel hunter served in place of someone else, who did not wish to serve in the military. You could do that back then.

It was claimed by several that Myers never saw battle and only worked as a nurse. However, in his old age, from the park bench Myers and his comrades spun graphic stories of thrilling Calvary charges, bloody engagements, death and destruction. These tales were vivid and detailed enough to make the hair stand up on the neck of any young listener nearby.

Perhaps these tales were stretched a bit, which cast a shadow of suspicion on the service of Myers and the others. In fact, Myers once claimed he was the sole survivor of the Custer Massacre. However, he was in Lexington at the time of his survival from that terrible battle. So the claim was easily dismissed.

Nobody really knew his military record and nobody cared. He was just old "Monkey" Myers to the people of Lexington. However, research reveals a different story…one of bravery, heroism and service.

George T. Myers was eighteen when he enlisted in Company L, 10th Ohio Volunteer Calvary on December 24, 1863. With this unit he saw action in Tennessee and Georgia, including the siege of Atlanta.

Twice more, during the bloodiest war in U.S. history, Myers joined the United States Army. He re-enlisted on September 30, 1864, in Company G of the Ohio Volunteer Infantry. Then he re-enlisted again in Company D, 45th Regiment, Indiana Calvary Corps.

His honorable discharge finally came through on November 26, 1864. However, he joined Company D of the Ohio Veteran Reserves in April 1867.

Myers, like other old soldiers, lived on a modest $14 a month government pension. In 1895, the pension was increased to $16 per month. To supplement this, he was a barber by trade. In addition to barbering, he took on odd jobs around town. In 1891 he was hired by the village to clean and light their coal oil street lamps each night. From downtown to the railroad station there were 20 of these at one time. Being rather short in stature, Myers had to stand on the oil cart he pushed to reach the fixtures, which were on wooden posts. He was paid 48 cents a night.

Myers was married and had three sons and a daughter. Sadly, the latter died in 1904, when she was in her teens. Two of his sons served in World War I. One of them, Clyde, came back from the conflict and it is said that he "was never quite right" again. The trench warfare and poison gas had left its mark. These two tragic losses must have affected the old soldier deeply.

Myers was a member of the Conger Post #330 of the Grand Army of the Republic, when it was organized by Col. R. C. Brown at Lexington in 1883. He was an active member and served the post in many capacities. This included being post janitor for their headquarters in Sowers' Hall, volunteering to help whitewash and paper their meeting room and serving in the rifle squad which marched on Decoration Day.

Sid Earhart snapped this picture of George Myers (left) and Jake Dennis in 1925. At the time, they were two of the few remaining Civil War veterans from Lexington.

In 1885 Myers was hired by the post to nurse comrade Samuel Stough through the night in the absence of a relief committee. This he faithfully did for 13 nights and received $17.50 for his services. In 1903, he was still available for this service, helping care for another comrade, Charles Bechter.

Once, when Myers himself fell ill, the post sent the family a sack of flour. The old soldiers stuck together and looked after one another as best they could.

In 1892, the Post Commander failed to show up on Decoration Day. Old George stepped in at the last minute and conducted the ceremonies. For this, he was gratefully thanked.

Myers was appointed Post Commander himself in April of 1899. However, as the ranks of living veterans grew thinner, the Conger Post decided to surrender their charter. George Myers presided over that last sad meeting in January of 1900. Then he and a number of others joined the GAR group at the Mansfield Memorial Building.

In his younger days anyone who called him "Monkey" had better be ready to run or fight. George Myers was nobody to fool with in those days. However, as he grew old things were different.

In his old age, youngsters around town thoughtlessly taunted him. However, they still were ever careful to stay out of reach of the heavy cane he always carried.

Once, while sitting on a park bench, a kid grabbed his hat and ran around and around the old bandstand as George made a feeble attempt to catch him. Such torments would send the old soldier into a rage and he would fire a verbal broadside of profanity that was unmatched anywhere in the village. In that sense, he was a teacher. He taught the kids of town how to swear. As one former student once put it, "old George knew all the right words and just how to use them."

In 1967 the writer interviewed Mrs. Barb Faust. The white-haired grandmother attested to the harassment of Myers. She recalled a poem the kids made up that she herself had used to torment Myers:

> *Monkey, Monkey, bottle of beer,*
> *How many Monkeys are here?*
> *1, 2, 3, Monkey, Monkey,*
> *Bottle of beer!*

She also remembered the time when as a little girl, she had been taunting Myers and he chased her home. She ran into the house…and he came right in after her. A terrible row ensued. Fortunately for Barb, her father was home at the time.

Almost to the point of tears, old Mrs. Faust confessed that after all those years she was still very ashamed of what she had done. "He was a nice old man and never hurt anyone," she said. Others echoed that sentiment.

The Civil War veterans, and indeed veterans of other wars, enjoyed spending time together at the local pool hall and bar rooms. Remembered are times when Myers or others were to be seen staggering up the street from these gatherings. In fact, in the late 1800s, the village appointed three extra deputy marshals to keep the peace on the day of the "Soldiers Reunion." There were quite a few of those veterans and the reunion was a time to have a few drinks and let off a little steam.

The disrespect of Myers continued in his last years. He lived in a small, one-and-a-half story house (it's still there) on the east side of Maple Street, which the locals referred to as "Monkey Avenue." A few folks today still call it that, even though three quarters of a century have passed since he lived there.

Private George T. Myers died on October 2, 1928. Part of his obituary is as follows:

George Myers, age 82 years, six months and 25 days died at his home in Lexington at 2:15 o'clock. Mr. Myers had been growing very feeble of late and his death was not unexpected. Mr. Myers was a lifelong resident of Lexington and Richland County. He was an old soldier having enlisted in the United States Army on three different occasions. Funeral services will be held in the family home in Lexington on Thursday at 2:00.

Unfortunately the story of disrespect doesn't end with his death. Through some error, his gravestone reads "George Myers, 1846-1950." In addition, on at least one occasion, when flags were placed on veterans' graves for Memorial Day his burial site was missed. His hated nickname may be the only part of Myers' that is still remembered.

History records the names of great leaders and famous battles. Will history remember the name of Private George T. Myers, the last of Lexington's Civil War veterans, and the battle for respect he fought on the streets of his own hometown? It was a battle he never won.

Every generation is indebted to the old soldiers from the previous wars. All veterans, those living or long dead, should be treated with great respect. The guilt of neglect and disrespect for these soldiers is a stain that may never be removed. It can only be lessened by atonement.

Jacob Dennis was remembered by the old-timers, not for what he did during the Civil War, but for what he reportedly didn't do. You see, old Jake did dutifully serve in the Union Army. However, he didn't enlist or wasn't drafted until shortly before the war ended.

Several old-timers remembered his story. Dennis was only in the service for 4 months and 2 days before the war ended. He never left the State of Ohio, never heard a shot fired in anger and, as he was fond of telling it from the park benches, "I never cocked a cannon." He served in Company "C", 101st Regiment of Pennsylvania Volunteers. He was discharged June 25, 1865.

Dennis was a member of the Conger Post of the GAR and a good friend of George "Monkey" Myers. He had farmed outside town most of his life. However, in his old age he moved to town, where he was well known and frequently seen on the streets walking with his cane.

When he moved to town, he lived next to the old Church of Christ on Delaware Street. He was often seen making one of his regular trips to the post office or Sid Earhart's pool room. A quiet man, Dennis wasn't known for the somewhat exaggerated tales spun by his comrades.

When he walked on hard pavement, the soles of his shoes made a peculiar slapping noise. As a result, behind his back, he was known as "old clap foot."

Jacob Dennis, born in 1839, was among the very last surviving Civil War veterans from the Lexington area.

Major Seymore Beach Conger
Col. Everton J. Conger

It's rather surprising that two sons of a Presbyterian minister from Lexington should have distinguished careers during the Civil War. The father, Rev. Enoch Conger, was onetime pastor of the Troy Presbyterian church (which was located at the corner of present-day State Route 97 and Gass Road). Only the cemetery marks the location today.

The two brothers enlisted in the West Virginia Calvary in September, 1861 at Wheeling, West Virginia. They were enlisted for service as independent scouts recruited in Richland County.

S. B. received a recruiting order, raised a company of men and was commissioned a Lieutenant, in October 1862. He was promoted to Captain and then in July 1863 he rose to the rank of Major in the 3rd West Virginia Calvary.

Major Seymore Beech Conger

S.B. was described as always being at his post, ready for duty and as a leader of men. He rarely failed to lead his men from the front, whether on the march, on scouting parties, in raids or in battle.

In 1862, he led his men at Strasburg, Harrisonburg and Cross Keys, all in the campaign of Gen. Fremont. During 1863, S.B. commanded his unit at Gettysburg and in the pursuit of Lee, in the campaign of General Mead. In 1864, his unit came to the aid of General Hunter at Lynchburg.

On August 7, 1864, he was at the head of his men when he was killed by a Confederate sharpshooter at Moorehead, West Virginia. He was 39 years old.

There are conflicting reports as to where the heroic Conger was buried. A story in the August 17, 1864, Mansfield Herald says that *his remains were brought to Lexington on last Thursday morning. He leaves a young wife and many friends to mourn his early loss." A funeral sermon was preached in Lexington in early October.*

However, a rare 1906 Memorial Day program lists S. B. Conger as buried on Southern Battlefields. (It is the writer's belief that by 1906 all family members had moved away. In addition, of the 112 area Civil War veterans listed, only 13 remained alive. So it is likely that none of these men could remember the actual location of his grave.)

In addition, a crude, hand-written 1864 letter suggests that he was killed in Maryland and buried in Plymouth Ohio under Masonic Order. Rev. Conger did serve churches in Plymouth, among other places. However, it is doubtful that the letter is accurate. (Ministers lived a pitiful life of poverty in those days. So it is quite likely that neither Rev. Conger nor the Major's widow had the funds available for a grand burial or headstone. At the time, some headstones were even carved from wood.)

Before the war, S.B. had attempted to build a brick house, but it fell down during construction. (The lime and sand mixture came into question.) He also owned some fine horses and 160 acres in the NE ¼ of section 10, not far from the old Troy Church where his father preached. (Part of this farm is now under the waters of the Clear Fork Reservoir.) So with ties to that area, it is quite probable he was laid to rest in the cemetery next to the church where his father was once pastor.

In any case, if he is buried in either the Plymouth or Lexington cemeteries, or quite possibly the Troy Cemetery next to the old Presbyterian Church, then he lies in an unmarked grave. No flag marks this heroic soldier's grave on Memorial Day.

Brother **Everton J. Conger**, born in 1835, was a dentist. He was working at Fremont when the war broke out and enlisted with his brother for 100 days service. Before his term expired, he too raised a company in Ohio and was commissioned a Captain. He was later promoted to Lieutenant-Colonel, serving in the 1st D. C. Calvary under a Col. Baker. Since Baker was absent much of the time, Conger had actual command of the unit.

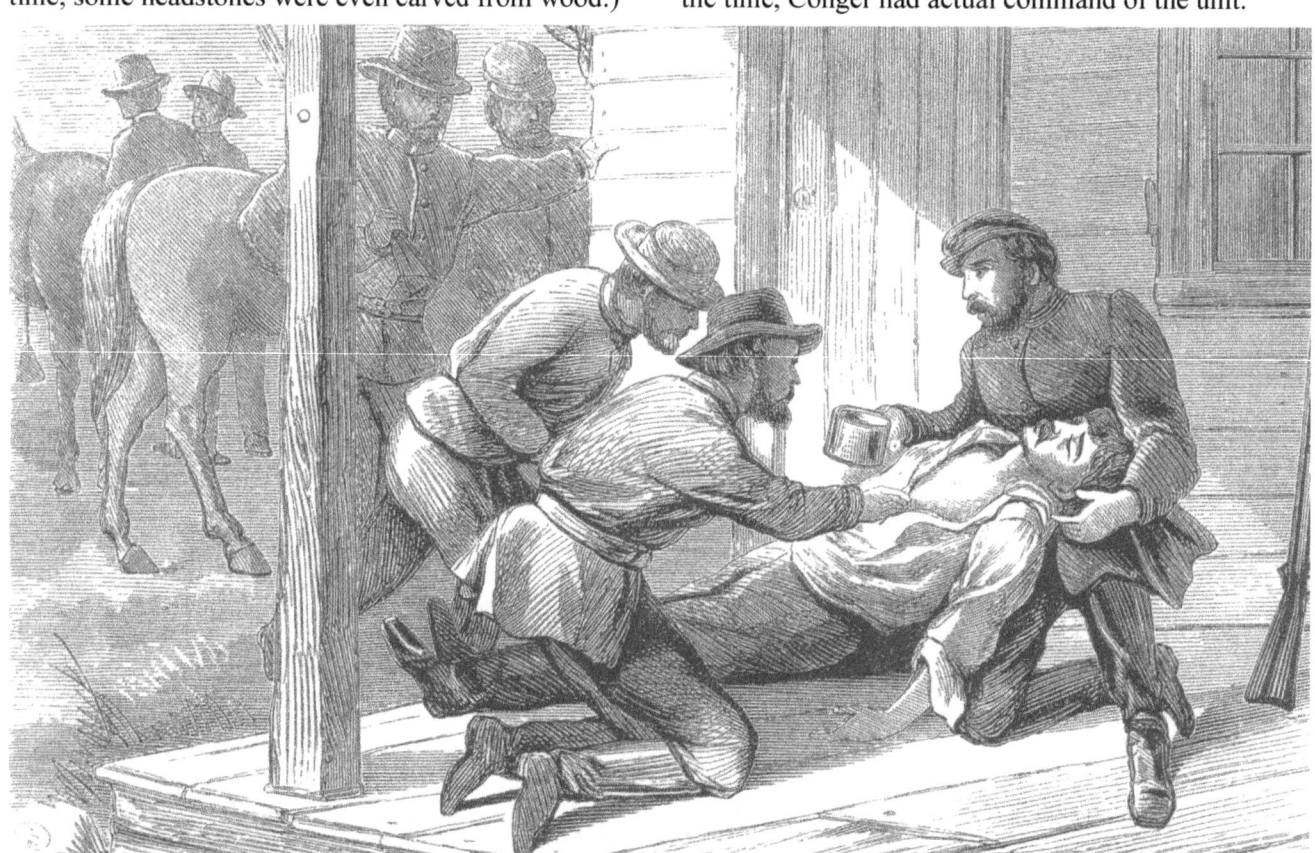

Artist's rendition of Booth's death, from the book "History of the United States Secret Service," by General L.C. Baker, 1867

E.J. fought at Petersburg and through the Richmond campaign and was wounded several times. In one action, his arm was nearly cut off by a broad sword. And he was later crippled for life, carrying a bullet in his body.

When Lincoln was assassinated, the then General Baker was head of what became the United States Secret Service. Twenty of Baker's men were detached to act under the command of Conger to go in search of John Wilkes Booth, Lincoln's assassin.

They finally found Booth hiding in a barn. When he refused to come out, the barn was set on fire to drive the assassin out. The attempt to take Booth alive failed, when one of Conger's men disobeyed orders and shot him.

Booth was carried to a nearby porch, where Col. Conger held the murderer's head and administered aid in an effort to save the dying assassin. However the effort was in vain, as Booth died before a doctor could be summoned. Conger and a few of his men took Booth's body back to Washington.

After the war, the Colonel tried to practice dentistry for two years. He then moved to Carmi, Illinois, where he studied law and was admitted to the bar in 1871. He was later elected Police Magistrate. In 1880, he was appointed to be a federal judge in the Montana Territory. He died years later, back in Illinois, at the home of one of his children.

Thus ends the story of the two heroic sons of Reverend Enoch Conger, onetime pastor of the Troy Presbyterian Church.

Samuel Strasbaugh was a private in the 102 Ohio Volunteer Infantry, which was formed at Mansfield in the fall of 1862. The regiment moved through Kentucky and Tennessee to Alabama, where it was involved in several engagements. In September of 1864, Strasbaugh was with a detachment of 400 men (200 of which were from the 102nd), when they were surrounded by an overwhelming Confederate force. After a fierce battle, the remainder of the detachment was surrendered.

Strasbaugh was taken to a rebel prison (either infamous Andersonville Prison in Georgia or Cahaba Prison in Alabama), where he languished for months amid the starvation, disease and death of those horrible confines. Thousands of men were crammed into small areas without shelter, good water or food in those prisons. Many of the prisoners died and were buried in mass graves.

A prisoner exchange was finally arranged, at long last, in April, 1865. And after riding in cramped train box cars and marching on foot, the prisoners were "paroled" at Vicksburg, Mississippi, as the war ended.

The Union Army gave the starved skeletal men food and they were able to replace their ragged, rotting clothing. Strasbaugh and approximately 2,250 of his prison comrades were loaded on board the steamboat Sultana for the trip north to home and freedom.

The Sultana was registered to hold 376 passengers. However, the greedy operators, seeing a chance for good profit, greatly overloaded the vessel. The boat left the dock at Vicksburg, April 24, 1865, with almost 2,300 people on board. (652 of whom were released Union soldiers from Ohio.)

Unfortunately, problems with the ship's boilers had only received temporary repairs. So the overloaded ship strained against the swift current of the Mississippi.

At 2:00 AM on the morning of April 27, seven miles north of Memphis, three of the Sultana's boilers exploded. The Mississippi was at flood stage at that time and it is estimated that the river was almost three miles wide where the tragedy occurred.

The explosions killed hundreds and set the wooden vessel on fire. Many more were burned to death or scalded by the steam. As the Sultana continued to burn, escape was impossible for the vast majority of very weak paroled prisoners.

It has been calculated from historical accounts and records that over 1,700 died in that explosion and resulting fire. Hundreds of weakened men drowned in the swirling water while attempting to swim the long miles to shore. It was the greatest maritime disaster in American history, surpassing even the sinking of the *Titanic*.

Of the 107 members of the 102nd Ohio on board, 71 were either killed out right by the explosion, burned to death, drowned or died shortly afterwards of injuries. How Strasbaugh died in unknown. Many bodies were never found or identified. Due to the flood levels and swift currents, dead bodies floated downstream for miles, some as far as the Gulf of Mexico.

One can only imagine the joy and expectation Samuel must have felt as he boarded the Sultana and was finally homeward bound. The anticipation of seeing family, friends and his farm southeast of town must have filled his heart with a renewed faith in God. For him the terrible Civil War was over.

Sadly, he never made it home.

Photograph courtesy of Tillie Taylor

Pictured here are former submariner Nelson Reel, wife Tillie and son Robert. Nelson was instrumental in starting the town park on Plymouth Street. Wife Tillie became the first female bus driver for Lexington schools in 1960. She was known as "the singing driver" for using sing-alongs to keep kids in line.

Nelson Reel was in the submarine service during World War II, serving as a machinist's mate. He served in the Pacific Fleet and his submarine was in the sea battles at Coral Sea, Midway, Java and the Macassar Straits.

Reel's sub had some close calls. His ship was depth charged one Christmas Eve 34 times and 27 more on Christmas Day. On another occasion, when they surfaced near a burning Japanese tanker, a Japanese cruiser was only about 100 yards behind them. They went down in a hurry and the cruiser narrowly passed over them.

Fortunately their sub was undamaged in these engagements. They had the satisfaction of sinking several Japanese ships during their campaign. And on one mission they rescued five United States pilots shot down and stranded on an island.

Reel had entered the service in December, 1940, when he was 17. He attended Lexington Schools and was always interested in sports. In fact he was so enthused by sports that, after the war, one of the ways he served in his hometown was along those lines.

Reel and his friend George Swigart put together a group of volunteers to build a ball field at the then new Lexington Park. The well-liked Reel put his friendly persuasion on folks and Swigart corralled any able-bodied man he found on the bar stools at Swigart's Café. Any healthy man who failed to show up on park work weekends was in for poor service and a lot of lip the next week.

Their leadership expanded into the community. Many willing hands cut trees, carved out the field and built fences. These fences were later rebuilt and improved, along with the addition of bleachers and lighting. And this work continues. Today, Lexington has a park system and sports program that is the envy of most villages its size.

It all started when a Navy veteran climbed out of a submarine, came back home and wanted a place to play ball. The main baseball field was recently named "Reel – Swigart Field" in their honor.

Robert L. Castor came from a large family of four boys and five girls. He and his brother Ed were drafted into the U. S. Army in 1941. Robert had worked at Gambles' Lunch Room and Ed for Brooker Brothers Trucking. They were together during basic training at Camp Wolters, Texas. After basic, Ed was sent to Georgia for paratrooper school. He later survived four combat jumps. Robert went to Camp McCoy, Wisconsin, for ski trooper training and then wound up in Europe.

Their two brothers, Charles, and William Jr., also followed them into service a short time later. Of the four, only three of the Castor boys would come home after the war. Robert was killed by a sniper's bullet near Brest, France, August 31, 1944. He was 26.

In 1967, a new Veterans of Foreign Wars Post was organized in Lexington. Several of founding members

Sgt. ROBERT L. CASTOR
Co."F"- 23rd Inf. Reg. - 2nd Div.
Killed In Action Aug. 31, 1944
BREST, FRANCE

of the Post called at the William Castor home. They asked permission to name the new Post after their son, Robert. Permission was gladly granted and Robert L. Castor VFW Post 5101 has become an important part of the Lexington community.

The Post's color guards for parades, programs on Memorial Day and graveside services for veterans are commonly seen. However, Post members are also quietly involved in support of numerous other activities in the area. In addition, and to their credit, the Post has attempted to maintain records of all veterans buried in the Lexington area cemeteries. In today's mobile society, that must prove to be quite a challenge. The writer has a copy of their list and it is quite extensive.

With this group as namesake, the Castor family will not be forgotten.

Charles Russell Heyser is another veteran that is remembered by older residents. A graduate of Lexington High School Class of 1930, he is recalled as being popular with the girls and having played an instrument in the band.

He always used his middle name, Russell, and lived with his parents on East Main Street, across from the Minnear Hotel. Russell worked with his father, Tod Heyser, who was the foreman of the section gang for the B&O Railroad tracks that runs through town.

Russell was 30, on March 24, 1942, when he entered the service during World War II. At Camp Forest, Tennessee, he was in the tank destroyer battalion. It is quite likely that he went from there to Fort Hood, Texas, where a Tank Destroyer Command had been formed.

It is unknown what battalion he served with or where he went in combat. Heyser never married and living relatives have found no record. Two contacts with the Richland County Veterans Service Commission have revealed very little. It seems all requested information was either "classified," could not be copied or, as the gentleman hastily shuffled through records, not found. To the writer it appeared that, like too many government servants, this bureaucrat had only two interests; quitting time and payday.

By the time Russell arrived in the service, the older design 75mm cannons used for destroying tanks had been mounted on M3 half tracks. There were also some Dodge trucks with a crudely mounted 37mm gun used for this purpose.

Then in 1943, a first standardized tank destroyer gun was introduced, mounted on a lightly armored M4 tank chassis. It could only withstand small arms fire. Improvement continued throughout the war, but bureaucratic bungling delayed delivery of a better design. This delay, and unwise field tactics, needlessly cost many lives. Survival of an encounter with superior armed German tanks often depended on who could shoot first.

There were 73 tank destroyer battalions by January of 1945, of which 53 were in Europe, the balance were in transit or training. Some of those battalions lost more than half their men in single battles. Heyser must have been in that awful European carnage.

Russell was "gassed" by the Germans during one of these long, bloody encounters. Those who knew him said that after he came back from the war, "he wasn't quite right." He would often carry on conversations with himself, when there was nobody around to reply.

Heyser went back to work on the B&O with his dad. In the evenings, he would often appear on the streets or at local businesses, where he would stand out among folks in blue collar Lexington. He was always neatly attired with dress pants, a nice shirt and sports jacket, with shined shoes and a gentleman's hat. When standing around town, Russell always held his hands behind his back observing the goings on.

His well tanned, clean shaven face wore a smile when anyone approached. With head nodding and mouth going, his conversations with himself continued after he was again left alone. When Russell drove through town, always at very slow speed which sometimes held up traffic, he could be seen talking even though there were no passengers in the car.

The teenagers and a few others around town called him "Speed" or "Speedy Heyser." And if someone shouted "Hey Speedy" as he drove by, he'd smile and wave. He didn't mind being addressed as such.

Folks trended to avoid or shy away from Russell. He was different. They didn't know his past. They didn't want to engage him in conversation. In retrospect, he must have been a very lonely man.

In 1966, he was admitted to the Columbus State Hospital for reasons unknown to the writer, and a year later the burden passed from his parents to his only sister, Bertha Bogner, who was appointed guardian. Their other brother had died when a teenager.)

In 1971, he was declared to need "aid and attending" when he was released from Columbus. At that time he went into one of several nursing homes. A Railroad Disability Pension was granted in April of 1971, and he received $216.45 a month. He had worked on the B&O for 29 years.

There are countless stories of veterans who suffered terribly in foreign prison camps before being released. One can now only speculate on the mental and physical condition of Russell. Did the memory of the horrors of that war haunt him all those years?

Although well-cared for, in his last years had the nursing home somehow become his prison, a prison from which there was no escape? His sister may have been his only visitor.

Ironically Charles Russell Heyser died November 11, 1978, Veterans Day, at the Griffith Nursing Home near Lexington. Perhaps for him, World War II was finally over. It was time to go home, free at last.

ROLLIN HEIDLEBAUGH wrote a story for the Mansfield News Journal in 1978, detailing his service during World War Two. It is reprinted here with permission, exactly as he wrote it.

In February 1941, as one of the first to be drafted from Morrow County, I was sent to Ft. Hayes in Columbus to be sworn into the army. In a few days 400 of us were put on a train and sent to Ft. Stevens, Oregon, as part of the coast artillery force. We were trained to fire the big guns that had been left there from World War l, which were still in thier original emplacement for harbor defense of the Columbia River.

After two years at Ft. Stevens and Ft. Columbia, Wash., I was sent to Santa Anna, Calif. for Air Force cadet school to become a pilot. Training took place at various air bases around the country to learn to fly everything from open cockpit planes to twin engine to the four engine B-17. After being commissioned a first lieutenant, I was sent to Grand Island, Neb., for training in the B-29 super fortress, a long range bomber.

Our 6th bomb group was sent to Tinian Island in the Marianas. Our 11-man crew flew 17 missions over 17

Rollin Heidelbaugh flew Army Air Corps B-29 "Blind Date" from the Tinian Island in 1945. The crew picked that name because they didn't know when they were leaving or where they were going. The first "Blind Date" exploded, killing all onboard, when another crew took it on a mission. His second plane of the same name was shot down on its 18th mission, over Tokyo May 24, 1945.

missions over Japan, (3,000 miles round trip over water) before being shot down May 24, 1945, during a fire raid over Tokyo. After spending three days in the hills of southern Japan before being captured, I was taken to Tokyo by way of an old Chevy truck and a box car. I was blindfolded and paraded through the streets to Kempi Tai prison and was beaten and interrogated by Japanese soldiers at the prison. There were 16 of us in a very small cell with no windows or vents. Guards were present 24 hours a day and we were not allowed to talk. We sat on a wooden floor 16 hours a day and slept for eight hours.

The only food we received each day consisted of three golf ball-size sour rice balls and a small amount of water. I lost almost 100 pounds from May until we were released in late August. There was not medical attention for any of us, and some airmen died in their cells.

In August we were moved to the Omori Prison Camp on Tokyo Bay. One of my biggest thrills was waking up on Aug. 29, 1945, at Omori Prison Camp, and seeing a white hospital ship with a large red cross on the side and watching the Navy boys come after us. This was the first knowledge that we had won the war. Another thrilling moment was watching a huge flyover by B-29s from the deck of the hospital ship and recognizing that many were from my squadron. I was on a destroyer near the USS Missouri, where the war treaty was signed.

We were sent to the Philippines for 15 days before being sent home. One of my fondest memories was looking up from the deck of our transport ship through the heavy fog and seeing the golden gate bridge. After spending a week at Letterman Hospital in San Francisco, I was sent home to Ohio for 100 days of sick leave. I then returned to Santa Ana, Calif., and was sent to camp Atterbury, Ind., for an honorable discharge April 4, 1946. The best moment of all was returning home to Ohio after five years of service.

Lieutenant Rollin Heidlebaugh was awarded the Distinguished Flying Cross, the Air Medal with Oak Leaf clusters, the Purple Heart, the pre Pearl Harbor badge, the Presidential unit citation, and the Pacific Theater of War ribbon with three battle stars.

He returned to his Morrow County family farm, which had a good-sized dairy operation. In addition to farm work, Rollin also drove a Lexington school bus for nearly 35 years. The last few or these years, he served as the school's Director of Transportation.

His combat service didn't necessarily end with the war however. Remembered is the time when Joe Prosser, a stocky country boy, was acting up in the back of Rollin's bus. Prosser refused several orders to move to a front and held tightly onto his seat. As the story goes, Rollin stopped the bus, turned off the engine, set the brake and went back after him. In the resulting tussle, the seat was torn clear off the floor. Prosser walked home that day and later rode in the front of the bus.

It must have been a comfort to parents to know their offspring were in the steady, no-nonsense hands of a former B-29 pilot. When he died in 2003, many of those former passengers, in some cases two or more generations, came to pay their respects.

Rollin was actually captured twice. First it was by the Japanese. Later he was caught again, by Gloria Ferguson, a pretty young lady from Mansfield. She knew who he was before the war and when he came back, friend George Clever arranged for the two to meet on a blind date. They were married in November of 1946, raised three kids and spent their lives on the family "Century" farm southwest of Steam Corners.

Gloria and Rollin Heidlebaugh photographed at their farm in 1966. Rollin was a former B-29 pilot and is well remembered as a Lexington school bus driver for generations of students.

Heidlebaugh also served as a Trustee of the Morrow Rural Electric Co-op for 36 years. Always active in the Farm Bureau, school, and community affairs, the Heidlebaughs were good friends and neighbors to all who knew them.

Lexington women have always helped on the home front. One example took place in Crestline.

When World War II was over, crowded troop trains headed east and west stopped in Crestline for engine service, car cleaning and crew change. The cars were packed with returning servicemen, but no food was available on the train. Crestline and Mansfield churches tried to feed the hungry men, but needed more help. Mona Schindler called Ruby Campbell and wondered if the Lexington churches should help.

It was Mona's idea. So she was put in charge of a loosely organized group of volunteers, mostly women, which was quickly assembled. Sloppy Joes, cakes, pies, cookies and the like were donated by the women from the Congregational, Presbyterian, Church of Christ, and Steam Corners Methodist churches. Two days were picked and the Lexington volunteers descended on the Crestline rail station.

All went well the first day. However, on the next day, after they had used up all their food on the first train of the day, word was received of a second trainload coming soon. So a mad dash was made to the get more supplies from local stores.

Unfortunately, the boys arrived before that second batch of Sloppy Joes was finished cooking. However, one hungry yet anxious soldier asked if the Sloppy Joes had any pork in it. "No," came the answer. And with that the GIs said they'd take the food as it was, even if only half-cooked. The train wouldn't wait and they were very hungry.

Some grateful servicemen left Crestline that day. Some weary, but happy women came back home.

Other local women served in more formal ways. **Ethyl Swank** is one such example. Ethyl worked for a high-ranking official at the Pentagon. Her service was important enough that, while she was home for a visit, the

At 96, Mona Schindler still fondly remembers when a group from Lexington fed the returning WWII soldiers at the Crestline railroad station. Wynonia Dill, Artie Heyser, Laura McIntire, Flora Wagner, Lucile Sowers, May Hoverstick, Jessie Pierce, Mrs. Hainer, Ruby Campbell and Mary Ann Campbell are just a few of those involved that Mona recalls.

Ethyl Swank worked for a very high-ranking official in the Pentagon. Home for a visit, the government sent an Army Air Corps plane to take her back to Washington. In the background you can see her "air taxi."

government sent an Army Air Corps plane to retrieve her. Exactly what she did is unknown. However, we do know that most of the military brass had to take a train when they took leave. That has to say something about her contribution.

Commentary:

Few veterans take the time to write down their service experiences. This is unfortunate. Their duty to the United States is seldom kept alive orally and that service should not be forgotten.

It matters not whether they were in combat or served in supply, hospitals, maintenance or the other support groups. These men and women gave of the time they were allotted on earth, for the benefit of their country.

Korea, Vietnam, Desert Storm, Afghanistan and Iraq, along with half a hundred other places, have witnessed the service of America's military men and women. Each one of these people has a story to tell. If they don't record those stories, their efforts will be lost to future generations.

Nearly all our servicemen and women have one thing in common. Their service to our country didn't end with their discharge papers. This is an important lesson that should remain.

To salvage what might also be lost to the pages of time when the writer is gone, below are contents of two Lexington Memorial Day Service programs.

Each is the only known copy of the event program. The first is from the 1906 Memorial Day service and the second from the 1916 service. These were found in the possession of Mrs. Ruth Chalfant in 1967:

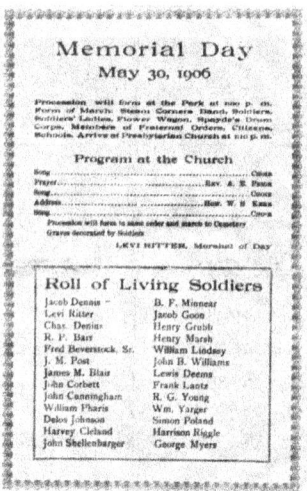 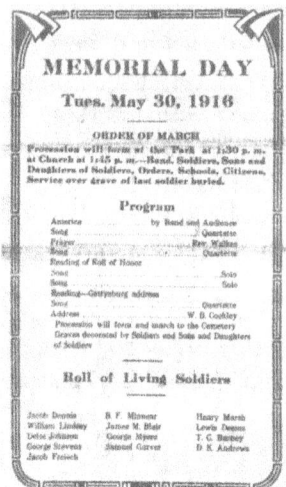

Rediscovered in possession of Mrs. Ruth Chalfant during 1967, these are the only known copies of the programs from Lexington's 1906 and 1916 Memorial Day Services. For clarity, the text has been transcribed and the soldier lists alphabetized on the following pages.

The uniformed Lexington town band was the pride of the village and replaced the Steam Corners Band for local events, such as Memorial Day ceremonies. The Steam Corners Band was hired to play at the 1906 Lexington Memorial Day Service, but our own Lexington Town Band was used in 1916. (Note the bandstand, which was located in the park on the square, in the background.)

MEMORIAL DAY
May 30, 1906

Procession will form at the Park at 1:00PM. Form of March; Steam Corners Band, Soldiers, Soldiers Ladies, Flower Wagon, Spayde's Drum Corps, Members of Fraternal Orders, Citizens, Schools. Arrive at Presbyterian Church at 1:10

Program at the Church
Song……………………………....Choir
Prayer……………….Rev. A. E. Proir
Song……………………………....Choir
Address……..............Hon. W. S. Kerr
Song……………………………....Choir

Procession will form in same order and March to Cemetery Graves decorated by soldiers.

Roll of Living Soldiers

R. P. Barr	Jacob Dennis	Simon Poland
Fred Beverstock Sr.	Henry Grubb	J. M. Post
James M. Blair	Delos Johnson	Harrison Riggle
Harvey Cleland	Frank Lantz	Levi Ritter
Jacob Coon	William Lindsey	John Shellenbarger
John Corbett	Henry Marsh	John B. Williams
John Cunningham	B. F. Minnear	Wm. Yarger
Lewis Deems	George Myers	R. G. Young
Charles Dennis	William Pharis	

Buried in Lexington Cemetery:

Soldiers of the Revolution

Amariah Watson   Samuel Colwell

War of 1812

Capt. Daniel Bailey	George Culp	Robert Serles
Silas Beverstock	William Damsell	Moses Sowers
William Blair	Daniel Keller	Henry Stewart
Ezekiel Boggs	James McIntere	William Stewart
George Carey	Thomas McIntere	Noah Watson
Justice Carpenter	John Milligan	Samuel Watson
Adna Coleman	William Richey	Cornelius Whitford

War with Mexico

Daniel Boals   John Carrothers
Joseph Boals   James Marshall

MEMORIAL DAY - May 30, 1906 (continued)

Soldiers of the War of the Rebellion

Wm. Anderson,	120th Ohio	C. D. Culp,	6th Oh.	Thomas Murray,	163 O B.
Isaac Baker,	102d OVI	Cyrus Day,	187th Oh.	J. P. Mount,	86th O C.
Oliver Barr,	86th O I	Samuel Dilly,	163d Ohio	James Narrence,	15th Ohio
Wilson Baughman,	86th O. C.	John Eastgate,	(Not listed)	Enock Numbers,	15th Ohio
Barney Beverstock,	163 Ohio B.	James Fergeson,	120th Ohio	James Palm,	163 Ohio B
Silas Beverstock,	144th	John Gailey,	163d OVI	Levi Rider,	120th Ohio
Samuel Blair,	111th OVI	Richard Gailey,	86th OVI	Squires Sanders,	58th NY
Thomas Bowland,	(Not listed)	John Goff,	(Not listed)	Edward Seither,	163 Ohio B
Col. R. C. Brown,	64th	J. J. Graham,	53d Penn.	Jacob Shambaugh,	2nd OVI
Alonzo Carpenter,	136th O.	Elias Heyser,	64th OVI	George Siley,	19th OVI
Miller Carter,	163d OVI	Henry Hiskey,	15th OVI	Samuel Stough,	64th Ohio
James Cass,	15th O. C.	Samuel Hiskey,	64th Ohio	W. C. Stough,	8th Oh. B
Silas Chase,	64th Ohio	James Keller,	163d Ohio	Zachariah Tanneyhill,	3d O
Wm. Chindler,	120th OVI	D. L. King,	6th Ohio. B.	Lemuel Timanis,	163 OVI
Allen B. Cockley,	10th O C.	Geo. Lewis,	163d OVI	Peter Tolhelm,	158 Penn.
Capt. W.W. Cockley,	187 O	James McCune,	64th Ohio	Carver Walker,	123d OVI
Lt. Jessie J. Cook,	64th Rg	W W. McJunkins,	64th O. C.	H. P. Washburn,	118th OVI
Logan Cook,	86th OVI	Bentley Meyers,	64th OVI	David Williams,	120th OVI
Robert Cornman,	64th OVI	D. P. Miller,	163d OVI	George Wilson,	(Not listed)
Elzy Courtney,	15th O C.	John Moon,	64th OVI	Wm. Wilson,	2nd Oh. Art.
Harness Coyner,	128 Ohio	H. S. Moore,	15th Ohio	Samuel Wolford,	(?) OVI

War of the Rebellion - Soldiers buried on Southern Battlefields

Simon Barnes,	McLaughlin Sq.	James Delamater,	92d Ill.	Abraham Marks,	32d OVI
Solomon Becthell,	159 NY	Jacob Eyerly,	15th OVI	Hamilton McClurg,	159 NY
Fred Beverstock,	3d WV Cal.	Robert Fix,	6th Ohio LA	Joseph Narience,	15th OVI
Issac Bonner,	McLaughlin Sq.	Matthew Grice,	15th OVI	Charles Newlom,	64th OVI
Martin Bowser,	64th OVI	Phillip Haflic,	15th OVI	Wm. Numbers,	86th Ohio
R. B. Cambell,	86th OVI	Wesly Hethrington,	64th OVI	William Palm,	64th OVI
Maj. S.B. Conger,	3d WV Cal.	P. L. Holton,	(Unknown)	Wm. Philip,	64th OVI
Wm. Coyner,	10th Ohio Cal.	Frank Jackson,	29th Iowa	Rev. Geo. Philips,	49th OVI
Charles Cracraft,	15th OVI	George Knox,	64th OVI	Jerry Ritter,	64th OVI
Jefferson Culp,	3d OC	Benj. Laman,	15th OVI	Thomas Shambaugh,	3d WV Cal.
				Avery Watson,	6th OLA

Spanish-American War

George Washington Coleman   8th Ohio Vol. Infantry

MEMORIAL DAY
May 30, 1916

Procession will form at the Park at 1:30pm, at Church at 1:45pm. Band, Soldiers, Sons and Daughters of Soldiers, Orders, Schools, Citizens. Service over grave of last soldier buried.

Program

America..........................by Band and Audience
Song............................Quarette
Prayer...........................Rev. Walker
Song............................Quarette
Reading of Honor Roll
Song............................Solo
Song............................Solo
Song............................Choir
Reading - Gettysburg Address
Song............................Quarette
Address.........................W.B. Cockley

Procession will form in same order and march to Cemetery. Graves decorated by Soldiers and Sons and Daughters of Soldiers.

Roll of Living Soldiers

D.K. Andrews	Jacob Freisch	William Lindsey
T.C. Barney	R. P. Barr	Henry Marsh
James M. Blair	Samuel Garver	B. F. Minnear
Lewis Deems	Delos Johnson	George Myers
		George Stevens

Names of Soldiers Buried in Lexington Cemetery:

Soldiers of the Revolution

Amariah Watson   Samuel Colwell

War of 1812

Capt. Daniel Bailey	George Culp	Robert Serles
Silas Beverstock	William Damsell	Moses Sowers
William Blair	Daniel Keller	Henry Stewart
Ezekiel Boggs	James McIntere	William Stewart
George Carey	Thomas McIntere	Noah Watson
Justice Carpenter	John Milligan	Samuel Watson
Adna Coleman	William Richey	Cornelius Whitford

War with Mexico

Daniel Boals	John Carrothers
Joseph Boals	James Marshall

MEMORIAL DAY - Tues. May 30, 1916 (Continued)

Soldiers of the War of the Rebellion

Wm. Anderson,	120th Ohio	Elzy Courtney,	163 Ohio Cav.	David P. Miller,	163d OVI
Isaac Baker,	102d OVI	Harness Coyner,	128 Ohio	John Moon,	64th OVI
Oliver Barr,	86th O I	Columbus D. Culp,	6th Oh. Bat.	H. S. Moore,	15th Ohio
Harris Baughman,	(Not Listed)	John Cunningham,	(Not Listed)	J. P. Mount,	86th O C.
Wilson Baughman,	86th O. C.	Cyrus Day,	187th Oh.	Thomas Murray,	163 Co. B.
Barney Beverstock,	163 Ohio B.	Charles E. Dennis,	184 OVI	Bentley Myers,	64th OVI
Frank Beverstock,	3 WV Calavry	Samuel Dilly,	163 Ohio	James Narrance,	15th Ohio
Silas Beverstock,	144th	Daniel Dye,	(Not Listed)	Enock Numbers,	15th Ohio
Samuel Blair,	111th OVI	John Eastgate,	(Not listed)	James Palm,	163 Oh B
Patrick Brannon,	(Not Listed)	James Fergeson,	120th Ohio	Levi Rider,	120 Ohio
Col. R. C. Brown,	64th	John Gailey,	163d OVI	Thomas Rowland,	(Unlisted)
John Carey,	(Not Listed)	Richard Gailey,	86th OVI	Squires Sanders,	58th NY
Alonzo Carpenter,	136th Ohio	John Groff,	(Not listed)	Edward Seither,	163 Oh B
Miller Carter,	163d OVI	J. J. Graham,	53d Penn.	George Siley,	19th OVI
James Cass,	15th O. C.	Elias Heyser,	64th OVI	Samuel Stough,	64th Ohio
Silas Chase,	64th Ohio	Henry Hiskey,	15th OVI	W. C. Stough,	8th Oh. Bat
Wm. Chindler,	120th OVI	Samuel Hiskey,	64th Ohio	Jacob Strausbaugh,	2nd OVI
Harvey Cleland,	(Not Listed)	Frederick Hoffman,	64 Regt.	Zachariah Tanneyhill,	3d O
Allen B. Cockley,	10th O C.	Daniel Keller,	(Not Listed)	Lemuel Timanis,	163 OVI
Capt. WW Cockley,	187 O	James Keller,	163d Ohio	Peter Tolhelm,	158 Penn.
John H. Coffman,	(Not Listed)	David L. King,	6th Ohio. B.	Garver Walker,	123d OVI
Obediah Coleman,	(Not Listed)	Geo. Lewis,	163d OVI	Chas. P. Washburn,	118th OVI
Lt. Jessie J. Cook,	72 OVI	James McCune,	64th Ohio	David Williams,	120th OVI
Logan Cook,	86th OVI	Robert McCune,	142 Ohio	George Wilson,	(Not listed)
Robert Cornman,	64th OVI	Thomas McCune,	(Not Listed)	Wm. Wilson,	2nd O. Art.
W. W. McJunkins,	64th O. C.	Samuel Wolford,	102 OVI		

War of the Rebellion - Soldiers buried on Southern Battlefields

Simon Barnes,	McLaughlin Sq.	Robert Fix,	6th Ohio LA	Joseph Narience,	15th OVI
Solomon Bechtoll,	159 NY	Matthew Grice,	15th OVI	Charles Newlom,	64th OVI
Issac Bonner,	McLaughlin Sq.	Phillip Haflic,	15th OVI	Wm. Numbers,	86th Ohio
Martin Bowser,	64th OVI	Wesly Hethrington,	64th OVI	William Palm,	64th OVI
R. B. Cambell,	86th OVI	P. L. Holton,	(Unknown)	Wm. Philip,	64th OVI
Maj. S.B. Conger,	3d Vir. Cal.	Frank Jackson,	29th Iowa	Rev. Geo. Philips,	49th OVI
Wm. Coyner,	10th Ohio Cal.	George Knox,	64th OVI	Henry Riggle	102 Ohio
Charles Cracraft,	15th OVI	Benj. Laman,	15th OVI	Jerry Ritter,	64th OVI
Jefferson Culp,	3d OC	Abraham Marks,	32d OVI	Thomas Shambaugh,	3d WV Cal.
James Delmater	95 Illinois	Albert McClurg,	159 NY	Samuel Strasbaugh,	102 O.I.
Jacob Eyerly,	15th OVI	Hamilton McClurg,	159 NY	Avery Watson,	6th OLA

Spanish-American War

Joseph Barnes	64 Ohio	Henry Grubb	163 OVI
Fred Beverstock	88 Ohio	William H. Hill	(Not Listed)
Geo. Washington Coleman	8th Ohio Vol. Infantry	James M. Scott	102 OVI
John Corbett	(Not Listed)	Thomas Scott	163 OVI
William Gass	86 OVI	John Shellenbarger	64 OVI
Jacob Goon	120 OVI	Jacob Shew	1 Maryland

Early Lexington Business

The building on the right (foreground) is the third water powered mill built in town. It operated for less than 10 years and was torn down in 1906. The white building on the left (behind bridge structure) was the old railroad station. The house across the tracks from the mill was built by Watson and the next building (barely seen behind Watson's house) was the Cook Tavern, which burned in 1899. This photograph was taken (around 1900) from the cemetery lawn (roughly), looking West toward the town square.

A Seed is Planted

Amariah Watson and his water-powered saw and grist mills were the first business venture in Lexington. As mentioned earlier, these were operating by the end of 1812 and soon the new mill created the need for a tavern to serve waiting mill customers. Jacob Cook answered this need with "Cook's Tavern" in 1815-16.

Adnah Coleman was the second owner of the Cook Tavern. He later opened a tannery south of East Main Street, along the Clear Fork, where he bought hides and made shoes.

It's interesting to note, that, of the original town plat, only two lots had been sold west of the square as of 1818. All cabins and business buildings were on East Main, near the mill, at that time. Records of that period are sketchy. However, it is probable that present-day West Main, Plymouth and Frederick streets, as well as the town square were still forest or tree stumps then.

Even all the lots on East Main Street had not been sold by 1819. You might expect that the erection of cabins and businesses, or perhaps land speculators would have ensured the sale of all East Main lots in the growing village. However, these were pioneer times.

To make a living in 1819 Lexington, you had to have a farm or a much needed craft. There were no large employers to support a "housing boom." The local economy was so small that it was a huge risk to open a business, especially if that business was not essential to the other settlers lives or if it faced competition.

Watson's mill had planted a seed that would grow into a town. However, that seed would take time to grow.

From Slow Growth to Boomtown

A stage line passed through Lexington in the 1820s. This helped put the new town on the map in the eyes of travelers.

According to the *1880 Richland County History*, John F. Adams and William Damsell opened a dry goods store in 1814. However, no trace of this business has been located in land or tax records until 1825. So there is reason to doubt the reported 1814 date.

In 1827 William Damsell was selling groceries and general merchandise in this "new" building. It later contained various types of businesses until the end, when it was known as "the old Hiskey place." This photo was taken from East Main, just East of Mill Street, looking to the South.

The large old building that once stood just east of Mill Street, facing East Main Street, was built by William Damsell in the late 1820s. There he operated a grocery and merchandise store in the basement. It would have been just outside Watson's original town plat. However, the building was on a property only 1¼ acres in size. This indicates it was not a farm and was likely designed as a business from the start.

Thomas Cook arrived in 1816, when there were but two houses within the town limits. However, by the early 1830s he had a store and was selling a wide variety of goods and services. An old account book from 1837-1859 lists shoes, wheat, beef, flour, corn, cloth, tools, nails, yarn, apples, coats, linen and silk among some of his stock.

Thomas Cook was a very early store owner, who lived in a fine house overlooking the valley. This photo was taken from the bottom of Maple Street, looking West on West Main. The Fire Station is now located at the bend in the road shown here. Cook's house was torn down when Grace Brethren Church was built.

He rented out horses, wagons, buggies and pasture for livestock, as well as doing plowing and hauling for customers. Cook also sold medicine, nursed a sick horse, hired women to sew and boarded hired hands. In addition, he taught school, was a Township road supervisor and the Troy Township Clerk for a number of years in the 1840s. He must have seemed like a one man band to the town and he was also a strong community leader.

The John F. Adams and William Damsell drygoods partnership eventually ended. In the late 1830s, Adams and his son went into business in the brick building, which was later enlarged to become the Minnear Hotel.

The new partnership firm of A. B. Beverstock and Moses Sowers opened a general store on lot 9, at the square, in 1836–37 and would prosper over the years. Both men were influential leaders in a growing town.

With the arrival of the Sandusky, Mansfield & Newark Railroad in 1850, Lexington was in some respects a boom town. If you wanted it, you could find it in Lexington or at least somebody could get it or make it for you.

The explosive growth of what Amariah Watson laid out next to his mill is captured in a rare business index printed in 1853. There were 26 business categories listed with some having 2 or 3 separate competing firms. Besides the usual general merchandise, there were wagon makers, coverlet weavers, cabinet maker, a watch maker and gunsmith, (a strange combination), a lawyer and an insurance salesman. Lexington seemed more like a city than a tiny rural town.

The coming of the railroad and the Civil War changed everything. Mail and newspapers came quickly. The lightning fast telegraph key in the SM&N (or later B&O) station master's office connected old Lex with the world.

A lot of the ordinary freight came and left the station, grain, flour, produce, live stock and so on. Unusual were the 300 walnut logs shipped in 1877 by Brown and Co. of Buffalo, consigned to parties in Europe. A tremendous amount of local timber had been used in building the railroad and fueling the early engines. Much more lumber from the Clear Fork valley was shipped north to Lake Erie and on to eastern markets.

An 1869 SM&N Railroad Directory provided a list of the growing and ever changing number of merchants and services:

LEXINGTON DIRECTORY.

Beverstock C H & Bro, (Chas H Beverstock, Frank Beverstock,) dry goods, groceries and produce, n e cor Public Square.
Boggs James A, stoves and tinware, Main.
Burtch Almon W, physician, Main.
Carey G W, physician, Frederick s Public Square.
Carey Manson, watchmaker and gunsmith, Main.
Cook William H, tailor, Main.
Cramer Jacob, wagon maker, Frederick s Public Square.
Culp C D, boot and shoe maker, Main w Public Square.
Daviese & Co, custom mill, Main and Clear Fork.
Delamater Mrs Harriet F, post mistress, Main.
Englehart & Co, (C Englehart, S W Blair,) hardware and groceries, Main e Frederick.
Fleming S K, harness maker, s w cor Public Square.
Francis Caleb B, cooper, Delaware.
Fry George M, attorney at law, Main.
Galbraith Robert, blacksmith, Main.
George William, druggist, Main.
Grubb George, painter, Frederick.
Guyselman Daniel, dry goods and groceries, Main.
Kelly J H, stoves and tinware, Main e Public Square.
Lindsley Samuel S, boot and shoe maker, Frederick s Public Square.

CX SANDUSKY, MANSFIELD AND NEWARK R. R.

McConkey John, tanner and currier, Main w Public Square.
Mansfield Gilead, photographer, Frederick n Public Square.
Miller Samuel, cooper, Short Alley.
Mitchell Samuel, cabinet maker, Main w Public Square.
Mosure Ben F, tailor, n e cor Public Square.
Rhodes Levi, boot and shoe maker, Main w Public Square.
Sowers M & Sons, (Moses Sowers, George M Sowers, Bloomer Sowers,) dry goods and groceries, Main.
Spalding House, Jarvis A Spalding proprietor, Main.
Stewart & Murray, (Geo. H. Stewart, Thos G Murray,) grocers; Main w Public Square.
Stough David, blacksmith, Frederick.
Stough & Haner, (David Stough, John Haner,) blacksmiths, Frederick, s Public Square.
STOUGH JOHN, furniture manufacturer, cor Delaware and Main.
Thuma J H & Bro. (Daniel H Thuma, Josiah Thuma,) groceries and provisions, Main.
Western Union Telegraph Co, C H Beverstock manager, n e cor Public Square.
Whitford L D, physician, Main w Public Square.
Williams John B, barber, Main.

This is rare copy of the 1869 Lexington Business Directory. It shows 26 business categories, some with as many as three competitors. (Note that this only covers Lexington proper, not the surrounding areas, as is the practice of current directories.)

The Mills

Mills were another attraction for the area. You might find the number of mills using water power rather surprising. The Clear Fork and Cedar Fork rivers and their tributaries had sufficient fall and volume in the early 1800s to provide numerous mill sites.

D. W. Garber's book *Water Wheels and Millstones* (Ohio Historical Society, 1970) cites the statistic that in 1840, Richland County had 82 gristmills, 106 sawmills and 2 oil mills for a total of 190 waterwheels furnishing power. This total does not include woolen, fulling, carding, plaster and other types of mills. It should be noted that Richland County was then the largest county in the state (nearly 30 miles square).

Ichabod Clark and son, Ezekiel, had a gristmill, sawmill and distillery near Gass Road and State Route 97 as early as 1831. It was later run by John K. Williams and in 1890 by W. G. Manner, although the distillery operation ended with the temperance movement. The mill pond is still across the road from the reservoir.

By 1832, Amariah Watson had built a second gristmill just north of town and another oil mill (linseed oil) and distillery for his sons-in-law, Sterling Graves and William Lewis. Watson's son, Asahel, ran a fulling or carding mill for the manufacture of woolen products. All three of these mills were just north of town. They were located along present Lexington-Springmill Road, between the bridge at the Lexington Park and Cockley Road.

Still another water-powered saw mill went up near the west end of Hanley Road, which the Watson family may have had a hand in building. Watson's son-in-law, William Lewis, owned the property for a period in the 1840s. It passed to a Mr. Easton who may have been the last owner or operator, although no record exists as to its demise. Water from the headrace was used by the SM&N Railroad for a water station in the 1850s. Remains of the headrace can still be seen from the Lexington-Springmill Road.

B. F. Mercer had two mills on Alta Road at the end of Griebling Road, a sawmill first and then a gristmill. Mercer sold the mills and property to Jacob Griebling in 1869. The Griebling family kept the gristmill operating until the summer of 1905, when a severe storm washed out the mill dam and operation ceased. The unused ancient building started to lean and finally collapsed on a quiet summer day in 1920. It was the last water powered mill standing in Troy Township.

The Thomas Logan gristmill site is now under the waters of the Clear Fork Reservoir. Francis McEwen built his sawmill in the deep valley just east of 97 and 314. Another early sawmill was at the bottom of the hill below Camp Avery Hand on Orweiler Road. All three of these opened in the 1830s.

"Griebling's Troy Mill," was located on the Alta South Road. It was built in 1833. The boy on crutches was Frank Griebling, Lexington's Postmaster from 1934-1967.

And let us not forget the Christian Klink distillery down on Mill Run Road along with an unknown number of small family stills. All these alcohol-producing operations had one thing in common. They all required the services of a mill (or had their own).

As the years passed more mills would have water wheels turning. George Miller built his sawmill with a lathe in the deep valley on Marion Ave. Jacob King was sawing logs on present Kings Corners Road, east of Route 42, while Thomas Mahon operated a good-sized carding machine and woolen mill up stream on the west side of Route 42.

Another gristmill, with a cider press, would be run by the Strasbaugh family. It would soon go up in the valley below the east end of Vanderbilt Rd., just inside Washington Township. While the mill was in operation, a road crossed the valley between SR 97 and Mill Run Road. Their mill was turbine powered from a 6' to 7' high dam and head race. The building fell down sometime around 1895. John Strasbaugh also ran one of the two sawmills north of Lexington in 1869, although it is not clear which one.

South of town, just inside Perry Township, one of the first mills built on the Cedar Fork was a log structure built in 1811-12 by John Herring. In 1814, it was sold to Josias Baughman. In 1833, the mill was sold to John Hanawalt, a miller from Galion who tore down the log building and erected a larger frame building with improvements for flour manufacturing. The mill burned in 1855 and was immediately rebuilt. The structure was located at the junction of State Route 546 and the Bellville-Johnsville Road. In an early day, Johnny Appleseed had a nursery a short distance to the north of the mill on what became the Baughman farm.

This photo, shows the South side of West Main street, the heart of the business district, as it appeared in the 1880s. Moses Sowers built the two-story brick building on the left. The offices of the Gailey Seminary, a small shop, Boggs Tinware shop and Wilson & Hamilton's drugstore have signs displayed. Other businesses up the street are unidentified. West Main was a busy place back then.

The 1855 mill building, the third one built on the spot, stood in the exact center of the cross roads. (Travelers just had to go around it.) The Hanawalt family owned it until 1906. After it was sold, the mill was sawed in half and moved to the northwest of the intersection, where it was used as a barn. In 1953, it was converted into a home by Jack Gleckner. At present, it is the residence of Mark and Barb Berry who've made additional improvements. The rest, a smaller portion, is part of another home across the road.

These water powered mills often did not withstand the test of time. Vibrations from the machinery nearly shook them to pieces over years. The waterwheels and wooden gearing often had to be replaced, at great expense, by skilled millwrights. On top of this, floods, water damage, low water in summer, ice in winter and friction fires were all a mill owner's nightmare.

The age of the steam engine, after the Civil War, brought with it manufactured machinery, which was more efficient and sturdier than wood. Turbines replaced the wooden water wheel and roller mills (with an improved bolting system for flour) replaced the old mill stones. However, the small country mills could not absorb the tremendous expense of the new machinery. Eventually the old water powered mills fell silent. Large commercial firms such as the Cockley Steam Roller Mill in Lexington, which bought grain and shipped flour by the railroad car, simply put them out of business.

Samuel Carter was operating what was originally the Watson/Graves/Lewis mill, north of town when the dam near Cockley road washed out during a flood in 1859. A newspaper reported that as a resul,t fishing in the Clear Fork had been much improved in town.

When Amariah Watson went west in 1835, his town mill was sold to Samuel Caldwell. The 1859 flood may have damaged that mill dam also, as Caldwell added a Hall & Allen steam engine to supplement its power. James Neely was the miller until he moved west after the Civil War. Water power was still used however and again in early February of 1877 two-thirds of his dam was washed out.

Bystanders watched a rather large workforce of fifteen to twenty men who were employed in its rebuilding at an estimated cost of $400, big money in those days. It must have been a cold, wet winter job and was finished by the end of the month. By 1870 ownership had passed to Dr. David "Daddy" Hahn who ran the mill until he died about the same time the dam gave way in 1877. His son, Rev. Benjamin D. Hahn of Springfield, Mass., continued ownership and leased the mill to others to operate.

The mill, the second at that location, burned on July 30, 1894 under mysterious circumstances. Several "thugs" had attempted burglaries in town and were suspected of arson. Surprisingly, Rev. Hahn leased the property and water rights to Charles McLane who immediately started construction of a new mill building on the old foundation. It was put into operation and ran until sometime around the turn of the century, but could not compete with the big Cockley Roller Mill just across the railroad tracks. It became a feed mill in its last days. By 1905 its rotting water wheel was a relic. The old mill was dismantled and torn down in April of 1906 by Albert Heskett who used part of the material to build a new house on the back of his property uptown.

As the forests gave way to farmland and the population grew, there was an itch in more than a few minds to move west. In April of 1858, the "Lexington Emigration Club" was formed with P. T. Coleman as president and Jess Shortess as secretary. The local group sent members west to look over or even buy land. Some area folks went west to visit and a few never came back. Businesses grew and changed hands as some failed or owners moved on.

Photograph courtesy of Harry Linton Collection

West Main Street, looking East, sometime around 1910. The buildings on the left burned in 1929

William W. Cockley

William W. Cockley posed for this photograph in 1902, while he was a member of the Ohio Legislature. He was also a Civil War Veteran, a progressive business leader and banker.

Early Years

William W. Cockley was a rather unique individual. The son of Benjamin and Fannie Cockley, he was born in 1840 and grew up in Lexington. His father died when he was only nine. So William worked at farming and for a wagon maker.

In 1862, Cockley enlisted in the Union Army and a year later was elected first lieutenant in Company C, 86th OVI. At Cumberland Gap, this regiment took 2,350 prisoners.

Cockley's subsequent enlistments and management ability saw him rise in rank to captain. Then in late 1865, he was appointed Asst. Inspector General of the Department of Georgia (187 OVI, under General John C. Croxton) with the rank of Captain. He later served as aide de camp on the staff of Major General James H. Wilson.

Mustered out in January 1866, Cockley returned to Lexington. Once home, he married Mary Urania Beverstock, the daughter of A. B. Beverstock.

Allen Barney Beverstock Sr. came to Lexington in 1837 and, along with partner Moses Sowers, ran a very successful general store. Beverstock posed for this photograph a few years before he died.

Mary Urania Cockley, wife of W.W. Cockley, was a daughter of Allen B. Beverstock. The two families were close and Mary was a well liked social leader in Lexington.

A. B. Beverstock and Moses Sowers had long been prosperous business partners in town. However, Sowers left the partnership and opened his own business on the southwest corner of the square.

After the marriage, Capt. Cockley farmed the large Beverstock acreage west of town. He then became involved in business activities in the village, where he ran a store. When A.B. Sr. died, Cockley and his brother-in-law, Allen B. Beverstock Jr., took over the Beverstock General Store on the northeast corner of the town square.

Life Away From Work

W. W. Cockley and his wife's family, the Beverstocks, were active not only in business, but also in the social and political scene as well. On one occasion, in the fall of 1881, Samuel J. Kirkwood and family were the guests of A. B. Beverstock. As a young man, Kirkwood was a promising Richland County lawyer who went west in 1855, and became the Governor of Iowa during the Civil War. He was elected for a second term in 1875 and was a U. S. Senator from 1877 to 1881. That year he was appointed Secretary of the Interior under President James A. Garfield.

The presence of a national officeholder in Lexington for a couple of days was the social highlight of the season. It must have made a bunch of local Republicans grin from ear to ear, even though President Garfield had just died a short time earlier. Kirkwood had been in Ohio for Garfield's funeral.

The Beginning of the Mill

With his business ability and growing financial interests, Cockley joined with partners S. B. Joslin, George Miller, both of Lexington, and a Mansfield capitalist. This partnership began construction of the Cockley Milling Company in the spring of 1881.

The mill project was the largest and costliest industrial undertaking the village had witnessed to that time. The flour mill was to be five stories high, cost about $20,000 and have the capacity to grind 500 bushels a day. The 300,000 bricks needed for the building were to be made on site, in kilns. The contractor hired local labor for the brick making work.

One mishap was reported during construction of the mill. This occurred the day of a freak July storm. It

The brick two-story Beverstock General Store on the north east corner of the square. It passed to W.W. Cockley and Allen B. Beverstock Jr. after his father's death. W.W. built a new brick home against the store a few years later. At the time of this 1962 picture, the building housed Armstrong's Royal Blue Market.

seems the strong storm blew off the boards covering the kiln, causing damage and scattering workmen.

When it opened in 1882, the mill was the town's first real industry. It bought and sold grain, seed and hay. This was in addition to the vast amount of flour and meal it manufactured. In fact, enough product moved through the mill that a steady stream of rail cars could be seen on the sidetracks beside the building.

The following year a cooper shop, for making wood barrels, was added to the operation. In addition, a storage warehouse was built at the same time.

The mill was the town's first major employer. At times the operation ran 24 hours a day and employed a dozen or more men. These jobs were a boon for the village and created a steady market for farmers.

The Millers War

William W. Cockley and partners were reluctantly pulled into what was called the "Millers War of 1884–1885." There had always been rivalry between the millers of the Clear Fork valley. However, the struggle to obtain the patronage of the farmers and their wives began in earnest about 1884. A good deal of animosity resulted from this competitive fight.

The owners of the Plank Mill, just above Butler, and the Rummel Mill, just down stream below Butler, voiced their differences in the Bellville paper. Plank had installed a

The Cockley Milling Company as seen from the southeast sometime around 1912. The small building on the right housed the cooper shop, used for barrel making. To the far left (background) rail cars on the coal chutes can be seen.

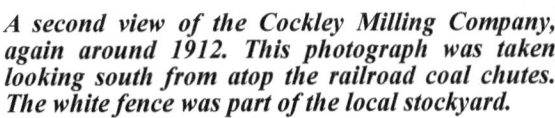

A second view of the Cockley Milling Company, again around 1912. This photograph was taken looking south from atop the railroad coal chutes. The white fence was part of the local stockyard.

roller system to modernize his mill and tried to claim greater patronage. Rummel stressed the superiority of the 1840 stone ground flour.

At about the same time, the head gates of the Stump Mill, west of Bellville, were destroyed by persons unknown. In addition, the Crain Mill, east of Bellville, was leveled in a suspicious fire. It was clear that matters had escalated from good-natured competition among these water powered mills to a take-no-prisoners fight for survival of the businesses.

The steam powered Cockley Mill in Lexington, with its larger capacity, was also a factor in this struggle. The fight grew so intense that Cockley was accused of putting alum in its flour, which would make bread rise more quickly. W. W. Cockley had to publicly deny and challenge the unjust accusation in the local newspapers.

The "war" eventually died out and the more modern Cockley Mill quietly outlasted its accusers. Progress had once again triumphed over tradition.

Always the Progressive

Cockley had the first telephone in town installed in his store in 1882. He later added a line from his store office to the mill, so he could keep tabs on its operation. This was a big deal at the time. By comparison, Johnsville and Mt. Gilead were not connected by wire until 1885. (Maybe there wasn't anybody worth talking to in those places. Sometimes progress was slow in coming to rural Morrow County.)

Cockley was a progressive and most eager to test the new. He had one of the first, if not the first, automobile in town. In the summer of 1904 he and his Curved Dash Oldsmobile were involved with a horse and carriage as noted by Al Moore:

Miss Effie Maxwell experienced the most thrilling and dangerous episode of her life when the horse she was driving became frightened by W. W. Cockley's automobile passing north on Delaware Street. Miss Maxwell was in the buggy and in front of the residence of George Hill when the automobile passed by and the horse gave a prodigious leap across the gutter and into the lawn and Mr. Hill caught the rein but the horse reared and threw the athletic young blacksmith off and about two rods further on north on the lawn in front of Fred

Walter's residence, the horse fell and broke a shaft and jumped up and made a sharp turn into the street and made a mad terrific flight south and finally stopped from exhaustion one and a half miles south of town.

During all this peril Miss Maxwell clung to the lines and displayed a nerve, presence of mind and skill that

W.W. Cockley's 1904 Curved Dash Oldsmobile must have been the first automobile in Lexington. Pictured here, college-aged son William "Bud" Cockley has the old man's car splattered with mud and evidently stuck on Plymouth Street. Bud doesn't look too happy about his predicament.

Photograph located by Elsie Simon from Galbraith descendant.

The Cockley & Galbraith General Store. The bank they operated was in the back room. Note the produce, clothing, carpet, cloth, and baskets. They also displayed wallpaper in the front window. The tailoring department was on the second floor. Shown here are George Galbraith (left), unknown (center), and son Robert Galbraith (right).

challenged the admiration of on lookers. The horse kicked and reared and tumbled and the buggy careened and onlookers had no other thought than that she would meet a tragic death and they stood with bated breath and pulsating hearts. In the exciting and dangerous ordeal the fair driver was seemingly the least disconcerted of all. She sat upright and seemed to have a fixed purpose to cling to the lines at any hazard.

It should be said that Mr. Cockley is never a scorcher. He had given the proper signal of his approach and was coasting slowly and had passed the horse before it started to run. The animal became frightened at another automobile and had run away and now scares at the sight of one.

Prosperity and Banking

In 1882, A.B. Beverstock Jr. sold his interest in the store. W. W. built a fine brick home attached to the store, on the northeast corner of the town square. However, the Mill and general store together were evidently more that he could handle alone.

So, Cockley brought in George Galbraith to be his partner and the firm became known as Cockley and Galbraith. This allowed Cockley to focus on the mill operation and Galbraith took care of the store.

At that point, a tailoring department was added, in addition to their line of groceries and general merchandise. The two also later added a banking business at the store. This too was the first in Lexington. The bank operated under the heading "Cockley and Galbraith" in association with the National Park Bank of New York.

Then in 1895, W.W. and his son Rollin, along with A. B. "Barney" Beverstock Jr., Edward Remy, and W. H. Taylor were the principal stockholders in the Peoples Bank of Bellville. Rollin ran this bank until he died in 1914. During that time, Rollin also organized the Lexington State Bank and built the building that now houses part of Vidonish Studios as the new bank's home.

The Lexington bank failed in the 1920s when a cashier embezzled a good deal of money. The Mansfield Savings Bank then bought the institution and it became one of the first branch banks in Ohio. In 1933 it was bought by First National of Mansfield and later moved to a new building on West Main Street, across from Kell Hardware. The bank has gone through several name changes in recent years.

In 1903, Cockley, who ran as a Democrat, was elected to the Ohio General Assembly 76th District, which included Richland County. He had served two years of his term when he died of cancer November 4, 1905.

W.W. had requested a simple funeral service and it was held at his home next to the store. During the service, a hundred or more local people paid their last respects, along with a delegation from the Ohio General Assembly. He was buried in Lexington Cemetery, along the main drive, and a beautiful, but simple monument marks his final resting place.

After Cockley's death, A. B. Beverstock Jr. took over the mill operation, which continued to thrive. However, on January 11, 1917, the mill caught fire and burned to the ground. The plant was partially insured and Beverstock pledged to rebuild. This rebuilding was accomplished the following year.

The rebuilt mill was put out of flour business by large corporate mills. So the operation switched to grain, feed, and seed milling for several years. However, this too failed in the 1920s. The mill was a landmark in town for nearly three quarters of a century. Twenty years after its demise, the site became Lexington Soy Products Co. in the 1940s.

Photgraph courtesy of Cockley Family

A view from the cemetery shows the Cockley Mill shortly before it burned to the ground. It was rebuilt after the 1917 fire and lasted several more years as a grain and seed mill. In the 1940s the mill was reborn as Lexington Soy Products.

Photograph courtesy of Elsie Simon Collection

The Lexington Savings Bank and Post Office were in a building built by Rollin Cockley. It was the most modern building on Main Street for many years. The bank failed in the 1920s, when a cashier embezzled a large amount of money. Note the water pump at the curb. Vidonish Studios now occupy the building.

Other Business Ventures

Railroad

The railroad was a major catalyst to the local economy. Obviously it provided transportation for inbound and outbound goods. However, often overlooked is the fact that the railroad provided a number of jobs. The line needed men for the engine crews, water towers, coal chutes and station operation. It was also a major consumer of local timber products.

A job on the section gang was hard work. However, it was a steady paycheck in a time when those were not common.

The section gangs were especially busy in the 1850s, 60s and 70s. These gangs maintained the roadbed, tracks and wooden bridges. During this period, the 112-mile-long line consumed nearly 40,000 wooden cross ties and 6,000 cords of firewood (to fuel its engines and heat railroad buildings) every year.

Much of this hand cut-to-size timber was purchased at local stations along the line and supplied by farmers or sawmills who then delivered it. This raw, untreated timber wouldn't last more than a few years as a cross tie and constant replacement was always necessary. Local gravel for the roadbed was hand dug from the pits next to the cemetery or north of town near Hanley Road. All this was a source of income for workers in the area

Dairy Products, Cigars and Power

In May of 1881, a group of investors started a creamery operation on the east side of Plymouth Street near the present-day park. The large amount of dairy herds in the area prompted the venture, but it did not last very long. After being shut down for a considerable time the building and equipment were sold by order of the directors in 1893. The Lutz brothers, William and Henry, bought the property and expanded a saw mill lumber business to include a planing mill, shingle mill and cider press.

In 1882 there were three cigar manufacturers puffing away. Mr. A. Heskett, A. Smaltz and Mr. E. Heskett each had their own shop. They were possibly one-man operations.

The turn of the century brought with it new industrial enterprises. Young Harry Smith and his father, Dr. Henry Smith, had started the town's first electric plant. When Harry returned from college with an engineering degree he founded the Smith Gas Power Company in 1904, and later the Smith Foundry in buildings on Plymouth Street along the railroad. More of that will follow in another chapter.

By 1910, the Indiana Condensed Milk Company was in full operation just to the north. It operated under the name "Wilson's" because Lowell Wilson was a nephew of the founder. It was claimed that 400 farmers sold milk to the plant, delivered by 23 route teams each month. The plant, which was capable of producing 50,000 pounds of milk a day, employed 25 people.

Indiana Condensed Milk Company operated under the brand name "Wilson's Milk." The plant, located north of town, bought much of the region's milk and was capable of processing 50,000 pounds of milk per day.

William Lutz (left) had a sizable lumber yard when this picture was taken. The operation had a saw mill, shingle and planing mill and a cider press. He also had five steam engines used to power portable saws and threshers at harvest time. Employees Oris Pollock (center) and Fred Lutz are also pictured. Fred had the misfortune to be killed in 1913, when he and a young lady were in a train-buggy accident. When the train finally got stopped, both were still on the front of the locomotive. She was holding his head.

The Wilson Creamery was a big operation and a real asset for local dairy farmers.

Women wrapping candy at Frye's candy factory. Each piece was coated to remove stickiness and then carefully wrapped by hand.

Frye's Caramel Candy

In 1905 G. V. Frye's caramel candy and condensed milk operation opened in a new three story building along the tracks south of Main Street. The 60 by 100 foot building was erected on the site of the 1851 Beverstock warehouse that had burned the previous spring. Eight thousand dollars worth of copper boilers, machinery and galvanized tanks for holding the milk went into the factory.

Frye developed a method of coating caramel candies, which did away with the stickiness and the need to wrap each piece by hand. He also found a method for making butter by treating cream with an electrolyte process. This did away with the natural souring of the cream. In addition, Frye invented a cosine plastic made from dairy products. He turned this invention over to a Cleveland firm for further development.

Frye was the son of Rev. George V. Frye, who had served as pastor of the Congregational Church from 1864 to 1871. G.V. grew up here, left and came back from Chicago where his main plant was located. It is believed that his coming back to Lexington was in part prompted by his wife, who was originally from Lucas and had relatives here, the Cooks. The readily available supply of dairy products was also an inducement.

The Lexington plant employed a good number of women and was a sizeable operation. The plant was designed to separate the men from the women. Frye found it necessary to open a boarding house of sorts to provide a place for out-of-town wrappers to live.

There was a housing shortage created by the job boom when his plant, Harry Smith's factory, and the Cockley Mill all expanded. There were job openings, but little in the way of lodging. As a result, eight new houses

Frye's Caramel factory employed women to wrap candy. They were separated from male employees. The sign on the building is no doubt the work of Seymore Lindsey. This photo was taken looking South from the railroad tracks near East Main Street.

Frye built an ornate summer home, the first ready-cut house in town, on the northeast side of the town square. It was torn down in the late 1950s, for bank parking. Seen here are wife Mayme Carey and daughter Kathryn.

were under contract by the firm of Bonham & Ritchie in the summer of 1906.

Bill Bonham, the local undertaker, also bought a new hearse for $1,100. Old-timers often commented that he drank like a fish and swore like a sailor, but was very well liked. (Except, maybe, by a few of the high nose church women.) Times were good.

In 1891, Frye had built an elaborate Victorian summer home on the northwest corner of the town square. His ornate house stood out from the rest of the community. It was often the scene of delightful summer social gatherings and entertainment, which were detailed in the papers.

A series of tragedies and misfortune nearly ended Frye's career. The Lexington plant burned down in 1907, while only partially insured. However, it was rebuilt the following year. Then the U.S. Department of Agriculture classified his butter process as oleo. Next the Cleveland firm developing his dairy-based plastic went out of business. Finally, his wife died after a long illness in the summer of 1908. Frye sold his home and moved to northern Ohio to live with his sister. It was a sad chapter in the life of a well-liked local businessman.

After George Frye's candy business closed, the factory housed a wood veneer and basket-making factory organized by a local minister. It too went broke. (Note the size of the local timber available in the early 1900s.)

After Frye's factory closed, a group of local investors converted part of the building into a wood veneer factory making baskets and furniture veneer. The wicker side baskets for the Halliday automobile were made there for a brief time. However, the venture was a financial failure. After it closed the building was used as a warehouse for farm supplies and fertilizer. It caught fire in the early 1920s and burned to the ground.

Rapid Growth

A fair-sized foundry that made engine bases, among other things, was built between the Smith and Wilson plants. The brick Kenny Foundry was sold after a few years to Samuel Cureton and a couple of stockholders named Cass and Cousins. Harry Smith used this foundry for his castings and may have owned it at one time. However, the ownership records are sketchy. The foundry burned down sometime after World War I. The writer interviewed old-timers in the 1960s who believed this fire was set intentionally, to collect the insurance. However, no evidence was provided.

Lexington changed drastically during the first decade of the new century. From 1890 to 1900 the population of the town had only grown by 16 to total 418 souls. By 1910 the number jumped again to 654, a growth of 46%. Manufacturing jobs and support business opportunities opened up in town.

In fact, opportunities opened up so much that it resulted in the housing shortage previously mentioned. So by 1907, of the 44 lots in the Sowers addition on Plymouth Street, only a dozen were unsold. New houses were also built on Frederick, East and West Main Streets. The town was no longer entirely dependent on agriculture for its economy. The Smith plant went to two shifts a day and started a building expansion.

Rapid Decline

But the rapid growth was not to continue. The candy factory had closed and the foundry burned sometime around 1916. In 1917, Harry Smith sold his electric plant to the Ohio Power Company. Sometime around 1912, he had sold the Gas Producer plant to his old college roommate, Charles Kettering of General Motors. (Kettering later moved the operation to Dayton.)

Finally the milk plant closed and the huge Cockley Mill burned in 1917. At that point the nearest blue color jobs were in Mansfield. Lexington, for all practical purposes, went into an economic slumber that would last until after World War II.

Art Hughes had a small factory near the Cockley Mill that made ornamental furniture, card tables, folding chairs, flowerpot stands and so on. In 1928, he shipped a railroad car load to Sears Roebuck in Chicago and thought bright days were ahead. Unfortunately the wrapping paper stuck to the fresh shellac and Sears rejected the whole shipment. That broke the company, which had only been in business about two years. Today a genuine "Hughes Lexington" is a rare find. The writer has one, hopefully worth thousands.

There were other small business changes. The age of the automobile would phase out the horses. Sam Homerick

The basket-making portion of the wood veneer factory.

opened a garage and started a bus service from Mansfield through Lexington to points south. For a time, he sold Ford and Studebaker cars from a building where the village hall now stands.

However, a disastrous fire in 1929 wiped out the Homerick garage, as well as many other businesses. That fire also destroyed Bauman's Pool Room, Ray Cashell's bakery and lunch room, the Lexington Hardware and two barber shops owned by Alan McNaul and Ed Smith. (The Smith barbershop shop had also been the waiting room for the bus station.) In addition, Maxwell's automobile garage and several apartments and were also lost.

The stock market crash of 1929 seemed to be the final blow to downtown business. Access to Mansfield by car became easier and much of the area's opportunity went to the city. Except for the addition of four new gas stations to supply the traveling public, Lexington's economic slumber truly began.

Character of the Town

Every town, valley or crossroads will have them. They are the remarkable persons that have a special knack, the personality or trait of character that sets them apart in some memorable way from the ordinary folks. The Lexington area was blessed with more than its share. Here are just a few sifted from the pages of time.

Photograph courtesy of Sid Earhart Collection
Monroe Taylor, sample case in hand, waves as he leaves the pool hall for another day on the road.

Monroe Taylor was a traveling salesman and a gifted orator. He appeared in Lexington in the late 1890s. Taylor worked at odd jobs and even taught high school for a brief period around 1900. He chewed tobacco and students remember his spitting through a crack in the floor boards for lack of a spittoon.

However Taylor was best remembered for selling Cloverine Salve, a cure-all concoction that is still made. From his Lexington base he trod over a wide area, selling to farmers and shopkeepers or anybody else he could corner.

His broad vocabulary and nonstop speaking ability made him the perfect target for a saloon or poolroom crowd. He could speak on any subject and quote long passages from the Bible. He was often goaded into making a speech with no advance preparation while standing on a make shift chair or soap box podium.

His alleged attentive audience did what they could to distract him. There were strange noises, cat calls, toots of excess gas, bodies falling off chairs or even fire crackers tossed under the speakers stand. All was to no avail. Monroe would just keep going. It was a contest, one he seldom lost.

Lexington could be rather dull at times. Taylor livened things up and was a major source of local entertainment. He spent most of his life here, but moved to Cincinnati toward the end and that's where Monroe died. Things got rather dull at the pool hall when he left.

Tom Lyons was a very old Delaware Indian. His Indian name was Kaschates, which in the Delaware language is the word for tobacco. As was sometimes the custom, he took the name of a white man that he admired, Tom Lyons. Who the original owner of the name is, why or even when Kaschates took the name is unknown.

Lyons passed through early Lexington at times on his way to Sandusky, although no specific record exists. Amariah Watson's granddaughter told the family story of Indians visiting and watching the first mill operation. He may well have been one of the visitors.

According to an early historical account, written by Dr. James Henderson of Newville, Lyons was murdered five miles south of town by three white men. The murderers had followed the drunken old Indian from a tavern in Lexington. He was reportedly beaten to death and his body hidden under a log.

Artist Tim McKee made this computer rendering of Tom Lyons, the 80-year-old Delaware Indian, from written descriptions.

Lyons, when drinking, would often boast of the white scalps he had taken, which may have prompted his death near Route 546 and the Bellville-Johnsville Road. No one knows for certain.

Carrying a string of dried strips of meat around his neck, Lyons claimed they were the tongues or scalps (the stories vary) of 99 white women. He said that he needed just one more to make it an even hundred and that made him a terror to frontier women. Old Tom was along the forks of the Mohican before, during and after the War of 1812. He was described as being *aged, dark, large for an Indian, of coarse features, high cheek bones, and large protruded lips. When ornamented with a silver clevis and double tree in each ear and one in his nose and smoking from the bowl and through the handle of his tomahawk presented a rather grotesque appearance. He was regarded by the whites as extremely homely and repulsive.*

He could speak some broken English and claimed to be 160 years old during the War of 1812. (He counted summer and winter each as a year, which accounted for his great age. However, he may well have looked just that ancient.) Pioneers agreed that he was the oldest, ugliest Indian on the frontier.

Here's where the story gets interesting. Did he really die south of Lexington? Can you believe everything you read in the history books?

Baskins *1880 History of Morrow County* states near the top of page 380 that Lyons was murdered by a man named Russell, who buried him in a swamp. He was murdered again 41 pages later in the same book by one of the Hardenbrooks. About that same time, he died again at the hands of Joe Haynes who threw Tom's body in the Leedy swamp south of Bellville.

In the *History of Seneca County*, Lyons was shot by two white hunters from Delaware. In the *History of Wyandot County*, at the bottom of page 291, he was shot by a Samuel Spurgeon.

The Amish country proved to be a dangerous place for Lyons. In Holmes, Coshocton and Tuscarawas Counties the bullets did fly. He was shot by a 16 year old boy, and again by Elias Hochstetler, once more by Jacob Mizer, and tradition handed down says a man by the name of Olinger killed Old Tom with a silver bullet, feeling he might be a bulletproof witch. Jacob Ammon and a relative also took time to kill him in Holmes County and again buried his body in a swamp. Did both shoot him or was it a joint effort? Then he was killed again by "someone" unknown near Berlin for reasons unknown. Had he also been causing trouble around that area?

The Douglas *1878 History of Wayne County* offers a different perspective on Lyons demise. A young boy went to Lyons camp and found him in a sick condition. This was communicated to his Indian friends at Upper Sandusky who came and took the old warrior back to the Delaware reservation. Days later word was received that the aged warrior had died. He died for the thirteenth time peacefully of old age among his own people, sometime during the winter or spring of 1823-24. He was no doubt well into his 80s.

And these are all the facts, straight from the history books. It's the true story of the killing of Tom Lyons just south of Lexington. If you believe what you read, his body is buried in six or seven counties in Ohio, including three swamps and under a log. He was murdered twelve times and died once of natural causes. You just can't dispute facts like that.

Hugh Fokner was a remarkable character, well-remembered by old-timers. Born on a farm in Nebraska in 1883, he came east to attend Oberlin College. Fokner took pre-college courses first and finally graduated in 1911 with a degree in Physical Education. He tried selling and then factory work, but his love of the outdoors ended those careers.

Hugh arrived in Mansfield in the 1920s and worked as a gardener and estate custodian for Dr. Johannes Jones. For many years he took care of Oak Hill Cottage, where he once met Louis Bromfield. Through that chance meeting, Fokner unknowingly became a character in

Hugh Fokner lived in a barn in Lexington during the 1930s-40s. He was a well-known outdoorsman and local curiosity.

three of the author's books, *The Green Bay Tree, The Farm, and The Forty-Niner*.

Fokner came to Lexington in the early 1930s. Why he came to Lexington is unknown, but we do know he sometimes went away, back to Mansfield. Fokner lived in a barn behind the home of Harry Linton on West Main Street. The Linton's had ten children, the largest family in town, but Fokner somehow gained use of their barn for several years.

Hugh was a friendly and interesting conversationalist.

The Linton children were very fond of him. Each weekday, around noon, Mrs. Linton would let him come into the kitchen and listen to a radio show called "Twenty Questions." Fokner was well read and could usually answer almost all of the questions.

Hugh was rather ordinary looking when he first came to town. However that all changed in 1934, when he joined the cult of outdoorsmen started by a Harvard professor. He never shaved or cut his hair after that. A man, slightly over six foot with long flowing hair and full beard, wasn't hard to locate when he walked the streets of the quiet village. In his early years, his long light brown hair must have been the envy of some women. However, behind his back, local kids referred to the mystery man as "Tarzan" or "Goofy."

Fokner often lived and cooked in the outdoors. He sometimes walked barefoot in summer and would frequently travel to Mansfield on foot. Louie Ryan recalled the time Fokner came into Darrenberger's pool room on a cold snowy day. As he stood by the stove, the melting ice from his beard and hair dripped all over the floor.

Fokner worked at odd jobs around town and sold cream pitchers with a flip top called "Handy-Mandy." (The first such vessel made from aluminum.) During the depression, he cut fire wood, which he sold in the area. Richard Linton and his sister Marilyn remember the old 1919 automobile, with the top and most of the body cut off, which was Fokner's make-shift delivery truck. The wood was gathered from yards and area wooded lots.

Also remembered is the time that Fokner was granted permission to cut firewood in the woods of the George Carter farm on Marion Avenue. The Carters knew him and later in the day old George walked down to see how the wood-cutter was doing.

As George peered thru the brush, his eyebrows must have raised. There was Fokner, stark naked, singing, and swinging his axe. Nothing like getting back to nature! Old George just turned around and quietly went back to the house. (After all, it's never wise to disturb a naked man with an axe.)

Sometime around 1940, Fokner started cooking in the barn behind Harry Lintons. Linton was afraid he'd set it on fire and told Hugh that he would have to leave.

Fokner went to Mansfield where he worked as a caretaker and house sitter for several estates. During World War II, he was hired in the fall as a watchman at the Dailey potato storage building between Lexington and Bellville. (With rationing some folks were stealing potatoes at night.) Hugh was to stay there and although there was no office and scant living conditions, there were plenty of spuds.

Self supporting as he was, Fokner was well traveled. In the early 1950s, he had a huge old Packard limousine (probably big enough to sleep in) and had been from coast to coast, made several trips to Washington D.C., and sometimes went to Florida in winter. He later traded the Packard for a brand new Volkswagen when they first came out.

Fokner was a good worker and self supporter almost to the end. Evenings were spent reading at the library, often with his dog at his side. The bearded one died in February 1968, after a short stay in the County Home. He was 84.

"Boots" Garverick was a local genius, who built a couple of automobiles. Most folks buy theirs. Boots made his own.

His nickname was picked up as a kid, when he wore a new pair of heavy winter boots to school on a warm fall day. His classmates teased him and called him "Boots." The name stuck. It was easier to remember than Maurice.

A well-known and likeable character, he ran a welding and repair shop in Lexington for 30 years. As an expert welder, he had a genius for designing and fabricating metal work.

The first car he built was in the hot rod style. It started with a 1932 Ford frame, a '41 Mercury engine and the body was of Boots' own design. The grill was from

Photograph courtesy of Lana Garverick Sluss
"Boots" Garverick and his homemade "Henry J Custom Roadster" attracted a lot of attention.

a 1930s sedan with a custom hood and open cockpit. This was followed by a beautiful boat-tail rear deck, fabricated from a '46 Hudson hood. Old Ford wire wheels set it all off. The engine wasn't all that souped up, but with the light weight body most folks figured it could easily take Mont Whitney's new Buick.

His next effort was a sports car that began with a $35 Henry J, which was not one of Henry J. Kaiser's greatest works. The Henry J was a rather ugly, early compact with the Cadillac style frogeye taillights, just not the Cadillac quality.

Off came the Kaiser's body and then Boots shortened the frame to 87 ½ inches. Next the Kaiser Jeep engine was moved back for better balance. A 1926 Whippet gas tank was mounted between the frame rails. The front fenders came from a '51 Chevy and were quickly followed by a custom fabricated grill, hood and doors. The rear fenders and deck were salvaged from a '53 Kaiser sedan. Boots made his own stainless steel windshield frame and rocker panels, as well as an interior to suit his own tastes.

He named his creation a "Henry J Custom Roadster," which was painted school bus yellow. The paint may have come from John Newcomer's school bus garage, where Boots worked part-time as mechanic. John was his brother-in-law.

The roadster was a man's car, equipped with only the basics. No need for fancy radios, plush carpet, velour covered seats or air conditioning. Those were for the fairer sex. Boot's creation had a floor shift, grease proof plastic seats, a canvas top in case of rain, outside mirrors to see who he had passed, a horn and windshield wipers. That's all a man needed.

He bragged the Jeep engine could propel the little yellow car to a blistering 72 miles per hour, while still delivering 26 miles per gallon. It cruised nicely at 55 to 60 and cornered like a billiard ball.

A summer evening would see him buzzing around area roads wearing his familiar flat hat, cigar in mouth and a look of satisfaction on his face. These trips usually ended in the parking lot at Swigart's Café, where he

Photograph courtesy of Lana Garverick Sluss
"Boots" ran a welding shop and Ada worked at the post office.

could enjoy a couple of beers and answer the questions of on-lookers.

What kind of a car is it? Where did you get it? How much did it cost? You simply couldn't find a car that would garner that much attention, at any price.

Garverick's welding shop, with blacksmith forge, was located in a barn on the alley between the Presbyterian Church and Main Street. Broken farm tools, worn plow points and damaged machinery all found its way to that shop from farmers and others who anxiously awaited repair or modification.

Boots genius for design started in 1935 when he built one of the first tractor-mounted mowers. He later designed and built a potato harvester that was used for many years on the Cockley potato farm, which is now the west part of town.

He was awarded patents for the harvester and a self-leveling stepladder. Boots built a small gas powered tractor for his son, Max, who became the envy of every kid in town. Young Bob Whitney motored on a Garverick tricycle until he got too big for it.

It was a good family. Boot's wife Ada worked at the post office and he taught welding at Tappan during World War

Seymore Lindsey, splattered with paint, was working on a large mural in this undated photo.

II. He served on the village council and fire department. His death in 1975 marked the end of an era. We now live in a "when it's broke, throw it away" society.

"Boots" Garverick, with his wry sense of humor, is fondly remembered.

Seymore Scott Lindsey was another Lexington character who may not be well-remembered by the present generation. Born in Lexington in 1848, his legacy as a skilled artist and painter lives to this day.

Lindsey was a house painter and interior decorator by trade. Although he had no formal training, Lindsey possessed a God-given talent for art.

He could take an ordinary sheet of paper and, using only scissors, cut a silhouette of a person or pastoral scene complete with trees, birds and animals in a realistic, but delicate fashion. Old-timers marveled at his ability. When finished, what started as a ball of paper in his hands would unfold, in one piece, to reveal a beautiful illustration. He often gave away these precious artworks.

One of these cut-paper masterpieces, sold at a 1997 auction for $1,375. The 10" x 12" work had the pencil inscription "Nov. 1878, this figure was cut by a boy of 10 years of age at Lexington O. without mark or pattern." The rendering contained a man and a tree with 22 birds and nests. (The first owner of this work had written the inscription in 1878. However, as the inscription said, Lindsey had actually created the piece as a child, in 1858.) Ten more of his silhouette cuttings sold for between $110 to $ 1,100 that night.

His early years were spent on a farm on Lindsey Road, just southeast of town. In 1985, Mary Williams, who was 99 at the time, recalled that Seymore and his mother once sold milk around town. Perhaps the close association and affection with his mother had some influence on his artistic upbringing.

For years, family members were always evasive when questions about the family and especially his father were asked. In a 1967 interview, the reason for the evasion finally came out. After some considerable hesitation, an 87-year-old churchgoing farmwife, Carrie Shuler, reluctantly explained.

She would only say, "There were two maiden ladies who had children out of wedlock. One of them was Seymore Lindsey's mother." And then the subject was changed. There was no further discussion. On a later visit, it was revealed that Shuler's mother and Mrs. Lindsey were good friends. The kind and very respectful manner she exhibited when speaking of Lindsey was memorable.

Each man stands on his own feet, ability and drive. Such was the case with Seymore Lindsey. He was a house and barn painter and widely known as an interior decorator. His specialty was painting artificial oak wood graining over pine or other wood surfaces. This was a popular finish in the 1880s and beyond.

His trademark, which wasn't always appreciated, was to paint a bird or animal into the finished graining of a door, cupboard or woodwork. A large bumblebee next to a doorknob, birds or squirrels on doors, kittens inside a cupboard door to keep mice away, or a large rat running towards a too small mouse hole in a baseboard were some of his prankish creations.

An early photo of Lindsey shows a rather dapper young man.

These two photos of Lindsey show him with his middle-age mustachios and in later years with his pet chicken. Both pictures show a hint of the devilish sparkle in his eyes.

When hired to do the interior of the John and Jennie Gribling home on Alta South Road, there were strict instructions from Jennie that none of his artwork should be used. When the job was finished, no one was home. Upon returning, they were greeted by the picture of a large owl, twelve inches high, on the kitchen wainscoting.

Yet another victim did not notice a baseboard corner rendering of two roosters fighting unless he almost stood on his head. That was three years after Lindsey left. He angrily stormed over to Lindsey's house, but no one was home. The owner never went back. After thinking it over, he realized how foolish he looked by taking three years to notice the painting. Lindsey would surely spread the word if they argued. So the customer just let the issue drop.

A church in Ontario hired Lindsey to decorate the interior of their sanctuary. He outdid himself. The backs of pews were illustrated with all kinds of birds and wild foul of every type. Beautiful to look at they proved to be a distraction as the minister sought to hold the congregations attention during a long winded sermon. The artist was called back to paint over them. What a pity.

An eyewitness to his artistic endeavor remarked that he simply used a small brush, a feather and fingernail to quickly create a bird or scene. It only took him a few minutes.

These quick creations became highly collectable years later. A six panel door with a large cat and bird on one side sold in 1997 for $2,200 at an auction house. Another door, with two doves on it, sold for $825. In 2007, a 40"x 46" framed Lindsey oil on canvas sold for $21,850. The painting was of a fox eating a chicken, with other animals in the background.

His artificial graining was done with a mixture of paint, varnish and beer. The beer gave the graining effect and

The original, un-restored, Lindsey barn painting shown here still resides on the side of a barn located on the south side of West Main Street in Lexington. Badly weathered and faded, it still shows the artists's talent. You can just make out the group of sheep in a meadow surrounded by woods. Sadly, a black and white photo just does not do this painting justice.

he was a master at making each board look realistic even with knots. Some of his work would look like real wood and was hard to detect except for the grain running across nail heads.

His murals were another well-remembered feature. Often livestock in pastoral scenes were rendered prominently in large scale on barns and outbuildings, which made those buildings a landmark for travelers. Sadly, these works have weathered and deteriorated over the years.

Efforts to repaint or restore and preserve them, however commendable, are not near of the quality of the original. Art student Natalie Prosser did a very fine job repainting one on the Robert Davidson farm south of town (the barn was torn down in 2005) and David Cochran from Steam Corners repainted one on Owens Road and several others.

Only a few of these masterpieces remain. They are all cherished and prized by their fortunate owners. The only untouched original mural known is on a barn on the south side of West Main Street in town. Badly faded, it is still something worth seeing.

Shockingly, Lindsey had no formal art training. According to a family member, Seymore was only four years old when he began his "scissors sculpture" and this rapidly developed his unusual talent. His paper cuttings were truly remarkable.

Lindsey's first attempt to capitalize on this talent was at the Centennial Exposition at Philadelphia in 1876. Seymore had a booth and spent two weeks in that space creating a masterpiece. When complete, Lindsey signed and dated the work. It was exhibited at the Centennial.

Speaking of this Centenial masterpiece, Lindsey once told his son Florian, "I could challenge the world with it." Lindsey willed the work to Florian shortly before he died, with the expressed wish that the son leave it to some institution in Richland County or the Ohio Historical Society. Sadly, the whereabouts of this masterwork are unknown at this writing.

Seymore Lindsey's paper cuttings are sought after by collectors. This masterpiece belonged to his son Florian. It was done with nothing more than one piece of paper, a pair of scissors and the artist's imagination. Note the intricate detail of the leaves, grass, birds in the trees and food the woman is feeding the birds on the ground.

The following year (1877) a news reporter commented that Seymore had sent a batch of his valuable paper cuttings to a Mr. Dunshee in Iowa. (Dunshee was a former Lexington resident.) As a result, Lindsey's art may be scattered around that state as well.

Seymore went to the World's Fair in Chicago in 1892 or 93, where he also had a booth. However, he only stayed three weeks before returning home because of lonesomeness. Evidently at heart he was a simple, small town boy.

Most of Lindsey's painting and decorating supplies were bought at Walker and Kell Hardware (later Kell Bros.). He was once hired to decorate the interior and front of their building. A plow with an American flag was a masterful exterior centerpiece he created for the hardware store building.

His regular order was for 100 lb. white lead and 5 gallons of oil for painting white buildings. He then mixed his own colors adding umber, sienna, Prussian blue, chrome yellow, vermillion, Van Dyke brown, and so on to get the desired effect. He could also buy a good variety of graining colors, walnut stains, oils and varnishes. The beer came from someplace else.

In October of 1877, Lindsey married Mary Miller, a local girl, and they raised two sons and a daughter. His son, Ralph, was born in 1880.

Ralph Lindsey married Verda Smith and was a well-known rural mail carrier for many years until retirement. He had inherited his father's "haw, haw, haw" laugh. Ralph died in 1950.

Daughter Isa married a Mr. Clint Schindler, but she died at an early age. Not much is known of her.

Florien V. Lindsey, born in 1891, started working with his father when he was 14. Florian remembered Seymore sometimes supervising a crew of four or five men as jobs required. His father's artistic talent evidently rubbed off. At age 17, Florian went to Cleveland to study art and then went to Brooklyn and later Chicago as a commercial artist. He worked for a number of firms that produced mail order catalogs – Sears Roebuck, Montgomery Ward, Spiegel, Gimbels and others. His firm sent him to Winnipeg, Canada where he worked for Eaton's, Hudson's Bay and several more until retirement. He did well and lived in St. Boniface, Manitoba.

For many years Seymores' half brother, William, ran a harness shop in town. William died in an unusual way. He passed away after a bath in a sitting position on a chair with his feet in a pan of water. Friend Sid Earhart later found him.

In the 1950s and 60s historian and writer D. W. Garber interviewed quite a number of people who knew Seymore. For many years, Garber wrote for the *Mansfield News Journal* and the *Columbus Dispatch* and authored several books. In his extensive research he once drove to Canada to visit Florian Lindsey. He spoke to Mr. and Mrs. Lee Logan, Mr. and Mrs. Dwight Smith, Frank Griebling and his mother Anna, grandson Rex Lindsey, Nellie Gatton Wade, Harry Miller, Carl Murphy, Mary Williams, Hoyt Cleland, Harry Smith and a number of others who were well acquainted with the man. Mr. Garber died in California in 1984 and his files were graciously loaned to the author by his grandson, Michael Cullen. From them and my own sources I obtained a wealth of stories about Lindsey.

Lindsey was described by several as a slightly small, rather shy-looking man with reddish brown hair, long mustachios and keen gray blue eyes that

This painting (in color) shows the Lindsey's versatility as an artist.

had a devilish twinkle in them. He was rather dapper in his younger years, but more careless in appearance as he aged. He had a wonderful sense of humor and an infectious laugh that brought smiles to anyone who heard it. All agreed he was a thoroughly liked man who enjoyed a good joke, a story or harmless prank played on a friend. Florian recalled a bit of humor his father painted on a board fence behind a rural farm house. "The reason the dog did not catch the rabbit," and showed the dog stopping to do his business.

The family belonged to the Congregational Church, but while his wife and mother attended, Seymore was not described as being very religious. Seymore was a fair singer and played a flute. He had tried to enlist during the Civil War but was too small and thin. He was told by a recruiter to "go home and eat mush." His wife, Mary, who was a rather quiet person, would sell his artwork and hold out for a stiff price. Seymore on the other hand, would happily give his artworks away to folks who appreciated them.

Mrs. Smith had a pair of life sized quail carved by Lindsey from a block of wood and painted realistically. His true to life wood carvings of birds and animals were another of his remarkable talents. It was remembered he deplored hunting and never killed a bird or animal.

Seymore was a Republican and was angered one time when son Florian voted for a Democrat for president. He kept pea fowls, and was particularly proud of his "White crested, black Polish chickens." These had a long feather, which drooped over the eyes. However, by cross breeding them, Lindsey eventually developed a strain without the drooping feather – they were almost erect.

Theron Texter, John Williams and James Timanus are

Larry Schumacher owns this sign. Lindsey painted it for his half-brother's Delaware Street harness shop. It is a very rare example of Seymore's advertising creativity.

three of the local men who are remembered to have worked with Lindsey.

Lindsey's house, at the point or corner of Delaware and Maple Street, was decorated with his paintings. The walls were covered with landscapes, animal, and bird figures. One scene recalled was a hillside scene with a flock of sheep. Another had a large tree trunk that rose from the baseboard, its limbs branched out with leaves, animals, and birds.

At the Gatton–Wade home near Bellville, Cy Gatton appreciated wildlife and the outdoors to the extent that the Lexington artist was given a free hand and spent part of the winter decorating the new home. One day about lunch time Cy was spotted coming in carrying three skunks. The scene was painted on the back of a closet door. On doors and panels were squirrels, a coon, rabbits, a Blue Jay (in color) and many quail. The house was filled with Lindsey's artwork, much of which still remains.

His reputation as a painter spread. He would often leave on Monday with his team and wagon, loaded with supplies and not return until Friday. News accounts reported him working in New London, Cardington, Caledonia, and other far off places. He evidently worked in a 30- to 40-mile radius of Lexington. For some odd reason, he enjoyed chopping wood on weekends.

When the Presbyterian Church varnished their pews years ago it wouldn't dry and panicking members believed they couldn't hold services unless they went to another church. God forbid they should do that! To Seymore they came for advice, which was "wash them down with stale beer and have the minister do it. You can't trust the members with the beer."

Harry Miller remembered Lindsey would enjoy a couple of drinks "and raise thunder" now and then. He was a regular guy and owned half interest in a race horse in 1883. Mrs. Lee Logan fondly remembered his hearty laugh and characteristic way to express his enjoyment when laughing. He would spread his arms wide and then clap his hands together as giving greater show of appreciation for the story or source of amusement.

The thoroughly liked man who gave so much color, art, laughter, and smiles to the village died September 16, 1927. He was 78 and is buried in Lexington Cemetery.

Maggie Colwell knew everything and everybody in town. She knew where they went, what they did and who they talked to. She was the town's telephone operator. And she could listen in!

The Star Telephone Company was the first to bring telephone service to the fledgling village in 1882. A night operator was necessary a year later as more subscribers came on. A line was later extended to Johnsville and Mt. Gilead in 1885. In March of 1900, it was necessary to stretch a line four miles west to Steam Corners. The prospects for progress in Steam Corners were enough to boggle the imagination!

But there was a problem. Several competing phone companies came into existence at that period (1880s and 90s) and the primitive equipment wouldn't permit a call to connect from one company's lines to another. A few folks, like a county commissioner who lived on Lexington-Springmill Road, had to have two phones. This meant they were sometimes imposed upon to relay messages…not a good arrangement.

In April of 1902, the new Mansfield Telephone Company was granted permission to begin operations here. res were to be strung on 40-foot poles, which were to be painted white. MTC took over the Star operations and installed the town's first switchboard. This switchboard went into the home of Mrs. John "Maggie" Colwell, on the southeast corner of Grange and Church Street. She was a widow and, in that day, would have been in dire need of some sort of income.

Maggie, seated on a swivel chair in her living room, was a whiz at the switchboard. In those days, there was no direct dialing. Every single call had to be put through by the operator.

While Maggie kept folks connected, it was an all day, all night job. Naturally, she had to have a substitute to fill in anytime she left the house. Laola Swigart was a frequent fill-in.

Everybody who had a phone knew Maggie and she offered cordial service and often times the latest news from around town. It's fair to say that Maggie became more of a friend than a just service provider to the phone users of the Lexington area. She was discrete with information she overheard and never repeated anything that would offend.

A person leaving their house to visit somebody could tell Maggie and any incoming calls would be directed to the phone at their destination. It was a real, live, personal service.

Call waiting, call forwarding, leave a message and information are nothing new. Maggie offered it all way back in 1900. Nowadays we get automated prompts and listen to impersonal computers.

Maggie held her post, and respect of her customers, for 30 years. She only gave way when the dial phone system replaced crank phones sometime around 1930.

Jay Ross was a curious character. Frank "Gee" Ross and his wife, Alice, lived on a farm out on Ross Road, west of town. They had two sons, Frank and Jay. Frank Jr. was a fine musician, well-liked, outgoing and generous.

Jay was the exact opposite. He was extremely penurious (that means frugal), or as folks described him, "tighter than bark on a tree." He wouldn't waste a penny on anything.

Jay farmed and raised a few head of cattle, but never owned a tractor or much machinery. He never owned an automobile, but would walk or ride his bicycle to town. If he had to go to Mansfield, he caught a bus.

At a distance Jay's clothes, dark blue coveralls, looked like new, but that changed when up close. They were somewhat black with dirt as he never washed them. His penchant for economy was extraordinary. He slept on a bed of rag balls, strips of rags wound into balls for making rugs possibly gathered by his late mother years earlier. He let the grass and weeds grow around

Maggie Colwell was Lexington's first and only telephone operator. Photographed here in the 1920s, she ran the town's switchboard, from her home, for more than 30 years.

his house giving it an abandoned appearance. Jay once told a neighbor he sometimes ate cattle feed mixed with milk, which he claimed "didn't taste too bad." What the heck, the cows ate it too.

He had few friends and his relatives doubtless stayed away. His somewhat hermit-like existence would have been lonely at best. Surprisingly when he spoke, one could see gold fillings in his teeth.

The writer once worked in Hugh Hiser's Sandwich Bar. On a cold winter day in 1953, Jay Ross came in and backed up to the gas heater just inside the front door to warm himself. Before long a foul odor began to permeate the premises. Customers began looking around and at each other. Hiser, a World War II veteran, who had served in the infantry but not the diplomatic corps, leaned over the counter, pointed towards the door and yelled at Ross, "GET THE HELL OUT OF HERE AND DON'T COME BACK TILL YOU TAKE A BATH!" Old Jay left, muttering to himself as he went. He never came back.

Jay died in April of 1954. Few mourned his passing. When they settled his estate they found $25,200 in bonds, 80 acres worth $6,500 and a ½ interest in 50 acres at $1,500. He wasn't poor.

What gave Jay Ross his peculiar trait of character is unknown. He came from a good family. Was it mental illness? Perhaps his God-given purpose was to re-teach the age-old lesson that friends and family are the most valued possession. How much or little we accumulate in our time here is of little importance. Like Jay Ross, we can't take it with us.

Aaron Moses Brown, Corporal, United States Army, World War I, came to Lexington sometime in the late 1930s or early 40s. He came alone and lived alone.

A rather homely man with coarse facial features, squinty eyes, and a deep raspy voice Brown worked at odd jobs for people all over town. He mowed lawns, cleaned up, washed windows and pulled weeds. Gladys Logan and her mother let him stay in an old chicken coop behind her house on Church Street and he took care of the yard work for her. With what little money he made he often walked out to the Corners Restaurant for a meal and sometimes they'd see him going through garbage cans out back.

Brown wore bib overalls and seldom wore socks, even in winter. In summer he wore the overalls, but no shirt.

"Brownie" watched the Memorial Day Parade from the sidelines for many years. Folks finally noticed he too was an old soldier and should be in the parade.

In winter, he added several layers of shirts and sweaters. He carried his things in an old orange sack.

Once people got to know him he was found to be friendly enough and would stop and talk. However, most women tried to avoid him.

The Logan chicken coop was just that and "Brownie" as he was called, fixed up a place to sleep. There was no heat and on cold frigid nights Bob Snyder, the local funeral director, would go get him. Snyder let Brownie sleep in the heated garage at the funeral home, where they kept the hearse and ambulance.

Bob and Dorothy Snyder were good people and often gave him a job to do. Sometimes when Brownie really needed a little money, Bob would look around and find something for him to do. Bob wouldn't just turn him away.

Few people knew that Brownie wrote songs. He gave fifty or more of them to Snyder to keep. He took several more to Smarts Music in Mansfield and had them copyrighted. Several of his songs were dedicated to young Sally Gibson. She was a warm, friendly person and had perhaps befriended him. There was no romance, Sally was a young woman.

Not much is known of Brownie's background. In the 1960s, Sid Earhart said Brownie had worked for the B&O Railroad, but got into some kind of trouble up

"Brownie" may well have been the last living WWI veteran in Lexington. The Robert Castor VFW Post recognized the error of omitting him from Memorial Day Parades. After that, he was a regular fixture of the event.

north and came to Lexington. Bob Snyder said that Brownie had a daughter living in New York and every few years he'd either catch a bus in Lexington or Snyder would drive him to Mansfield and he'd go visit her. When he came back he'd be cleaned up pretty good.

In his later years, Gladys Logan let him live in a garage behind a house at the end of East Main. There was heat and a stove. One time it caught fire. There was heavy smoke and panic as the call went out, "Where's Brownie?" At first he was thought to be dead, but he later came walking along from uptown wondering what the fuss was all about.

In his last years, Brownie read of a concoction of limburger, garlic or other things that if worn as a necklace it would keep germs away and promote good health. It smelled so bad that it kept people away or at least upwind. He stayed healthy enough, although the way he smelled a few folks thought he might be dead.

The details of Brownie's military service are not known. However, he had joined the Robert Castor Post of the VFW. And on Memorial Day, dressed in his best clean clothes and wearing his Post Veterans cap, Brownie was always standing on the sidewalk as the parade passed. A few folks finally noticed that this seemed a bit odd.

It turns out that Brownie may have been among the last, or possibly was the last, World War I veteran living in Lexington. The VFW Post saw their error.

The next year Brownie was in the parade, riding to the cemetery in Bob Snyder's magnificent yellow 1953 Packard Caribbean convertible. Amid the applause of the crowd, he finally got the recognition he deserved. The old veteran was a familiar figure in parades after that.

When he died friends and veterans laid him to rest and saw to it a marker was placed on his grave. It reads, Aaron Moses Brown, Cpl U.S. Army, WW I, 1890-1977.

Pete Bikar was a big man, a real big man. Standing a bit over six feet and weighing somewhere around the 340 pound mark, he was a veritable giant in town during the 1950s. Imposing in stature, he surely made the list of "men with whom I wouldn't pick a fight."

Pete had lost an eye in an accident. A replacement glass eye, coupled with his huge size, big hands and well tanned complexion, made him a real eyebrow raiser when met for the first time. However, he was a gentleman, a good businessman and well liked, with a wide circle of friends.

Pete was in the blacktop paving and road oiling business. He had his office across the street from the railroad station at the old bulk gas and oil plant. Some of his oil supplies were delivered by rail. Lexington Asphalt Paving was a good local business and did many driveways in the growing local developments.

A memorable business calendar he put out one year had a dual picture on it. One photo showed Pete standing beside the company's new 5 ton roller. Beside that was another picture, showing Pete sitting on the same roller. The second photo had the caption, "The Company's new 10 ton Roller."

To keep costs down, Bikar did most of the upkeep on his trucks and equipment himself. Well remembered is the time Pete came up to John Newcomer's school bus garage next door and wanted to borrow an engine hoist. He needed the hoist to take the motor out of a Chevy cab forward truck he owned. Newcomer was sorry, but he didn't have one to lend.

A few days later Bikar came back again and wanted to know if he could get a little help putting the engine back in the truck. "How did you get it out?" came the question. "I just reached in with my hands and picked it up" was his answer.

Putting the engine back was a different proposition. A very powerful man, he could lift an engine. However, he needed help lining up the shaft for the clutch, the transmission and the motor mount bolts, etc. That took extra hands.

Pete was a popular figure at Swigart's Café in the evenings. Usually still dressed in his tar stained work clothes, he was the delight of the working class folks. His right hand man and longtime helper, Al Jones, was the exact opposite of his boss. Jones was very short, and thin but a good reliable worker. Together they were the "Mutt and Jeff" of Lexington.

When Bikar and his wife retired, they moved to Florida. The business was then sold to Jones, who moved it to Galion.

Capt. Levi Rumsey was a rather suspicious character who arrived in town sometime around 1879. His actions led many to believe he was associated with the western outlaw Jessie James gang. He came from Union County, or so he claimed, and was looking for a farm to buy.

He approached John Graham who had a farm on the north side of Steam Corners Road, just over the hill from present-day Route 97. It encompassed much of what is now know as the "Clear Fork Hills" allotment.

In 1880 Graham wasn't interested in selling, but Rumsey insisted he name a price. In an effort to get rid of Rumsey, Graham set a figure well in excess of the value of the 221-acre place. Graham thought that would end the matter. To his great surprise, Rumsey reached in his pocket and paid the full amount in cash.

Rumsey dressed well, seemed to have plenty of money and rode a spirited horse named "Yellow Boy." He seemed friendly, but was always on the alert. He avoided letting anyone get behind him if he could help it. Rumsey viewed any strangers he met with suspicion. That coupled with the habit of squatting on his haunches and moving around so he could keep an eye on those present, was another unusual trait.

Morris Graham was born and grew up on his father's farm before Rumsey bought it. In a 1956 interview, the 88-year-old Graham related much of the information about Capt. Rumsey's time in the Lexington area.

Rumsey was always referred to as "Captain" although no military record was known to the locals. He was a dealer or trader in horses and from time to time some rough-looking characters visited his place, which the locals thought might be outlaws in hiding. He bought strings of local horses and allegedly took them out west to sell. He would often return with a different bunch, some of which were unbroken or wild. These he sold locally. Some folks believed a number of them were stolen, although no proof was forthcoming.

After Graham sold the farm and moved to Bloomington, Illinois, Rumsey would stop and spend the night on his trips west. He would be offered a second floor bedroom where he always slept on the floor instead of the bed. Graham believed it was so he could keep his ear to the floor and detect any strange noises from below.

The "Captain" was in a July 1881 altercation that Lexington's colorful news correspondent and onetime medical student would stretch for maximum interest (and pay). He incorrectly spelled his name "Ramsey."

Morris and Jenny Graham knew the details of Captain Rumsey and the Jesse James Gang.

A few days ago when the rays of the solar orb were glinting the tree tops with golden light, Captain Ramsey and Dillon McKee, a tenant on Ramsey's farm between whom much bad blood has been engendered, caused by litigation about business affairs, met on a stack of wheat and after exhausting the vocabulary of abusive epithets, an altercation ensued in which McKee struck out from the shoulder in an admirable manner, giving the Captain a sledge-hammer blow at the base of the right auricular appendage, making a deep abrasion of the cuticle and causing a liberal effusion of the rich crimson fluid of life, and sent him cavorting in mid air to the terra firma, followed by McKee, who walked up and down the entire length of his vertebra column, wretched his cervical vertebra and dealt him several blows in the region of the occipital bone, and would no doubt made a "cadaver" of the valiant Captain had not bystanders interfered. McKee then left the scene of the affray which was made crimson with the blood of the chivalrous Captain, and voluntarily appeared before Justice (of the Peace) Custer and paid his fine. This did not please the wrath of Ramsey, and he had his assailant arranged before Mayor Blair's tribunal to answer to the charge of assault and battery.

Five months later McKee, who was then living in Bellville, sued Rumsey for $10,000 claiming damages for malicious prosecution. The case dragged on to the Supreme Court.

Rumsey had a steam powered sawmill in operation at the farm in 1882. Two young men, one from Mansfield and the other a young a Lexington area relative of the Mansfielder, stole a small quantity of lead pipe feeding water to the mill boiler. They were caught, but mill operation ceased for a few days. Rumsey must have been annoyed over that.

Horse traders in the 1880s were generally viewed with the same distrust and suspicions as present-day used car salesmen. Folks no doubt kept an eye on Captain Rumsey as the horses came and went. Adding fuel to the fire was a local April 1882 newspaper report of the fatal shooting of Jessie James, by gang member Robert Ford. Ford had shot James in an effort to collect the $50,000 reward offered by express and railroad companies and the Governor of Missouri. Ford and his brother Charles gave themselves up and claimed that they were detectives. However, they were jailed. Robert Ford was convicted of murder, but immediately pardoned and paid by the Governor.

Jessie with his wife, two children and part of the gang had been living in a shack outside St. Joseph, Missouri. They were reportedly planning another raid when the Jesse met his fate.

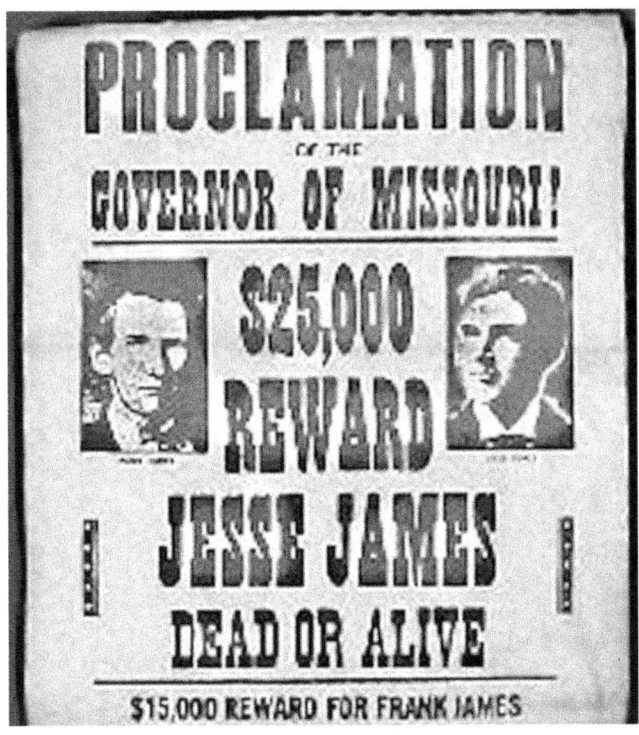

One of a series of Wanted Posters for Jesse James.

In March of 1883 another news item from the pen of Al Moore would also raise a few eyebrows:

Mr. James, of Texas, was recently the cynosure of our citizens, as he is a cousin of the Missouri bandits, Frank and Jessie James, but has not their blood letting propensities, and we are informed, he was once involved in lariating on the plains of the Lone Star State with Captain Ramsey, of Troy. Morris Graham claimed Perry James said he was a Texas Ranger and on one occasion was brought to Rumsey's farm to recover from wounds received in a gun battle. He and Rumsey demonstrated a warm friendship and James was allowed to ride "Yellow Boy" during these visits.

Augustus Loveland lived on the adjoining farm to the east and Rumsey boarded with them as there was no woman in his household for cooking or domestic chores. The Loveland's had raised a girl by the name of Alice Numbers and the Captain became enamored with her, a romance developed, and they were married in October of 1883. It was a choice news item for Al Moore:

Captain L. Ramsey, having passed the meridian of life, was thought to be unsusceptible to the wiles of our young ladies, but last week he led to the altar the genial Miss Alice Numbers of this vicinity. Rev. McFarland officiated at the wedding rites at the residence of the valiant Captain which overlooks the fertile expanse of more than 200 acres one mile north of Lexington.

It was an apparent happy union and the Captain provided his wife with fine clothes and jewelry. His new father-in-law once rode "Yellow Boy" from the farm to downtown Mansfield in 35 minutes, a feat that made the local paper.

In 1883 for some unknown reason, Rumsey sold his farm to W. W. Cockley who put the deed in his wife's name. Perhaps Mary U. Beverstock Cockley had inherited funds from her father's estate or the deed was in her name as protection against lawsuits. It was the basis of what was extended years later to become the largest land tract in Troy Township, encompassing more than half of the present village. It is possible Rumsey continued his horsetrading business from his former farm through an agreement with Cockley, who lived in town, or the Rumseys may have moved into the Loveland place. Nothing is known.

Captain Levi Rumsey again left for the west shortly before May 1, 1885. Weeks later nothing had been heard from him. It was then that Alice noticed her jewelry and part of her wardrobe missing. It was apparent that the scoundrel was not coming back. What became of him is unknown. With the money from the farm he could start anew. Or did the rascal meet his fate at the wrong end of a gun barrel or hangman's rope while procuring more horses?

Poor Alice evidently returned to her maiden name. In the 1960s, older members of the Congregational Church could still remember her. Whether she remarried or moved away could not be determined. Her parents had moved to Colorado.

Left behind was the suspicion that Lexington may well have been a haven for outlaws and members of the notorious Jessie James Gang. That legend will never die.

Jesse and Frank James, seen in a photo taken in Carolinda, Ill. during 1872.

Lexington Awakes From a Slumber

Turning Over in Our Sleep

Not much had changed in the business district in the first half of the 1900s. The buildings, those that survived the several fires, were occupied by new tenants from time to time, but growth was limited.

Photograph courtesy of Ester Hildebrand Collection
Maxwell's was on the southwest corner of the square.

Sowers' General store, on the southwest corner of the square, passed to Hugh Maxwell. After Hugh died in 1910, his wife and son George continued to operate it until 1915. Next David Ireland ran the business until the 1930s, when it became one of Barney Kroger's stores. Yes, Lexington had a Kroger store. Currently, the building is occupied by American Pie Pizza.

At the opposite corner of the square, what originally in the 1840s had been Sowers & Beverstock's general store, evolved to just Beverstocks'. Then with A.B. Sr.'s death in 1882, the store passed to son A.B. "Fred" Beverstock and son-in-law William W. Cockley. Those two teamed up until George Galbraith bought out Beverstock's interest, at which point the store became Cockley and Galbraith's. Cockley's other business interests grew and he sold his half interest to Galbraith as well, who ran the store until he sold out to I. W. Garverick. Garverick in turn sold to Charlie Koogle. Richard Armstrong bought out Koogle in 1946. And so the deeds did go around and around, always new owners, but in the same old building.

The Culp Building held McNaul's Meat Market and a variety of business efforts over those years. The first Kroger store was there during the late 1930s and early 40s. George and Kenny Clever opened a duck pin alley (a miniature bowling alley) after Kroger moved down the street. It was a popular hangout for teenage kids, but closed when the two brothers enlisted during World War II. There wasn't much for young people to do downtown after that.

Other shopping or businesses were Aten's Meat Market, Derrenbergers Pharmacy, Charlie Hartenfelt's High Speed Bulk Plant, Butch Castor's Sohio Service Station, Kell Hardware and Koogle's Grocery. Gladys Logan ran a restaurant in Whitney's Mobile Station, next door to Mrs. Lee's Home Cooking or you could get a short snort down under the Minnear Hotel. John McNaul ran a slaughter house on Maple St. behind the funeral home, which was on Delaware Street.

Photograph courtesy of Elsie Simon
McNaul Brothers Meat Market was in part of the Culp Building, on the now-empty lot next to Deckers on W. Main

In 1931, Charlie Sowers had a small hatchery and chicken butchering business on Delaware Street and ran a Sinclair Service Station on East Main. His brother, Art, worked in the chicken slaughter barn. Art was rather small, crippled and mentally slow. He was hit and killed crossing Delaware Street one day, which ended the chicken slaughtering business. Women were saddened by his death as they depended on him for chicken feathers for pillows. Oddly enough, Green's Hatchery was just up the street from the chicken slaughter barn. That must say something about the natural cycle of life.

The only new buildings downtown were the Lexington Savings Bank building, with the post office inside as well, which opened about 1910.

Photograph courtesy of Ester Hildebrand Collection

Hugh Maxwell's (on the left) grocery and dry goods store was the place to shop in the early 1900s. In this early picture, George Maxwell (on the right) is seen as a young clerk. George was the proprietor after his father died.

Irwin "Butch" Castor's Economy Garage sold Red Crown gasoline in the 1920s and 30s. Butch and his son-in-law, Adie Young, were good mechanics and kept folks old cars running.

There was also a Texaco Gas Station built shortly after the 1929 fire. It was the first new structure in nearly 20 years.

Mont's West Main Mobile Station

In 1932 Mont Whitney moved his family to Lexington from Cardington, where he had worked for the Hart Brothers. The Hart Brothers were the new owners of the Lexington gas station on West Main. The brand of the station was changed to Secony Mobile and the well-liked, hard working Whitney ran the station until January of 1956.

Mont's two sons, Lloyd and Robert, grew up in that station environment and worked with their dad when they were old enough. Robert, the youngest, became a prominent trial lawyer in Mansfield and has served on the Lexington Board of Education as member and President longer than anyone else. Lloyd served the town as a part-time Policeman and Volunteer Fireman for many years. He had other exploits as well and these are detailed in a later chapter.

Sometime around the summer of 1947, a Chevy panel truck with a Red Cross sign on the side stalled across the street from Kell Hardware. An anxious young woman in uniform walked to the gas station for help. Mont went down, opened the hood, climbed in and spent quite some time tinkering. After repeated tries, he finally got the truck going again. The delighted and much relieved woman, purse in hand, wanted to know how much she owed. "Red Cross money is no good in this town", replied the smiling Whitney. He tipped his hat and walked back to the station. Mont was that kind of a guy.

By 1956, the million or more trips from the gas pumps to the cash register were taking their toll on Whitney. Paul Fisher took over the station. Mont later dabbled in insurance, real estate, worked at Stevens Manufacturing, and finally sold cars for John Jagger in Mount Gilead before retiring.

Swigart's Café – Buck's Friendly Tavern

During World War II, Roy Swigart opened a bar and restaurant in what had been the old Derrenberger Pool Room. By the end of the war, he moved the business to part of his home (two doors away) and thus Swigart's Café was born. Its location on Main Street made it a popular stopping place and Roy was a likeable character.

Photograph courtesy of Swigart Family
Leola and Roy Swigart opened Swigart's Café in the brick Derrenberger building during World War II. At the end of the war, they moved the café to part of their home.

To most it appeared Roy ran the place as a means of support, which was understandable. However, his true love was hunting and fishing. That was undeniable.

Roy once told the story of duck hunting on the Clear Fork. He took his boat out very, very early, crossed the lake, shut off the motor and let it slowly drift. It was still pretty dark and misty…long before sun up, when the law said hunting could legally start.

Then ahead in the mist he spotted a row of ducks, just waiting to be bagged. He just couldn't wait. "Boom, boom!" went his shotgun. Roy noticed after the first shot that none of the other ducks tried to fly away. He had just started to realize that not fleeing was an odd reaction for the ducks. When he heard a voice from out of the weeds, "What the hell's going on out there?"

Roy had shot up several decoys that belonged to Fred Laubie, the Ford dealer from Fredericktown. There were evidently profuse apologies and more than a few free drinks and food to smooth over that mistake.

Roy and his son George ran a good business. It was the town's favorite watering hole and hangout. It had one of the first TV sets in town, which gave folks an excuse to go watch the ballgames on a 10 inch screen. Roy had opened another tavern in Butler, which his son Jack ran for 37 years.

Mont Whitney explains the virtues of Mobile Oil to a customer in this posed advertising photo. The customer just happens to be his son Lloyd. Mont took good care of his customers, for over 24 years, at the West Main Street station, where the current Marathon stands.

Swigart's was a popular tavern, as was the bar room under the Minnear Hotel next door. Laughter and good company were found especially on weekends.

After Roy died, George and wife Jean ran the place a few years and then bought John Newcomer's school bus business after John retired. Swigart's Café was sold to Buck and Betty Burkepile, who changed the name to "Bucks" and expanded the restaurant. It was later resold to Larry Proto.

Buck's was a favorite place to eat in town. Famous for its "Big Pete Burger" (named after local near giant Pete Bikar) and an order of fries that could feed a family, locals kept the place filled. On the weekend, race crowds and out-of-towners helped keep it jam packed.

Sadly, in a heart breaking 1996 fire, Buck's was burned beyond repair and was torn down. Lost in the fire were many autographed photographs and souvenirs accumulated over the years from celebrity customers. Larry Proto said he wanted to rebuild at that site, but plans

Photograph courtesy of Swigart Family
George Swigart worked with his dad and took over after Roy died. Wife Jean was a ready helper during busy periods.

John Newcomer owned and operated the Lexington school bus system from 1930 until the firm was sold to George Swigart. The school district later took over transportation, bringing the system in-house.

never materialized. Present-day "Bucks" is a delightful place, combining dining and recreation and is a real asset to the town.

Polly Kunkle opened the "Atmosphere" for private parties in 1959. She was an excellent cook, cake decorator, and host for gatherings. For a while she and her family operated in a remodeled barn just outside town, but a fire ended that.

Charles Ink opened a drive-in root beer stand at Orchard Park also in 1959, the first in the area. He ran the popular hangout until 1975.

In December of 1945, Louie Ryan came back from World War II and bought the Sinclair Station on East Main from Charlie Sowers. Was it an easy way to make a living? Twenty years later, he was stillworking 15 hours a day, seven days a week. But it was a family affair as his father Frank and son Gary helped out for a few years. The station was remodeled in 1965 and in 1972 sold to Walter "Mick" Cashell. It was torn down when present-day "Bucks" was built on that spot.

The Minnear Hotel and Kell Hardware were the only two businesses that remained in the same families.

All of this is to make the point that Lexington really changed little during those years. All the job prospects were in Mansfield or elsewhere. In a very real sense, Lexington's economy was asleep.

Awakening

The slumbering village in the valley was to encounter a change after World War II that was beyond imagination. The national "move to the suburbs" craze landed in old Lex.

Mailman Lloyd Clever and plastering contractor Joe Wilson each built new houses on the hill just beyond the Rt. 97 and Steam Corners Road intersection in 1947. A couple more went up east of town and couple more on Steam Corners.

In 1955 an announcement that Rollin Cockley, Wright Armstrong, and George Texter had platted 10 acres for 10 residential lots on Steam Corners Road was surprising. Wright Armstrong and Cring Reality had already produced seven new homes.

Two years later, in 1957, retired engineering genius Harry F. Smith was to write, "Within a ½ mile radius

The village councilmen, meeting on the partitioned off stage of the old town hall, considered tearing down the little used building during the 1940s. They had no idea of the changes that lie ahead. (L to R) Ted Welch, Leland Armstrong, Ed Wilson (hidden), Robert Arehart, Mayor Lowell McIntire, Robert Carter Sr., Simon Seif and Walter Shafer.

there are no less than 14 housing developments under way. The largest of these is the Clear Fork Hills Addition on land formerly owned by Mr. William B. Cockley and extending along Route 97 from Lexington to the Clear Fork Dam."

In November of 1956, John L. Morley, President of Midwest Houses, announced the start of a 1,000 home development on 550 acres of land northwest of town. A plan had been drawn by the firm of Seward H. Mott of Washington DC and was Morley's third and largest development. Some folks were rather skeptical to say the least when they read that in the local paper. Grading for the first 60 lots and streets started two months later. Clear Fork Hills was born.

Morley was a remarkable businessman who left a legacy that will long be remembered in this area.

Born in Detroit, he grew up in Bloomfield Hills, a fancy suburb with well-to-do parents. His father didn't give him everything like his friends who were from wealthy auto empire families. If John wanted something, he had to work for it. That's the way he was raised. It was the start of a work ethic that always stayed with him.

He once commented that his friends never amounted to much, a lesson for today's parents.

Morley dropped out of Michigan State College (it was boring) and worked for the New York Stock Exchange for seven years. He said that was his education. He then worked for Great Lakes Steel, where he was involved in locating fabricators for steel products used in housing projects.

John came to Mansfield during World War II, working for a firm (Jones & Brown) that made Quonset huts for the Navy. He was able to sell the idea to the Army too. After the war, he left Jones & Brown, which had two plants, and took over their Midwest Fabricating operation at Alta. Morley started building prefabricated components for housing contractors all over the state. Then one day he thought "why not build houses himself."

With the post war building boom, Morley's Midwest plant soon outgrew its space. So, in 1956, he purchased the former United Implements building in Lexington. The structure was expanded and a rail siding put in. The new facility could prefabricate over 100 different styles of homes in an assembly line fashion.

Photograph courtesy of Rollin Cockley
William "Bud" Cockley, potato farmer and owner of land soon to become housing developments.

Midwest came in, but it was time for the cows and potatoes to go. William B. "Bud" Cockley's Wiliben Farms sold his premium grade herd of 118 cattle and 5 bulls in November of 1956. All but two of the cattle had been born on the farm. The auction attracted buyers from all around the United States. One of the prize bulls was flown to South America.

In 1956, the last of at least 30 years of potato crops grown on the Cockley farm was harvested. It was the end of an era. The bulldozers and earth movers moved in and started grading part of the 550 acres Morley bought from Cockley.

Morley's experience with housing developments before the war enabled him to find the right people and build a well-planned community. Streets were nicely laid out with a wide variety of housing styles and sizes. Landscaping was included with 80% of the trees and shrubs raised in John's own nursery.

Daughter Adelle Morley did all the color coordination on his homes, selecting interior and exterior finish, siding, brick, shingles and so on. Their success went beyond Lexington's Clear Fork Hills. A development in Marion was just as big. Others were in Mansfield, Ashland, Willard, Mt. Gilead, Norwalk, Mt. Vernon and Bucyrus. Buyers could generally always sell a Morley home for more than they had paid for it.

Tom Edge, Midwest Staff Architect, introduced a new concept in 1957. Called a "split level ranch" it featured three bedrooms, two baths and claimed it would sell for $15,000 including the lot. They built a bunch of them. Some cost a little more however.

Morley was not a suit and tie guy. Dressed in khaki-colored work clothes and wearing a straw hat, he was seen daily checking work crews and solving any problem that came up. His "hands on" approach was respected by those who worked for him. One person told the writer years ago, "When you work for John Morley, you work for John Morley." He was a no nonsense guy.

Morley died in 1985 at age 75. In his forty years in the North Central Ohio area, his company built more than 2,500 homes. He helped make Lexington the beautiful community it is. That is his legacy.

There were other housing developers. Templeton Terrace by Bill Templeton along with Lex-Gate Village and several other housing developments out of town, such as Walnut Hills and Orchard Park, soon joined the building boom. Orland Thomas, Walter Brown, Dwight Schumacher and Jack Morrison along with a quite a few other contractors had all the work they wanted.

The growth brought changes in what was then the business district. Crep's Meat Market was forced to close in 1957 and an amazed bunch of onlookers watched as the building rose up and rolled down West Main Street. It's now the two story apartment building next to the fire station.

The Creps brothers were two popular young men who ran a good store. They were displaced by a Sunoco Station, where Jim Sherman was hired as manager. After a few years the Certified Oil Company bought it and the brand changed. The station lasted until after Interstate 71 opened and it is now the main part of Decker's. If you have lunch there, you're sitting in the old Sunoco grease rack. (However, it's doubtful that's where the term "greasy spoon" originated.)

Decker's is a very popular spot for a most unusual clientele. If one wanted to judge the character of the village, then Decker's is the place to go. That's where most of the local "characters" hang out. Amid the complaints,

Hugh (right) and Marie "Mert" Hiser (center) ran the popular Sandwich Bar. They were known by more school kids than anybody else in town. Shown here, they take a quick break for lunch.

the bull, the gossip, stories and laughter is found the latest news of the area…long before it hits the papers.

Decker's interior décor is remarkable. One customer identified it as "advertising flea market." The exterior hiding its Sunoco heritage is something else. To some folks, Decker's is the heartbeat of the village, but to others it's the heartburn of the village.

The Lexington fathers once tried to pass an ordinance banning the outside row of pop machines lined up like soldiers across from city hall. However, that caused a local uproar and the wise politicians provided Decker's a "grandfather clause." Where else could one get a can of pop for a quarter this century? You don't mess with folk's pocketbook.

Nearly every community has a place like Decker's. A person in dirty work clothes need not feel out of place. He'll get the same friendly welcome and service as the guy in a three-piece suit. Low overhead equals low prices and this attracts the common man. You can pour your own coffee.

Joe Clark bought the business in 1990 from Max Decker and aims to keep it that way. Certified Oil owns the property and would have to remove the tanks under the building if they sold the place. That would be expensive. Clark is reluctant to remodel a building he doesn't own.

Prior to the arrival of Max Decker in 1982, the town's popular hang out was Hiser's Sandwich Bar in part of the old Culp building. The place was originally opened by "Red" Bishop after the war and called "Reds", a name that hung on for years even after he sold the place to Wilbur Wade and Dick Roberts.

Hugh and Marie Hiser bought the business from Wade (Roberts was out by then) in December of 1950. The

Hiser's ran it for the next 17 years. It was a combination news stand, restaurant, sandwich shop and ice cream parlor all rolled into one. At one time they even sold a small variety of groceries.

The school kids and people of all ages flocked to the place. Hugh and Marie liked the kids, so they put up with the jukebox music and noise. Marie, or Mert as she was known, was a pleasant, smiling, hard working woman. In her early years, she had worked as a waitress in the Corners Restaurant at Orchard Park. Hugh had his leg badly injured in an industrial accident and a change of career was in order.

The two were a great team. Hamburgers were a quarter, Cheeseburgers a nickel more and the ever popular Hires Root Beer barrel filled frosty cold mugs right out of the freezer. Life didn't get any better than that! They hired teenage kids for after school and evening hours. The place was supposed to close at 10pm, except on home basketball nights.

In 1952, the pay was 60 cents an hour and all you could eat. That's when the writer went to work there. A year later he got a nickel raise.

As a promotion, Hugh Hiser handed out 300 free Boston Coolers (root beer floats) in April of 1956. Everybody in town knew the much loved couple. It was a

Mert Hiser and employee Phyllis Sherman pause for a break. Both Mert and Hugh worked long hours at the sandwich bar. So they grabbed a quick break when they could. Note the Lexington ball scores that the Hisers always posted on a chalkboard.

Hugh Hiser serves one of his famous Boston Coolers (root beer floats) to Linda Whited (front) and Lisa Walker.

sad day when the Sandwich Bar closed for the last time.

Richard Armstrong built a new Royal Blue Super Market in the lot behind Whitney's Mobile station. That meant Vanderbilt's repair garage had to disappear.

Armstrong ran the town's first supermarket. Prior to that you told the grocer what you wanted and he or she went and got it for you. It was a nice system. Years later, the Brown family bought the store from Armstrong. However, they were eventually forced out of business by competition from the big chain supermarkets. After it closed, the building was remodeled into the Lexington Library.

A new First National Bank building went up across from Kell Hardware on a long vacant lot next to the park. It was a welcome modern 1950s addition to the downtown. Later the bank would tear down the old Frye Victorian home and add drive-thru service. Its name has been changed a couple of times in recent years, but that seems to be a trend in banking.

In 1960, a very old house was torn down on Short Street to make way for a new post office building. According to Harry Smith, the house had been occupied in the 1880s by a Mrs. Jackson.

Mrs. Jackson's Native American linage traced back to the Colonial Wars in the United States. She was descended from Tom Green, a renegade during the Indian wars in New York State. In 1782, Tom Green established Greentown, a mostly Delaware Indian village in Ashland County.

Sterling Green (also a descendent of Tom) arrived in Lexington in 1836. Two years later, he married the daughter of Rev. Cromwell, a pioneer Methodist minister in Troy Township. Sterling was a stone mason and bricklayer, who had worked on buildings that are still standing in town. He lived a mile or so out Lexington-Ontario Road, near what the old-timers called Black Bridge (wherever that was located). He was also an early leader in the anti-slavery movement in the Lexington area.

Frank Griebling, seen here in the new post office on Short Street, was the Lexington Postmaster for 33 years. He also ran a local newspaper for awhile.

Growing Problems

The rapid population increase was not without its problems. 1957 was a pivotal year. Lexington schools were crowded to capacity and a series of new buildings, both elementary and high school, would keep bond issues before the voters for years.

Part of the attraction for young families to move to Lexington was its good school system and affordable new housing. So the town found itself stuck in a vicious circle. More home building led to more students and school overcrowding. Overcrowding led to higher taxes for school construction, which made the town more attractive again.

From 1949, with 534 students, the school enrollment had more than doubled in eight years to an estimated 1,200. In that summer of 1957, officials commented that in one day 10 new sophomores were registered.

There were not enough seats or desks, classes were held in the cafeteria, music room, home economics room, teachers lounge and auditorium. A 12-room addition to the elementary school was under construction, but would not be adequate when finished. Things would get worse.

That same summer, Lex-Gate Village held an open house to show off their first houses. In one week 4,000 people came through. John Morley's Clear Fork Hills were showing their first four homes a week later. The population of Lexington was still only about 1,400, but many, many more were coming and everybody knew it.

With all this came heavier traffic and a lack of parking downtown. Harold Kinton and Robert Moyer opened the new Lexian Restaurant next to the old town hall in '57. The truck traffic was also very heavy through town on Route 42 until Interstate 71 opened in 1960.

The opening of the Appleseed Shopping Center helped take away part of the parking problem…and a good deal of business with it. In a few years, the town would have its own shopping center.

Other nerve wracking decisions fell to the village fathers. The formerly dead-end Third Avenue was being connected to Holiday Hill by a new development in between the two. A street name was suggested, but it would mean that a finished street only six blocks long would have three names. Good grief!

With the wisdom of Solomon, the village fathers settled on Holiday Hill for the entire street. It had the most houses. No doubt there was some real crabbing and complaining from the Third Avenue bunch. Their street was there first! The houses in the middle weren't finished and therefore didn't get much say in things.

The last potato crop was harvested in the fall of 1956. All the open land seen here is now covered with houses from Clear Fork Hills.

Midwest Houses Presents New Split-Level Prefab

Introduction of a new split-level prefabricated home to be produced by Midwest Houses, Inc., Mansfield, Ohio, has been announced.

The new multi-level house was designed by Tom Edge, Midwest staff architect. It will sell in the $15,000 price range complete with lot.

"One unique feature of the new model is its versatile front entrance hall," Edge explained. "Open architecture at the entrance emphasizes interior spaciousness. And the location of the hall provides easy accessibility to all parts of the house.

"We've capitalized on the trend to indoor-outdoor living with a rear living room that opens onto a patio," Edge also points out. "And the lower level features a practical 'mud room,' with an outside entrance for youngsters.

The house features bathrooms on both upper and lower levels, three ample bedrooms, generous inside and outside storage areas, maple kitchen with space for eating, and an adjacent family room.

Initial presentation of the new design was made at the recent Ohio Home Builders Convention in Cincinnati. Production of the house will begin shortly at the firm's New Lexington, Ohio, plant.

The NEWS of LEXINGTON

VOL. II NO. 18 — WEDNESDAY — FEBRUARY 6, 1957

An Independent Weekly Newspaper published by the Snyder Printing Co., 30 Delaware St., Lexington, Ohio. Phone TU 4-1711.

Application for Second Class Mailing pending at U. S. Post Office, Lexington, Ohio.

SUBSCRIPTION RATES
$3.00 per year .... Locally
$3.50 per year .... Elsewhere

ROBERT & DOROTHY SNYDER
Editors and Publishers

New Type Home To Be Fabricated In Lexington

Tom Barber (left) and Bill Poff, Midwest Houses Inc. Sales Managers, show off the new "split level" homes planned for Clear Fork Hills and other developments.

Post-War Industry

New people were moving to town at a fast clip, but for the most part their jobs were in Mansfield or elsewhere. Lexington was referred to as a "bedroom community" starting in the late 40s.

Bill Templeton – United Implements

William "Bill" Templeton and wife Lillian had a large dairy farm in Greenville, Pennsylvania. However, they lost it to the government during World War II, when Camp Reynolds was expanded.

Bill came to this area after meeting Jim Gorman in Florida. He and Gorman opened a very large potato farm between Bellville and Lexington. It was an operation that expanded after the war, shipping spuds by the semi load to Columbus and large grocery concerns. However, the two partners had a falling out and Bill left.

Photograph courtesy of Gene Wirick
Templeton's first front-end loader, mounted on a borrowed Farmall tractor. It survived until a couple of years ago.

Most of the loaders United Implement sold were for Allis Chalmers tractors like this one. The loaders could lift a ton and were easy to install.

photograph courtesy of Gene Wirick Collection

In 1947, Bill opened United Implements. The company employed a number of men in part of the old foundry building on Plymouth Street, which had been used for potato storage.

Although Bill wasn't an engineer, with his farm experience he designed, patented, and manufactured hydraulic front-end loaders for farm tractors. They were good, rugged, and easy to assemble units, which were shipped to dealers throughout the region. These loaders were sold from Pennsylvania to Wisconsin and Kentucky to Michigan.

Gene Wirick started working for Templeton when he was still in high school. He worked with Lewis Worley on the new sandstone house Bill was building at the corner of Plymouth and Holiday Hill. Bill took a liking to Gene and offered him a job after graduation in 1950. Within a short time, and at only age nineteen, Gene became the company's only salesman.

Bill bought a new truck and sent Gene all over the country demonstrating the easy installation of a Templeton

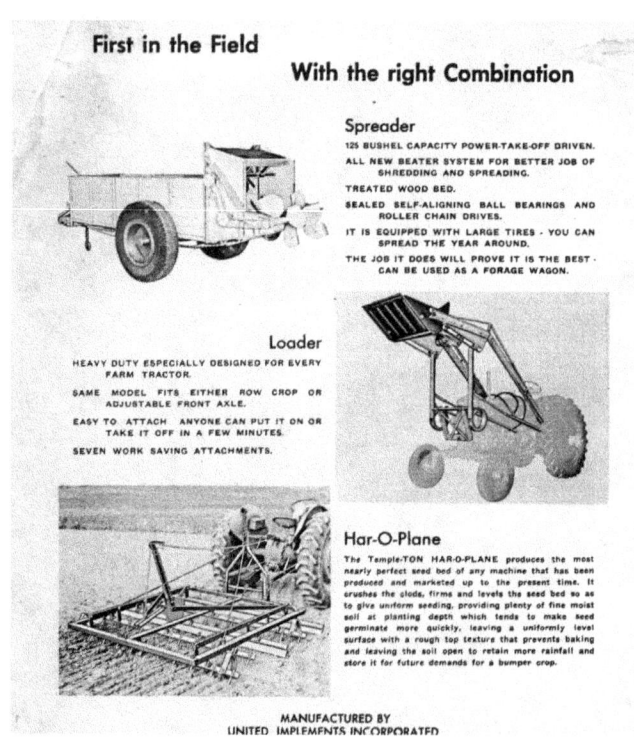

Gene Wirick saved this United Implements ad brochure.

Dan Fuhrer still uses a nearly 60-year-old Templeton loader on his farm. Fuhrer's father bought one of the first units made.

loader. It only took a short time to do the demonstration on a dealer's tractor. He called on tractor and implement dealers far and wide…usually coming away with an order. Sometimes the orders were for as many as a dozen units.

The loader was designed to easily fit Allis Chalmers WD tractors, but would also fit most other tractor makes, including Farmall, John Deere, Case, Oliver, Silver King, and so on.

Wirick went to the Allis Chalmers factory when the tractor manufacturer made model changes. He got to know their engineers, who were impressed with Templeton's loader. In fact they were so impressed that company officials flew to Ohio and offered to make Templeton's loader their exclusive option. The offer included the tractor maker putting in a rail siding, so United could more easily ship the units.

All Allis Chalmers asked in exchange was that the loaders be painted "AC orange." (The loaders were painted yellow.) However, after painting, United could attach a plate explaining that they, and not Chalmers, were the manufacturer.

Templeton refused the change. He was described by Wirick as bull-headed and wouldn't budge. Wirick and other employees pleaded with him to accept the offer, but to no avail. Later the tractor maker came back a second time, and offered to buy Templeton's company. Bill once again refused the offer.

So Allis Chalmers went to Templeton's biggest competitor and made a deal with them. That was the death knell of the Lexington Company. However, in addition to losing his biggest customer, Templeton had other problems.

He and his wife divorced. And since she had owned the Pennsylvania farm, she got the money. Also many of his dealer customers had not paid for the loaders that had already been delivered to them. In addition, he was expanding the product line to include a large heavy duty manure spreader and was tinkering with a side mount tractor mower. It all ate up money. The

United Implements Company finally went broke sometime around 1954.

Templeton was down, but not out. He had also developed a company called Brickcrete, which produced brick-sized colored cement building blocks. The plant was in a new building on Orchard Park Road, where he also sold rebuilt parts for his farm implements. He remarried and built two Brickcrete houses on Hanley Road, living in one and selling the other.

John Hoffner had been a 14-year-old orphan when he went to work for Templeton on the Pennsylvania farm. In 1951 he came to Lexington to work for Bill again and he spent most of the next 10 years at the brick plant. John's sons, Ed and Jack, worked for Templeton during high school. Sometimes they worked at the brick plant and other times delivering loaders, sometimes even outside the state.

Paul Cullen was Templeton's nephew and also moved here from Greenville. He was another longtime Templeton employee.

Bill wasn't the easiest person to get along with and neither was his new wife. Eventually both of the longtime employees quit. Cullen bought the Corners Restaurant.

Gene Wirick went into the military service in 1953 and when he came back the company was about finished. With his experience, he went on to work for Mansfield Tire as their youngest salesman.

In 1960 Templeton Terrace was Bill's next brain-child. The Mark IV partnership housing development would carry his name, though not many living there remember the man. Eighty homes were planned for the 25-acre site.

Shortly before Bill died, he finally acknowledged to Gene Wirick that the Allis Chalmers decision was a huge mistake.

Still you can occasionally see an area farm tractor equipped with a Templeton front-end loader or big manure spreader. They were good units, some of which are still in service after half a century.

Stevens Manufacturing Company

Walter Stevens grew up on a farm in Lexington -- Lexington, Georgia that is. He got his electrical engineering degree from Georgia Institute of Technology. Walter then went to work for Westinghouse, first at Pittsburgh and later at their Mansfield plant. While working there, he met and married Toby Ehrlich, a pretty local girl. He left Westinghouse in December of 1945 and started out on his own.

With nothing more than a handshake, Lew Hartman, of Hartman Electrical Manufacturing, let Stevens use a corner in his plant to design and build thermostats. Walter soon outgrew his allotted space and moved his 35 employees to a building on Walnut Street in Mansfield.

His business expanded rapidly and soon, it was time to find more space again. With the encouragement of Harry Smith, Ralph Lutz, Avery Hand (of First National Bank), branch manager Dave Snyder, and a local Realtor, Walter moved a portion of his growing operation to part of John Newcomers' school bus garage on Mill Street in Lexington.

Smith and Snyder were on the Industrial Committee of the Lexington Men's Service Club and had prepared a brochure listing all the local assets and the names of over 500 available women workers.

Photograph courtesy of Stevens Family
Walter Stevens of Stevens Manufacturing. Walter and his faithful dog Sandy were inseparable. Sandy became known as the "company dog" and her passion for ice cream bars was well-known among the Stevens workforce.

The recruiting effort paid off. Plans were soon underway to build a new building on Plymouth Street, in the former pasture field owned by William B. Cockley, an old friend of Harry Smith.

The new modern steel structure was air conditioned by circulating well water, which was a system pioneered by Harry Smith. The growing company moved into their new plant in July of 1954, while carpenters and painters were still working on the interior.

Stevens had a good quality product line of bi-metal thermostats and the company was constantly growing. By November of 1956, there were 362 people on the payroll and the new building would undergo several expansions to handle the growth.

Stevens Electrical Manufacturing, Stemco as it was known, was a family friendly industry. The majority of employees were women who, with their deft fingers, could quickly handle the small parts. The labor-management relations were quite good and for several years a full page in the local paper titled "Stevens Contacts" was written by employees and published weekly.

In 1956 Walter Stevens personally awarded service pins to 5- and 10-year employees. Promotions, birthdays, weddings and even special honors for a person who became an American citizen were celebrated. News from the day and night shifts brought the company family together. Indeed, several whole families did work in the plant including Stevens' two sons, Walter Chandler Stevens and Robert Hutch Stevens. They were known as Chan and Hutch.

Then there was the company dog. Walter had a Britney Spaniel, named Sandy, which was much attached to his master. It came to work with him, stayed in his office and grew rather fond of ice cream. To that end, a special collar was fitted with a small pouch that could hold a couple of quarters. Sandy would trot back to the vending machines and bark or make a fuss, until some tenderhearted employee fished out a coin for a chocolate covered ice cream bar. Then the treat had to be held while the dog licked and ate it. Sandy often arrived for "work" in the front seat of a Mercedes convertible.

One time when Walter was away on business a few days, Sandy became so unruly that Mrs. Stevens called the plant to ask if somebody could come and get the darned dog. Son Chan told his mother to put a couple of quarters in the collar and he'd come get the dog. Arriving at the plant, Sandy first checked the boss's office and then headed straight for the vending machines.

The only other animal visitors were cows. One night, four or five got through the fence from Cockley's Wiliben Farm and wandered in the open back door. They must have thought it was milking time. The plant manager called the farm manager and Stevens, but they still had a hard time getting the cows back out. It was nice, clean and air conditioned in there.

The company growth was exceptional. By the mid 60s there were nearly 600 employees in Lexington, plus approximately 200 more in a second plant opened in Canada.

An attempt to unionize the Lexington plant had been made by Local 709 International Union of Electrical Workers, but had only been partially successful. Their contract with Stevens was about up and Walter wanted to get rid of the union. Local 709 wanted the shop to be totally unionized. So the resulting negotiations between the two went nowhere.

On May 11, 1967, the union called a strike at the plant and, as might be expected, it was only partially effective. Slightly less than half of the workers were union members and work continued with those who crossed the picket line and a contingent of college students Stevens hired as replacements. The latter came through the picket lines or backyards and over fences to get in. They needed college money. Chan Stevens recalls that production was back near 90% at one time.

At that point violence erupted, caused by out of town union "observers", as they called themselves, from General Motors, Mansfield Tire, the steel mill, Westinghouse and elsewhere. The attempt to shut the plant down by force led to violence, a clash between police and outsiders and a division between workers that was the most unfortunate and disgusting episode in the history of Lexington.

Overwhelmed Lexington police had most of the Richland County Sheriffs Department, Highway Patrol and police from Bellville and Ontario trying to maintain order. Tear gas and a fire hose were used at one episode June 22. Mayor Emery Armstrong called Columbus and asked assistance from the National Guard, but to no avail. So he ended up closing Plymouth Street to all traffic.

THE PLAIN DEALER, FRIDAY, JUNE 23, 1967

DOUSED PICKETS—Pickets at the Stevens Mfg. Co. at Lexington, O., near Mansfield were doused with firehoses by township firemen in the wake of strike violence. AP Wirephoto

New Violence Feared in Lexington Strike

News of the strike and riot went beyond Richland County. Cleveland and Columbus papers reported on the troubles as well.

Arrests were made, cars damaged, including two that were upset in the street by outside union thugs. One car belonged to young Jim Traxler, who lived on First Street. Neither he nor any member of his family worked at Stevens or had any connection with the company. Members of the Fire Department were deputized and at one point turned a fire hose on an unruly mob that refused police orders to disperse.

At that time, Stevens had to hire a helicopter to get out of the factory and was forced to set up temporary offices in a tenant house at his farm. A group of workers even went to Columbus and met with Governor Rhodes' chief aid for help in an effort to get back to work.

Unknown to either the union or non-union workers was the fact that the Essex Wire Corporation of Ft. Wayne, Indiana had tried to buy the business earlier. Stevens thanked them, but refused the offer. They came back some time later with a better offer. Again Walter declined.

To Stevens' surprise, Essex came back a third time, during the strike, with a much better offer and were unaware of the labor troubles. Stevens figured when he informed them of the strike situation that would be the end of it. To his astonishment, Essex said the strike didn't matter…they had a man who could handle it.

Walter Stevens had a decision to make. He was 64 and looking to retirement. When the strike was settled, and eventually it would be, the plant would have a bitter hate-filled workforce. That's exactly the way it turned out. Many good friendships were lost. Chan later said what hurt his father the most was when he saw good friends and employees on the picket line, including a few he had helped financially or kept on the payroll when they were unable to work.

If he sold the company, he and his boys would be fixed for life. Essex offered him a five-year contract to stay on with a buyout option and his sons ten-year contracts. It was too good of an offer to pass up. So he sold the company. The 44 day strike ended a few days later.

In hindsight, there were no winners. Walter Stevens lost a business he built and loved. He would have left it to his family. Perhaps he should have been more flexible in the beginning.

Local 709 gained nothing. They settled for basically what had been offered before the strike. Plus a number of their members had been arrested. They still didn't get the full union shop they wanted, only the new hires.

Union strikers, or outside union "observer" thugs, upset a car near the plant on Plymouth Street. One has to wonder what example they set for the young boys watching. The car belonged to Jim Traxler, who had no connection with the company whatsoever.

Organized labor got a black eye that, in some cases, it carries to this day. The actions by union outsiders seemed to come from a 1930 era mentality. Little wonder unions have difficulty organizing new plants to this day. The 44-day strike ended with the fear Essex would move the business.

The 570 employees (only 70 were men) got a seven cent an hour raise and better life insurance. The 110 college students could stay on the payroll until school started. They painted, cleaned up, did maintenance jobs or worked at the Stevens farm doing anything and everything to keep busy. Stevens knew they needed money for school and wouldn't let them down after they worked during such strife.

Walter Stevens stayed on with Essex and was sent to check their various plants. He reportedly felt that he was more of a visiting dignitary, rather than doing something useful. He left after one year and went to work for the Richland Foundation, where he helped guide that charitable fund for quite a few years. Hutch and Chan stayed on for a couple of years after their father and then took a buyout and left for other endeavors.

Among other things, the Essex Wire Corp. made magnet wire used in electric motors. It was their chief product. They wanted to get into the motor control business, which was why they bought the Stevens plant. They thought a plant that made thermostats could easily get them into that motor overload business. What they underestimated was the huge cost involved to set up and test that new product line. And to their dismay, they found that another company already had that market well covered.

The Essex Corporation was a poorly run business. At one time, they decided to go into the trucking business by buying up small truck lines before they understood Ohio PUCO territorial regulations. They bought an aluminum extrusion company that had a contract to furnish all the aluminum trim on the revamped restyled Sohio gas stations in Ohio. That was profitable only until the stations were finished. An attempt to get into the plastic extrusion business was another misguided adventure as was the purchase of the Stevens plant.

After a few years Essex sold the plant. When it later belonged to United Technologies, employment dwindled. Then the EPA discovered that dangerous chemicals had been dumped, or somehow leaked into the ground, and were thought to be headed toward the village water wells. The plant was closed for good.

The empty abandoned building is, and evidently will be for a long time, a village eyesore. A badly leaking roof, contaminated ground and broken windows present a sad picture of a once promising industry that is now empty. It can't even be sold, due to the chemical contamination liability that would accompany the deed.

It stands as a monument to the seemingly brainless union outsiders who helped fan the flames of hatred and divide a company and community.

For the record, the writer is a retired member of the International Brotherhood of Electrical Workers union, Local 688.

Hartman Electrical Manufacturing Company

In May of 1962, Albert W. Hartman announced the 58-year-old Mansfield firm would start a $500,000 expansion in Lexington on a 62-acre lot. The new building on Castor Road (which in the 1920s was known as Pig Road.) was to be a very high-tech plant designed to make a new line of electrical relays. The plant would have one of the first "white rooms" (clean room) in the area, where workers could assemble tiny, delicate parts of their relays in a dust free environment.

The plant opened with another first, a natural gas "jet engine" powered generator. This generator delivered special high-voltage electricity, which was used for building aircraft equipment, as well as the building's heat and lighting. The whole operation was space age modern at the time.

Opened amidst great hope, the engineering and sales efforts did not meet expectations. The huge gas bill ended the self-generation plan and the relay found little market value. Hartman reluctantly closed the plant and the building was sold to the Lexington schools. It was remodeled to become Eastern Elementary.

The effort was a disappointment to the company and the community.

Neer Manufacturing Company. Inc.

Neer Manufacturing made its debut on Mill Street, in the new Lexington Industrial Park, in the fall of 1961. Electrical fittings were manufactured in the new 10,000-square-foot building, which would employ 25 people by spring.

This firm had a good product and grew and expanded its plant. Neer's popular electrical fittings were shipped all over the country. As recently as 2006, Neer had the distinction of being the first successful postwar Lexington industry. The plant has been an asset to the area and no doubt an example for others to locate here.

Sadly, as this was being written, the plant closing was announced. The company cited competitive pressure, especially from foreign manufacturers, as the cause.

The Neer Manufacturing Company on Mill Street closed in 2007, after 46 years.

Snakes by the Tale

A few readers may get the urge to throw the book away when they reach this chapter. Snakes are a nasty reptile. Our dislike of reading about them, no doubt, has its roots in the Bible. Over the years various writers have taken advantage of that fear and stretched each story a bit. Often the length of literary snakes grew to monstrous proportions.

In Lexington, that tradition all seems to have started when the railroad sold the swampland east of the cemetery. An 1858 edition of the *Mansfield Herald* carried the following:

The Great Serpent of Lexington!

It is a veritable snake, of prodigious dimensions (thirty feet long) inhabiting a large swamp on the outskirts of the village.

That such a giant reptile as this is now holding forth on the outskirts of the village is firmly believed by knowing ones of the village, and is a fact, which is left on the record that Mr. A. B. Beverstock, a respectable merchant of this place, under the impression that this monster reptile is not imaginary, but real bona fide serpent, has procured a deed of the animal, secured by him and his heirs by the R. R. Company.

Squads of men with guns and pitch forks reportedly scoured the dismal swamp in a fruitless attempt to kill the beast. In 1869, several "reputable men" saw the giant reptile on another occasion lying asleep with its head in the top of a tree that had blown down. The giant beast had crawled across the muddy road and left a groove in the mud. When measured, the groove proved to be more than eleven inches across. Its length was described as being nearly four fence rails long (or about 30 feet).

In 1899 news correspondent Al Moore put another spin on the legend:

Its size and appearance were variously described according to the fear and elasticity of the imagination of those who claimed to have seen it and heard its loud hissing and bellowing. Its length was variously estimated from 10 to 15 feet and some described it as having huge blazing eyes, a forked tongue and several tails, its body mottled with black and green and yellow and on its back was a row of sharp spines. It has been seen entwined along fences and about trees and moved over the ground as fleet as a man. It is said to have gorged itself with sheep and hogs and squads of men with guns would grope cautiously about to kill the reptile lest it strangle them in its slimy coils and swallow them and their fate remain a mystery to their friends.

If you should visit the cemetery or one of the businesses along the swamp, be sure and look under your car before you leave. The monster reptile might be chewing on your tires or trying to get into your trunk.

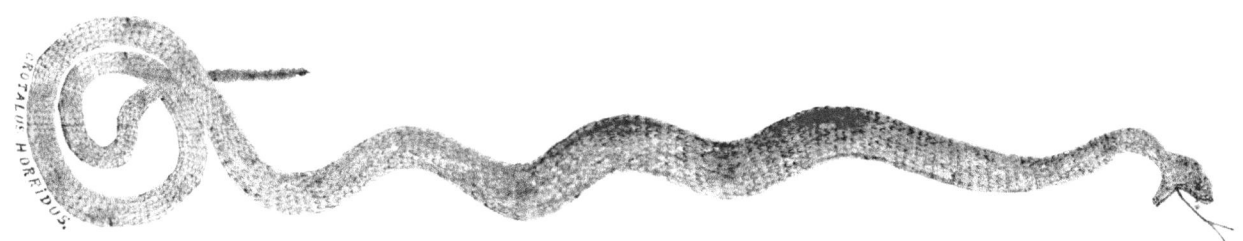

This picture of the "great snake" was hand-drawn on the side of the 1858 deed purchased by A.B. Beverstock

The Smith Family

Without a doubt, Dr. Henry H. Smith and his son Harry Smith left their mark on Lexington. Few have matched their contribution to our town. Theirs is a remarkable story that deserves to be remembered.

Doctor Henry Smith

Dr. Henry Howard Smith lost his parents when he was an infant and was raised by his grandparents near Loudonville. After finishing school, at age 15, he became an apprentice cabinetmaker. Working at Mohicanville, Smith stayed in that profession for three years. Then he decided he wanted more education. So Smith enrolled in the Vermillion Institute, a private high school, in Hayesville. Later, in 1870, he attended the Ohio Medical College in Cincinnati.

While in Cincinnati he ran out of money. So for 18 months worked at the cabinetmaking trade in Auburn, Indiana. While there, Smith organized a singing group, which performed at socials and other gatherings. A slightly tall, thin young lady by the name of Emma Ford, who played the piano for the group, captured his heart. Months later after graduation she became Mrs. Smith.

While in Cincinnati, he applied for and received a scholarship to the University of New York. In 1875, he would graduate from that school with a degree in medicine and surgery. He had also studied at the Boston Conservatory of Music.

The young couple settled in Columbus Grove, Ohio, where he began his medical practice. A son, Harry F. Smith, was born there in 1877. The doctor didn't like the climate in Columbus Grove, as it was too wet to suit him. So the young family moved and, for unknown reasons, he selected to set up practice in Lexington. Perhaps he had visited here in his youth.

Sometime around 1958, Harry Smith wrote a brief biography of the Smith family. He recalled those early years:

I was only 2 ½ years old when this move was made so I have only vague recollections of the home at Columbus Grove. In Lexington our first home was a rented house on Main Street next door to the drug store The four years we spent there brought the closest approach to Family happiness we were to experience. Father

Photograph courtesy of Helen Smith Steiner

In 1880, Dr. Henry Howard Smith moved his wife, son and medical practice to Lexington from Columbus Grove.

and mother both took an active part in Village affairs. Mother was organist for the local Presbyterian Church and father led the choir. We had a small "melodeon" on which mother would play and teach me simple – and not so simple – songs which I used to sing for the edification of the members of the choir on "practice nights". There I learned to read and perused the pages of St. Nicholas Magazine with its marvelous description of the building of the Brooklyn Bridge and Palmer Cox's Brownies. And mother would let me comb out her long silky hair with a big hard rubber comb – which I still have as one of the few mementos of that happy time.

From there I started to school in the primary room to Jane Shelenbarger and quickly bypassed the Chart class and the Primer and first reader.

Then disaster struck. Mother had been ailing for a year or so, and now it developed that she had that dreaded "white plague" tuberculosis.

Each evening - just before bed - mother would do the bookkeeping. She would get from dad an account of the day's business and make proper entries in the day book and ledger. She was the financial brains of the firm. Dad would sit by and draw plans for the house they were planning to build as soon as cash was available. I remember dad always put a fountain in the front yard, and a picket fence and a gate across the front. It was mother's greatest ambition to live in a home of her own but time was running out.

Dad so much wanted to satisfy this one ambition and so in the spring of 1884 he bought the old house on Frederick Street that was to be their last – and only home. I remember well the high adventure of moving in and of the rapid and thorough renovation that made the place livable. And then after a few sunny days, came November and mother died.

That was the end of the world for us. She was buried in the old Evergreen Cemetery at Auburn, Indiana, beside the other Fords that had gone on before. Grandmother Ford had with her a son of an older daughter who had also died at life's beginning and so agreed to take on Emma's son as well – so father came back alone.

My recollection of the months that followed is exceedingly hazy. I cannot recall whether I stayed through the winter or not. An attempt was made to start me to school but I can recall only a day or two. Cousin Tom Patterson was an inveterate tease, which didn't help much. I remember falling down stairs in Grandpa's woodshed and landing on a bunch of glass cans that grandma had setting on the steps, with a resulting long gash in my hip. Uncle Doc ford was called to patch me up and wanted to take some stitches but I made such a fuss that he finally settled for a couple strips of adhesive tape.

I guess that was the last straw for Grandma, for shortly after that I was shipped back to Lexington. I recall very vividly my arrival. Father was down to meet the train and when I saw him I began to laugh, and was unable to stop laughing for an hour or more.

Father had procured the services of a widow lady, Mrs. Alma Spaulding to keep house and she was in charge for a couple of years. During that time I had gotten going in school again. I seemed to be afflicted with some sort of instability because for many years I could not complete the school year. By the time the spring term came around I was so completely exhausted that Father took me out and let me rest and play.

Through the summer I had no difficulty in picking up all I had missed in 2 months so I was able to start in with the rest of my class in the fall. Father concocted several toys for my entertainment, one of which was a miniature train, with locomotive, coach and track, large enough that all the little dolls in the neighborhood could take a ride. Later, he concocted a larger railway by laying 1X2 strips down the edges of the board walk that led to the barn and wood shed. A small car with flanged wheels with broomstick axles would hold a couple of small boys. For bad weather I had a foot powered jig saw on which I finally learned to make more or less useful article. The most pretentious was a walnut stand I made for grandma Ford and which has survived to date.

For summer he made me a small boat with which I could navigate the old mill dam. In spite of all this constructive "Physiotherapy" I still had endless troubles in school. First, I could not master the multiplication table. I was completely stalled by common fraction. Father made a small blackboard and took me out of school for one whole winter which was spent learning all about common fractions at home. This curious mathematical blind spot seemed to disappear when I finally finished grade school and got to high school. Higher Arithmetic, Algebra and Geometry offered no special difficulty.

A couple of years after I returned from Grandmother Fords, Mrs. Spaulding left and father married again. My stepmother (Margaret Hainer) formerly ran a dressmaking shop in Lexington. She was of German decent, an excellent cook and as thrifty as Germans usually are. Her advent was the signal for a lot of refurbishing. Father procured a small building from a man who owed him a doctor bill and moved it to the corner of our lot for an office. A new kitchen and back porch was built onto the house and a 'consultation room" built into the side of the office. Father removed all of his medical equipment and activates to the new quarters.

Stepmother was of the opinion that youngsters should all contribute to the family welfare, so I had the job of clearing the table and washing dishes after meals. This continued for some time much to my disgust. However

Doctor Smith's office was a small building located on the southeast corner of the town square, adjacent to the SE square park. Note the lean-to shed attached to the rear of the office. This was his son Harry's first work room.

fate intervened. Our kitchen table was of the drop leaf design and usually stood against the wall with one leaf up and one down. On one occasion when we had "company", there was an unusually large number of dishes to wash and when I started the job the center part of the table was already filled with this and that, so I started to stack dried dishes on the leaf. Shortly, the leaf became overloaded and the whole table full upset onto the kitchen floor. The damage to Stepmother's "company china" was terrific, and I was forthwith banished.

Thereafter I came into the house only to eat and sleep. Dad's new office soon acquired a lean to shed along its east side which served as a fuel storage place and soon housed my jig saw and other activities. Stepmother would have no part of "keeping house" so far as the office was concerned, so I took over the chores for this part of the premises. There was also my blackboard and study room. The office was heated by a small stove set exactly in the middle of the "reception room". Light was furnished by a single oil lamp mounted on a side wall bracket and provided with a concave reflector. Light was sufficient for reading only on a spot about 6 foot in diameter where it was focused.

We seldom had enough of anything. Doctors bills were usually paid - if at all, by donations of a load of hay for the horse – a quarter of beef at butchering time – a few bushels of potatoes, cabbages or turnips, etc. Clothing was difficult. I never possessed a dress up suit nor a change of shoes, rubbers or an overcoat. A cash allowance for youngsters was entirely unknown, so spending money was always a problem..

I used to make fancy gadgets on my jigsaw to peddle to our more affluent neighbors. I also used to gather coal along the railroad, transport it by boat to the mill dam and sell it to the miller for 10 cents a bushel. The boat also helped me trap muskrats whose pelts were marketable at 25 cents each.

Dad was a great reader but his selection of books was beyond my abilities. I read and digested most of "Gray's Anatomy" having in mind that I would probably study medicine. Once, dad brought me a copy of Quackinos' "Natural Philosophy", which I promptly devoured from cover to cover. Frequently in summertime I would ride with him on his rounds to visit his patients. With only an old horse for motive power this was a slow job and he took advantage of this opportunity to impart some of his knowledge of nature – whether the woods and plants or the stars over head. We were both very lonely.

Somewhere I picked up a mouth organ and learned to play – very much to my surprise and delight - that I could pick out recognizable tunes. One of the neighbor boys had a guitar, and soon the two of us had a band.

Margaret Hainer Smith was a good seamstress, which brought in a little money, and was a good mother to both Harry and his brother Boyd. Very active in the Presbyterian Church, she played piano and organ for the congregation. An interview with granddaughter Helen Smith Steiner of Medina brought forth a wealth of stories about the family.

Living with Dr. Smith was something else. He loved animals and, in later years, he would cut a big slice of steak (or whatever was for dinner) and carry it outside to feed some dog or cat. This greatly annoyed his wife. Knowing where supper came from, it was not uncommon to see him walk down the street or through the square with two or three dogs and a couple of cats following along behind.

Dr. Smith was a very good doctor and once served as President of the Ohio Medical Association. He won numerous awards from his peers and was a much-admired family doctor.

His political views were, shall we say, out of the ordinary. In a small town fairly well divided between

In addition to his cabinet making, Dr. Smith hand-crafted violins. The Smith family still has one of them.

Republicans and Democrats, Dr. Smith was a strong supporter of the Socialist Party. This rankled more than a few feathers.

In the election of 1903, he was the Socialist party candidate for Auditor of State of Ohio. Naturally he lost by a very wide margin, except in Lexington where many admiring friends voted for him. Those Lexington folks remembered him coming to their aid, at times on horseback, regardless of the weather and never refusing to help. His pay, if he received anything at all, might be a bag of potatoes or other farm produce with grateful thanks.

The writer's father told of Dr. Smith operating on an aunt who was laid on the farmhouse kitchen table. While Grandfather Carter held a kerosene lamp, Smith removed her appendix. She lived on for many more years.

Smith gave out pills in paper envelopes, because he couldn't afford the glass bottles other doctors used. One old-timer remembered when he only charged a dime for an office call. His habits and willingness to accept little pay would always haunt the physicians who came after him.

Dr. Smith was also a genius and he tinkered with the ideas that crossed his mind. He made furniture and handcrafted beautiful violins. In 1893, when teenage son Harry wanted a bicycle, a fad that had swept the country, Henry said he couldn't afford to buy him one. They cost nearly $100. As mentioned, in those days doctors were seldom paid with cash. And perhaps it was a fatherly nudge to see what an energetic son could do with his own mind and hands. Harry would have to build his own.

To that end, Dr. Smith knew of a patient who couldn't pay his bill but had an old metal lathe. Several neighbors worked at Shelby Seamless Tube and they could procure scrap metal pipe. A scrap pile behind Delos Johnson's blacksmith shop was another source. The foot-powered lathe and a homemade forge used to bend and shape the metal became part of the town's first bike shop in the lean-to addition of Dr. Smith's office. Needed castings were made in a foundry at Bellville from wood patterns likely crafted by Dr. Smith.

Harry Smith

Bicycles were normally 26- or 28-inch in size. Harry's height and long legs dictated he design a 30- inch with longer pedals. With strength gained pumping the foot lathe he became the fastest "wheelman" in town. Others came to him for bikes or repairs and soon he was in business. Reporter Al Moore commented in May of 1895:

Harry Smith's miniature foundry may yet develop into quite a bicycle plant. He recently finished three wheels that are of quite ornate finish. Tuesday he wheeled to Bucyrus and back, covering a distance of 50 miles in less than three hours on a wheel nearly all parts of which were forged by him and all of which he adjusted with admirable precision. Our streets are becoming thronged with wheelmen. The young feminine element are practicing and may yet design to exhibit their radiant beauty and grace on their silent steeds.

The foot-powered lathe was time consuming and it was decided that a gasoline engine would be more efficient. A 3 ½ horsepower engine was procured which solved that problem.

In late 1893 Harry went to Auburn, to visit his grandparents, and spent time with relatives who worked at a steam-powered electric plant. That opened doors to a new world and he came home with an idea to use his gas engine in the evening hours to run a dynamo, an electric generator. He and his father bought the equipment, strung wires, and a ray of the future came to Lexington the first week of July in 1897.

Al Moore reported the historic occasion:

Dr. H. H. Smith received his dynamo and his office and residence are now illuminated with incandescent lights. The bulbs have 16 candle power and their brilliant white rays is in marked contrast with the pale yellow glare of kerosene lamps in the adjoining stores and it is an innovation for which Dr. Smith receives much credit and the whole village may be illuminated with the same mystic agent.

Shortly, the Smiths had their first customer. A single light was strung up over the intersection in the town square and that prompted George Galbraith to add one to his store which eliminated the need to clean his kerosene lamps every night. Walter Walker had the third light placed in the hardware store (now Kell Hardware). Several households also wanted this new source of light.

When Harry graduated from high school in 1897, he had a teaching certificate and a job teaching at the one-room Vine Hill School. That, with the bike shop and running the power plant, kept him busy.

Dr. Smith (left) and son Harry (second from left) with the bicycle Harry made from scratch. The two on the right are unidentified.

The May 1900 electric bill for the Minnear Hotel. They had three lights at 50 cents each for a total of $1.50.

Photograph courtesy of Robert Snyder Collection

The 75 horsepower engine that ran the Smith Electric Light Plant had nearly six-foot flywheels. It was located in a building behind the doctor's office.

The following summer Harry had a contract with the village, by ordinance, to furnish nine street lights and erect the necessary poles. The lights were to be turned on at dusk and run until 10:30pm except on moonlit nights. Also by ordinance, the saloons were to close by 9:00pm weekdays and 10:00pm on Saturday, so that the elbow benders would get home before the lights went out.

Chestnut poles were brought from the Schindler farm on Mill Run Road and with the help of his younger brother, Boyd, the poles were set and wires strung. With several more customers and his contract with the village and income of $40 a month it was enough for Harry to go to college.

After working most of the summer of 1898 on the new light plant Harry would cycle 63 miles to Ohio State University at Columbus and pedal back on weekends to run the plant. During the week Dr. Smith and younger brother Boyd kept the light plant going.

As Harry would tell the story in 1959, a devil was waiting to wreck his college plan. Gasoline cost 6 cents a gallon delivered, from Kell Hardware, in 53-gallon wooden barrels. This amounted to $3.98 about once every two weeks. With the age of the automobile, the price of gas jumped to 12 cents a gallon in 1898, wiping out his profit margin.

At the college library Harry read of a man in Germany who had developed a means to extract gas vapor from coal. Further research and drawings developed a plan to convert the power plant engine.

Two large boiler shells were purchased and transported to Lexington. Jim Leppo had a machine shop in Bellville that wasn't used much. So by dickering with Jim, Harry arranged to use the facilities of that shop. Daily trips by bicycle, or walking down the B&O tracks, soon produced the various castings and machined parts needed to convert the old engine from gasoline to coal vapor.

Disconnecting one of the engine's two cylinders completely, the gas vapor was injected into the other cylinder under high pressure. The result was that the engine produced more power from one cylinder running coal vapor than it had before on two cylinders using gasoline. Although it knocked and pounded fiercely at first, further tinkering and adjustments smoothed it out.

The capacity of the original plant was 35 bulbs, each delivering 16 candlepower. However, a 1901 trip to Cincinnati brought back a larger capacity, used two cylinder engine and dynamo. A larger shed addition and foundation was built.

The Smith Electric Light Company had a simple electric rate for their customers, 50 cents per bulb per month. There were no other electric appliances in those days and the carbon fiber bulbs didn't last long. For that 50 cents, electric was supplied from dark until 10:30pm.

Sputtering arc lights were later used on the expanded village street light system. They were lowered by a pulley mechanism for adjustment. Soon, the electric hours were extended until midnight and in winter the village requested that the street lights to be turned on at 5:30am.

Before entering Ohio State, Harry was familiar with his father's medical books and had planned to study in that field. However, the only financial aid he had came from the electric plant. It would not be enough for medical school, so he switched to engineering studies. Harry found his Lexington High School diploma was viewed with skepticism at OSU (his was only the second class to graduate), but he was enrolled "on condition."

Graduation from OSU in 1902 found him teaching school, running the growing electric plant with his father and tinkering with bicycles. The income from the electric plant was now $60 a month, enough to get married. Al Moore reported the news of the wedding in September of 1903:

Again have maidens lustrous trusting eyes beamed through bridal veils here, the hope of every maiden's heart. Miss Carrie Hainer is the maiden blushing as a violet and radiant and fragrant as a rose, and Harry F. Smith is the cavalier, who wooed with knightly gallantry and won her gentle, fervent, loving heart.

They were married in a simple ceremony at noon on a Wednesday at the home of the bride's parents, Mr. and Mrs. John Hainer, north of town. Harry taught 8th grade and his new wife taught 7th. You might say their romance began while they were in school.

There was a problem. A severe housing shortage existed in Lexington and there was no place for the couple to live. In what must be the landmark real estate deal of the century, Harry bought four acres of land at the end of Short Street, with a beautiful view across the valley, from the Sowers family for $200.

Harry then turned around and borrowed the $200 back. His father had received payment for medical bills in the form of lumber and labor. With the money, materials and help, Harry, Carrie and Dr. Smith built a new house. It was nearly finished by December of 1903. (This house is the basic center section of the beautiful home that sits diagonally across from the present-day post office. It was expanded in later years.)

Several inquiries had been made about Harry's gas producer and visits were made to the Smith Electric plant. Recognizing the market, in the spring of 1904 Harry decided to go into the manufacturing business. He contracted with a gas engine company in Springfield and modified the engines to work with his gas producers. The producer units were to be made in Lexington, with needed castings and parts supplied by other firms for the first few units.

In 1966, John Satterfield, one-time employee of the Smith Gas Producer plant said, "The town wouldn't do anything to help Harry Smith get started." Maybe the local banking firm of Cockley & Galbraith was skeptical of the unit's success. Or maybe a family political difference was behind the lack of local backing. Dr. Smith, a Socialist, had run against Democrat W. W. Cockley for school director. Cockley won, with Smith finishing second.

In November of 1904, the Smith Gas Producer Company was incorporated for $50,000 by Harry F. Smith, Dr. Henry H. Smith, and Dan Struble of Fredericktown. Struble and his son owned a prosperous banking business and, as it turned out, had the foresight to invest in Harry's plans.

By the end of the month a large number of men and teams were excavating and starting construction on a 45' x 75' building, which went up rather quickly. A pattern shop and molding building were included. A dozen or more men were working in the Gas Producer plant by the spring of 1905. However, orders came so quickly that an addition to the main building was needed by July and more workers hired.

By 1907 the Smith plant was working two shifts a day and had difficulty keeping up with the orders. Some of

An early photograph of the Smith "Gas Producer" plant. The Buildings were later expanded several times and a foundry was built.

Smith built a two-story office building as the business grew. To the left, in the background is the foundry.

the first gas units went to Texas and Mexico. Men were hired to set up the units for customers and found themselves all over the country, Washington, New Jersey, Chicago and Milwaukee to name a few. Carl Larsen, Wilbur Lawrence, salesman Tom Cureton and others spent many days away from home. Patents were granted for improvements in his design and Harry Smith was widely considered the town genius.

An early photograph of the Smith Gas Producer plant day shift employees. Pictured are: 1) William Mull, 2) Ray "Red" Ogg, 3) Alex Knapp, 4) Harmon Wiles, 5) Dwight Palm, 6) Fuller Temple, 7) Chester Chalfant, 8) Mr. Chatterton, Foreman, 9) Wilbur Lawrence, 10) Sam Homerick, 11) Sidney Earhart, 12) Clarence Koheiser, 13) Harley Temple, 14) Chris Shuster, 15) Lonie Wentz, 16) Calvin Stiffler, 17) Bill Wentz, 18) John Fighler, 19) Harry Applegate, 20) Ira Beverage.

Haddie Levering was the office girl in May of 1919. A desk lamp, pencil and manual typewriter were all the technology she needed.

Catalog courtesy of Dave Foust

This is a page from the Smith catalog. They built many large units for industry. Note the group of men standing in front of the Gas Producer in this photograph.

Dr. Smith was always the perpetual tinkerer. Newspaper accounts usually identified him as the owner of the electric plant and he may have been its chief operator when Harry and Boyd were busy. He even designed new electric and gas controls. During the summer of 1903, he sprinkled the dusty streets with water. He installed 1,000 feet of pipe and a pump driven by an electric motor to wet down the streets in four directions from the town square. Property owners who got the benefit of this wetting paid for the service, which kept the dust clouds from horses and wagons out of their stores. Dr. Smith was in the process of ordering a much bigger 75-horsepower engine for the growing electric plant when disaster struck. The old engine gave out in October of 1906 and for three weeks the town went dark.

Harry and Carrie Smith had four children: Howard Wayne Smith became a doctor; Edward Malcolm Smith was a mechanical engineer; Helen Emma Steiner was a nurse; and the youngest was Henry Ford Smith. The latter possessed the mechanical ingenuity of his father and grandfather. His sister Helen remembered the time at age six when he took a pocket watch completely apart and put it back together. And it ran!

Unfortunately, little Henry Ford Smith came home from school one day in 1914 with what proved to be scarlet fever. The fever grew much worse and he soon became delirious. Dr. Smith with all his skill was unable to save him. Young Henry died a few hours later. He was nine. One can only imagine the sorrow felt by the family and especially Dr. Smith. He must have carried that sadness until his own death in 1922.

Harry Smith had to keep busy. The workload and ever increasing sales of his Gas Producers was something the town had never imagined. Units large and small were shipped all over the country. The gas was not suitable for cooking or lighting, but was used in industrial applications and powering engines. Large units

Photograph courtesy of Helen Smith Steiner
Harry F. Smith, pictured here sometime around 1912.

Photograph courtesy of Helen Smith Steiner
Carrie Smith and son Henry Ford Smith. Henry possessed the genius of his father and grandfather, but died at the age of nine from scarlet fever.

were installed at the Ford Motor Co., (the largest) International Harvester, Trenton Pottery, General Electric Lamp Works and Standard Sanitary to name a few.

Somewhere around 60 men worked in the plant on two shifts. There were also installers and salesmen on the road and personnel in the office. Business was booming, but Harry was smart enough to see there were problems ahead.

Gas wells had been drilled in the Butler area and in the summer of 1907 an 80-man crew was laying an oil pipe line north of town. That pipeline stretched from Illinois to eastern refineries for the Standard Oil Company. Natural gas lines were reaching larger cities, including Mansfield, in an expanding web. This would eventually make his gas producers obsolete.

While Harry was a student at OSU, for a while he had a roommate by the name of Charles F. Kettering. Both were engineering students and after graduation in 1904, Kettering went to work for the Inventions Department of National Cash Register Company in Dayton. There Kettering developed the electric driven cash register and other inventions. In 1909, Kettering and Edward Deeds left NCR and formed their

Dr. Smith and wife Margaret are shown with a new 1916 Studebaker that son Harry bought for them.

own company, Dayton Electrical Engineering Laboratories Company, later shortened to "Delco."

Their interests varied, but their first thrust was to improve ignition systems in automobiles. Next came the development of a self-starter. Harry Smith would tell of being on the sideline one day while Kettering was working on that first starter in the loft of a barn. The motor worked on a test bench but would do nothing in the car. It was Harry who noticed that a mounting bolt was too long and was shorting the motor windings. They used a shorter bolt and the engine started.

Kettering hit the jackpot with this much needed improvement and in 1909 the first starters were offered on cars by the Republic Motor Car Co. In 1912, 12,000 Cadillacs were so equipped. In 1914 the Delco Farm Lighting system came on the market, another huge success.

Charles Durant offered to buy Delco in 1916 and later merged the firm into what became General Motors. Kettering was paid in GM stock worth a reported value of $9,000,000, a tremendous sum in those days, making Kettering the largest GM stockholder. As part of the agreement to sell there were four conditions: he was to stay in Dayton; he wanted no authority or responsibility; he was not to be held accountable for money spent on research; and was to be appointed head of the GM Research Division.

Flush with cash, he came to his old roommate Harry Smith and bought the Smith Gas Producer plant and moved it to Dayton in 1918. The Smith family also moved as Harry had gone to work for the research department of the Frigidaire Division of General Motors in Dayton. The electric plant had been sold to what became the Ohio Power Co. in 1917. The Gas Power Plant, now part of General Motors, closed in 1927.

Photograph courtesy of Helen Smith Steiner

The Smiths added to their home while in Lexington. When Harry returned, in so-called retirement, two more small additions were made. One of these made his the only house in town with an elevator.

Photograph courtesy of Helen Smith Steiner

The basement workshop was well equipped and a place to think and tinker. The table Harry is resting his feet on was an old grand piano at one time.

This was a big blow to Lexington and a tough decision to make. But the possibility for the company's future existence was dim.

At GM, Harry once said he averaged at least one patentable idea every two months. He was always thinking ahead and was working on inventions such as air conditioning long before anyone else saw the market for it. He became an expert witness for GM patent infringement cases and claimed he never lost a case. He would take on big corporations (Tappan was one of them) but never small firms if it would ruin the company.

Harry never forgot his hometown or his friends. After the stock market crash of 1929 and the ensuing depression, a number of families and indeed the entire Lexington Savings Bank were in dire straits. Some people were going to lose their homes. Harry came in to the Lexington bank and quietly bought up their mortgages, which took pressure off the institution and saved the homes by giving people time to recover.

In Dayton, through Kettering, Harry became acquainted with Wilbur and Orville Wright and their sister Catherine. He visited with them many times over the years. The brothers were shy and shunned publicity. Catherine was well-educated and handled their correspondence and affairs. Their mutual friendship was no doubt based on something the men had in common: their inventive genius and they had started their careers in the bicycle business. One has to wonder what interesting conversations those three had.

After nearly 25 years with the Frigidaire Division, Harry retired at age 60 due to arthritis in his knees. He moved back to Lexington in 1939, after buying his former home back from a doctor who had owned it. He remodeled the place, built an addition and installed hardwood floors. It also became the only house in town with an elevator, because of Harry's bad knees. It remains to this day one of the finest homes in old Lexington.

Harry never fully retired. He did consulting work for several area firms and began promoting a pet project he had been working on for years. Mansfield had been taking water from wells they drilled in the Clear Fork Valley. They had a series of wells running from

Photograph courtesy of Harry Smith Collection
The view from the Smith side yard was across the beautiful valley. The houses in the distance were at the end of Third Avenue in this 1947 picture.

Alta south to near Lexington. The wells they had in the Rocky Fork Valley were inadequate and some in the industrial area had become contaminated by the steel mill, Ohio Brass, and other plants.

As Mansfield grew, more and more water was drawn from the Clear Fork wells. The result was that the water table dropped as much as 10 to 12 feet. So wells in Lexington went dry and had to be drilled deeper. Outside of town the wells of the sprawling Cockley farms also had to be redrilled. All across the valley, farm springs went dry for the first time.

Harry had grown up and gone to OSU with William B. "Bud" Cockley, who later became a very prominent and wealthy Cleveland attorney. The son of W. W. Cockley, Bud had inherited part of his family farm. So in 1916 he started a dairy operation with half a dozen purebred cattle he purchased in Columbus. He practiced law with his firm for 40 years and expanded his land holdings over that time to 1,000 acres covering six farms. It was the largest single farm in Troy Township.

By 1956 Cockley had 130 head of dairy cattle and a large potato operation going with plans to expand. However, he found it would be difficult to compete with the area's rapidly growing manufacturing firms for labor and he had problems hiring farm help. Bud decided it was time to sell it all, including his beautiful summer home locally known as "Cockley's Mansion." He was 73 and time to retire to his home in Chagrin Falls.

Cockley carefully considered his farm sale. A 550-acre parcel went to John Morley only after a well planned development was envisioned. Walter Stevens bought the home and another large acreage.

Sadly Katherine Cockley died in India while the couple was on an around-the-world tour in 1962. She had donated the land for the Lexington Park. William Cockley was 85 when he died in 1968 and is buried in Lexington Cemetery.

The friendship between Smith and Cockley had been maintained and both men had affection for their old hometown. Harry, the engineer, understood the water problem, and Bud Cockley knew the law. The two collaborated and came up with a solution.

According to Ohio law, a municipality in one valley or watershed could not draw well water from another. It was as simple as that. Mansfield was in the Rocky Fork. A lawsuit filed by persons in the Clear Fork Valley could make Mansfield pay for every drop of water or shut down their wells. The only legal out for Mansfield would be to build a reservoir in the Clear Fork Valley as a water supply and to replenish the underground aquifers.

In March of 1945 Cockley sent a seven-page letter to Mayor William J. Locke and other city officials from his Cleveland firm of "Jones, Day, Cockley & Reavis" (the letter head carried the names of 41 more partners and staff lawyers in smaller print). In that letter, one paragraph must have hit like a lightning bolt and caused the good mayor to sit ramrod upright in his chair:

Photograph courtesy of Helen Smith Steiner
Harry Smith went on the road speaking to groups explaining and selling the plan to build Clear Fork Reservoir.

To an industrial city it goes without saying that an abundant and cheap supply of good water is absolutely essential, both for existing industries and their growth and for future industries. It is precisely here that Mansfield is and always has been at a great disadvantage. **It never has and does not now either own or control its water supply.**

The letter, no doubt with input from Harry Smith, outlined possible legal problems and also suggested methods of financing the building of a reservoir by the City of Mansfield. It also impressed the need to act quickly as little Federal assistance would be available for 10 years or more. Mansfield could afford to build one on their on.

Smith and Cockley had them over a barrel. Although Mansfield officials had little choice, at least the solution was laid before them. Lexington and Mansfield were in the same boat so to speak. They both faced a future water problem.

It was Harry's idea. He had worked several years on a plan and quickly agreed to help promote the project and act as an engineering consultant for Mansfield. It wouldn't be easy. It would take him a year of public, political, industrial and business group meetings to sell the project. The need had to be explained and the project sold. Then it would be necessary to get permission or approval of nine different governmental agencies; federal, state and local before work could begin. The financing and bonds also had to be arranged and land purchased.

Harry had surveyed four possible locations to erect a dam for the reservoir:

The first was a 60-foot high dam at the edge of Bellville which would back water up almost to Lexington, flooding 4,600 acres. It would require relocating six miles of B&O Railroad and require pumping water a great distance to Mansfield.

Number two was to dam the Cedar Fork between Bellville and Johnsville. This would flood only 1,200 acres, much of which was prime farmland, and the distance from Mansfield was still great.

Option three was to build a dam at Lexington between the cemetery and the present city buildings on Plymouth Street with a secondary low dam at the East Main and Rt. 97 area flooding 575 acres. This would have made Lexington a lakeside community. The hang up with this option was again relocating the railroad or having it bisect the lake and also rerouting Lexington-Springmill Road.

Option four was where the reservoir, the Clear Fork Reservoir, is today…almost exactly as Harry Smith envisioned it several years earlier.

Harry went on the road, so to speak, and appeared before every group from which he could wrangle an invitation. His presentation included maps and geological charts to explain to ordinary people both the need and solution. News stories appeared in the area papers.

Mansfield officials got their act together and hired the Columbus firm of Jennings-Lawrence. Negotiations with landowners began. Some good, hard-working people were going to lose their homes and farmland, which put Harry in an awkward position. He was an active member of the Presbyterian Church as were a number of families who were being forced to sell and move. His understanding manner and the respect he carried from the Lexington community enabled him to maintain friendly relationships with all involved. Most were understandably opposed to the plan for the "damned dam." But, it was for the public good.

Things did not go quite so smooth as far as Mansfield was concerned. They hired a rather arrogant lawyer by the name of Les Wagner Sr. who ran roughshod over the landowners telling them they better take what the city offered or they would lose through eminent domain proceedings. Most were hard-working farm folks with limited education unable to afford hiring a lawyer to fight Mansfield and caved in.

Robert and Georgia McFarland were both college educated schoolteachers and held out for a better offer, which they got. They and friend Harry Smith convinced planners to relocate Route 97 to where it is now rather than further south through the middle of what was left of their farm. Mansfield also had to agree to keep timber and brush cut so they would always have a view of the lake from their house. In her later years Georgia McFarland often commented how poorly the city lawyer treated a few of their neighbors and failed to give them a fair settlement.

If a farmer lost just part of their farm, there wasn't enough left to make a living. The McFarlands had to give up a field below their house, but made the city agree to sell it back at the same price if it wasn't flooded. It wasn't and the city wouldn't sell it back. So the McFarlands took the city to court. Before the case was heard, they found out their lawyer and the judge had gone to school together. They fired their lawyer and went to Ashland and hired another. They got their field back.

There were a number of good-sized farm parcels and buildings sold. D. K. Wittmer sold 169 acres, J. A. Wittmer 100 acres, Dr. Otis Wiles 264 acres, W. R. Sanderlin 106 acres, E. S. Eaton 204 acres, E. W. Thomas 130 acres and numerous smaller parcels. Several folks reserved the right to live in and move or salvage houses until January 1, 1947. Proceedings were started against those who refused to sell. More than 5,000 acres were acquired in total. The township lost $2,200 a year in tax revenue, which was big money in 1947.

Move or Swim

Young Bill Volz Jr. was still in school and two days away from being drafted when the draft ended in 1946. He had raised a bunch of hogs on the family's modest farm and sold them for $800. His dad, William Sr., always looking for a way to make a buck, took the $800 and went to G. L. Rogers, the International dealer in Mansfield. He bought an army surplus military halftrack. These 12-ton powerhouses had a tremendous pulling capability and would be just the thing to move a house. William Sr. had an old Allis Chalmers and Earl Weirick hired on with his 1937 John Deere A. With that, Bill and his dad were in the house moving business.

Walter Streib was their first customer. They faced a tough choice. A long trip or they had to cross a swamp and either had to float the house across or drag it through. They jacked up his house, put it on log skids and dragged it through with water coming up to a couple of boards on the siding. They moved it clear up on Blooming Grove Road.

Volz's Army surplus halftrack was an $800 house mover.

Photograph courtesy of Lynn Wiles Leitschuh

The beautiful old Wiles' home was a victim of the new reservoir. Only the white, center, single-level kitchen portion could be saved and moved to higher ground.

Walter Streib was their first customer. They faced a tough choice. A long trip or they had to cross a swamp and either had to float the house across or drag it through. They jacked up his house, put it on log skids and dragged it through with water coming up to a couple of boards on the siding. They moved it clear up on Blooming Grove Road.

The Loren Wiles home was unusual. The 1840 era two-story brick had a wood frame, one-story kitchen addition to the rear. This addition was separated and moved to Lexington-Ontario Road. The old brick part of the house was demolished and a new house was built onto the former kitchen after the move. It now looks like a 1950 ranch.

One of the toughest moves was the Neal home on Wiles Road. The two-story, seven-room house had to be hauled up a hill on Marion Avenue and professional help was needed. They hired a Mr. Baumgard from Mansfield who had a big truck with a winch. Using the halftrack as an anchor they winched the house up the hill. The pull was too much at one point and the halftrack slid into a ditch and upset with Bill Jr. in it. Bill Jr. also had to cut the guardrail off a bridge to get through as well as a few trees. He later went back and welded the rail back in place.

Land clearing and construction began on the nearly $900,000 project in 1946. Records show Harry Smith

Photograph courtesy of Harry Smith Collection
When the new reservoir was built, construction delays or a miscalculation left the Bowers Road bridge under water.

heavily involved during construction as a consultant to the City of Mansfield. At times he recommended changes, negotiated with engineers and suppliers on the project, and was involved in meetings with the general contractor. There were almost daily visits to the site. He traveled out of town to meetings with government officials and engineers on behalf of Mansfield. His Buick spent a lot of time on the road.

He had offered his services to Mansfield for free, but city officials insisted he be paid. He was paid $1 per year for the three or four years he was involved with

Harry Smith photographed finish work on the dam before filling began.

the project. His records indicate he may have only been reimbursed for travel expenses. His daughter Helen said he had been working on the plan for 11 years starting in the 1930's. He must have had a great feeling of satisfaction as the reservoir began filling in 1948. It is remembered he could predict the water level week by week. The Clear Fork Reservoir was born.

But that wasn't his only effort. In Lexington, Harry was instrumental in forming the "Men's Service Club" during World War II. Its membership was open to anyone interested in promoting the welfare of the village. The club set up an industrial board and helped locate a doctor in the 1950s. In 1957 they published the town's first directory for newcomers, which included a brief Lexington History authored by Harry. Men from this group were instrumental in founding the "Boosters Club," which developed the village park and ballfields on Plymouth Street on land donated by Katherine Cockley. Smith, no doubt, had a hand in that too.

Lexington area residents selected September 14, 1953, to honor their "favorite son." Organized by the Men's Service Club, more than 500 people were guests at the school where tributes to his life and work were heralded. He was presented with a plaque in appreciation for his devotion to his hometown and several speakers gave interesting talks on his background. His good friend Charles Kettering was unable to attend. However, Harry related the story of being on the sideline when "Ket" was working on his invention of the self-starter. To the audience he maintained that the future was in education and engineering to which there was a great round of applause. No other citizen of Lexington has been so honored to this day.

His beloved wife Carrie died in 1950 and her sister, Ludella "Dot" Hainer, a retired schoolteacher from Pittsburgh, came to live with and keep house for him. In his will, she was granted use of the house as long as she wanted.

Harry F. Smith died in June of 1961. His daughter Helen, a nurse, was at his bedside holding his hand. He was buried in the family plot next to his wife along the drive on the west side of Lexington Cemetery.

No grand monument marks his final resting place, just a simple small gray marker with the inscription "Harry F. Smith, 1877 – 1961." However, if you seek his true monument, drive west and take in the beauty of the Clear Fork Reservoir. The next time you take a drink of water, remember Harry Smith.

Photograph Courtesy of Helen Smith Steiner

Carrie and Harry Smith in the late 1940s.

Commentary on Our Water Supply

When Harry Smith died, the estate evidently sold his personal files to an antique collector named Howard Young. Years later, teacher Jan Dunlap, who then owned Young's former house, discovered that they had been left in the attic when Young died. The writer was fortunate enough to be given these files by Dunlap, as he prepared to move.

There is a lesson in those papers that relates to the present. Harry Smith could see the future. Harry said the reservoir would silt up, over the years, and it has done so. The reservoir has the same water level, but less volume. It's becoming a shallow body of water.

Smith pointed this out starting in 1945. The last time this point was made formally was in a 1972 engineering report from Finkbeiner, Pettis and Strout to Mayor William McCarrick and other elected city officials including City Engineer George Cunitz.

Howard Young had obtained copies of the 1972 report. In it, a suggestion was made to raise the height of the spillway by one foot, which would have provided an additional 29 days of water supply. Three to five feet additions to the reservoir height were also each proposed. However, an engineering firm suggested the cost of land acquisition would be too high and Route 314 would have had to been bridged...obstacles that left the suggestions unheeded.

However, Route 314 is bridged now and always has been. The cost of land would also have been much less in 1972 than it is today. A proposed alternative idea was a second storage dam to the west, above Route 314. However, nothing has ever been done with that suggestion either.

At present, most of the water supply for Mansfield, and all of it for Lexington, comes from the series of 1945 wells, plus several new ones near Plymouth Street. Lexington officials, asleep at the switch, somehow even let Mansfield drill a new well almost in the village park.

A Mansfield filtration employee informed the writer that reservoir water is more expensive to treat, so well water is their preferred source. They typically use 40% well water, unless the Clear Fork is cloudy or algae and temperature are a factor. Then it's mostly well water.

A second dam and water supply could be built on the Cedar Fork as outlined in 1945. This was suggested again in 1972. Nothing has been done.

The engineer's 1972 report also stated: "The existing reservoir will provide sufficient water storage to satisfy the surface water demands during periods of minimum flow until approximately 1990. At that time the demand for surface water will have reached the maximum allowable regulated flow during drought periods and a new source of supply must be obtained."

Lexington will soon have grown into a city. With the population expansion both communities have gone through, Lexington and Mansfield will soon face the same problems they had in 1945. One has to wonder where the water table is now. The question is whether the elected officials from both cities will act while there is still time...or ignore the issue until a drought comes and the wells go dry?

Harry Smith is gone, but his lessons remain. Will anyone listen to them?

Seen here in 1945, Harry Smith speaks on plans to provide both Lexington and Mansfield with a desperately needed adequate water supply. If action isn't taken soon, the same problem will shortly face both cities again.

Politics

Oh God, not more of that! Well a short look at early political campaigns in Lexington might be a change from the neverending bombardment of political television ads we endure today.

The campaign of 1880 was the most intense campaign ever waged in Lexington after the Civil War. Both Democrats and Republicans held rallies and parades in the town square. Al Moore, Lexington's Republican correspondent for his *Republican Newspaper* devoted a whole column in an October 7, 1880, issue covering a Republican gathering on a previous Saturday evening. In part he wrote:

At 5:00 pm there was a popular pole erected on the north-west side of the town square, on which was placed on the utmost top a beautiful streamer thirteen feet in length with the inscription "Garfield and Arthur" which was presented by the ladies of the town, elevated to a distance of some eighty feet, which shall wave until the winds and storms shall rent it from it's place.

A large group of mounted horsemen from Lexington and Ontario, led by a band, escorted the speaker, Col. Cooper of Mt. Vernon, from the railroad station to the square. He spoke for an hour and fifteen minutes, but had to quit early in order to catch the 8 o'clock train back home. The horsemen and bands marched Cooper back to the station where they met 50 more uniformed horsemen from Mansfield and then the whole crowd, most marching on foot, paraded the half-mile-long procession through the principal streets. It was a grand Republican success as seen through the eyes of a Republican reporter.

Now the Democrats just didn't lie down and take this without reply. They had their own big rally with speakers, erected two similar poles with banners every bit as high and, they too, paraded with band and mounted horsemen. There was no Democratic correspondent covering the event and, as one might expect, a one-sided coverage remains. Moore dryly noted Lexington's Richard Gailey Jr., who had recently switched to that party, was one of the principal speakers.

In one of his lopsided reports of another Democratic parade he commented: *They made great preparations for this wonderful event (with their mouths) for some days and the decorations were such as a windy Democrat could be proud of. There were three houses on Frederick St decorated with 10 flags, 2 saloons, 1 shoe shop and 1 barber shop with flags out and not one on Delaware St. The procession in the evening consisted of a marshal band and about twenty men and boys carrying torches and was 32 ¼ seconds passing any given point. They could have made 10 seconds better time but one of their musicians was afflicted with rheumatism brought on by hard work (he is now expecting a pension).*

The Republicans did well in 1880, Garfield was an Ohio boy, and to celebrate they erected another pole (they only had one, the Democrats two) on the northeast side of the town square--more horses, big parade and speeches. Moore noted some young Democrats in groups were yelling and whooping and interrupting the speakers. Perhaps enough was enough for everybody. A month later came this suggestion from Moore, *"We move that the Democrats and Republicans cut down their campaign poles and cut them up for fire wood and give them to our ministers.*

Neither party could ever really claim Lexington. It has see-sawed back and forth to this day. From Lexington, W. H. Earhart, a Republican, was elected to the State House of Representatives in 1902-03 and was defeated by local Democrat W. W. Cockley in 1904. But back during the historically noisy election of 1880 there wasn't much to do on a Saturday night in October and politics became, in some ways, a form of entertainment.

That is unless your party lost.

A Business Variety

The Entrepreneurs

A number of business ventures deserve mention as they have added so much to this area. Here are just a few.

Kell Hardware could almost trace its origin back before the fire of 1885, which wiped out the north side of Main Street and some of the south side. In the 1870s, James Boggs had a tin shop in a building on the west side of what was then lot #11. Tinware, cups, buckets and roofing were made in his place. The space between his shop and the brick Sowers building had been filled in with space for a shoe shop, bakery, and at one time, the office for the Gailey Seminary.

The 1885 fire wiped out everything except the brick Sowers building. Sowers owned the lot and a new wood frame tin shop building went up for Boggs & Son in 1886. A limited line of hardware was added. Several years later, Boggs must have moved on or kicked the bucket. John G. Walker, a farmer from west of town, had taken over the shop by 1889. Walker evidently expanded into the general hardware business.

Walker entered the business with confidence and did well until 1896, when he retired due to poor health. He died two years later. His son, Walter Walker, and a new partner named Marshall Kell took over the business.

The new firm of Walker and Kell prospered. In 1899, they built a two-story tile building on a lot near the railroad as a place to store building supplies, cement and roofing materials, as well as to rent out as a saloon.

Old-timers who knew both men told how they lived in bachelors' quarters on the second floor at the rear of the store. They were members of Lexington's famed Bachelors Club. As the story goes, one day in the spring of 1903 Marshall Kell entered the sea of matrimony without consulting his partner. This was a shock to the members of the club, as well as his partner Walker. Al Moore reported the incident this way: "Martin A. Kell the hardware merchant is the winged victim of the winged little Gods cunning wiles and Miss Ella Bachelder is the lady whose queenly grace and witching smiles set aflame with tender passion his cold stony heart….Mart was the main financial guy of the Bachelor's Club and his desertion from the ranks has created fear and consternation among the vagrants."

Two's company and three's a crowd may have been the reason Walker dissolved the partnership in 1903. In any event, Walker went across the street and opened his own hardware. Marshall's brother Thad bought Walker's interest in the original store and it became known as Kell Brothers Hardware.

Seymore Lindsey was a regular customer. Note the wide variety of goods Kell sold in 1901.

Photograph courtesy of Harriet Kocheiser Curry

Pictured here are (L to R) Thad Kell, brother Martin Kell and Walter Walker. Kell Hardware is Lexington's oldest business. At the time of this photo in 1890, the store was known as Walker and Kell Hardware.

A year later, Walker was working on the slate roof of Martin Touby's big, new, brick home on Route 97 south of town. Walker fell off and was laid up for part of a year, but slowly recovered. Later he was doing so well with his new store that he bought the whole block on the north side of Main Street. The town had two good hardware stores.

Looking at old 1900s inventory records from Kells' store, the list of goods is amazing. They carried everything from horseshoes, harness, woodstoves and furnaces, roofing, to plumbing. They also sold coal, farm implements, kitchenware and even built wagons and sleds to order. Seymore Lindsey bought his paint supplies there. They also did shingle, slate and tin roofing. Oil, gas, dynamite, and hundreds of needed items were always available. When Route 42 was paved with concrete, railroad cars filled with bags of cement came from Kells'. It was a profitable partnership.

The brothers hired Seymore Lindsey to paint the inside and decorate the outside of the building with two of his murals. A large mural on the second floor had an American eagle with an American flag in the background. The other was an oval picture of a horse drawn plow and above that was a Kell Brothers advertisement. They were landmark paintings that may still be hidden behind newer siding that went up many years ago.

Thad Kell died in 1930. A year later, Marshall turned the business over to Arthur C. Kell, Thad's son. Art grew up with that store and for the next 30 years guided it with good public relations and his ever-present cigar.

Art was always a supporter of village projects and the one constant in the business community. During his time, he was to see nearly every business in town close or change hands.

Photograph courtesy of Harriet Kocheiser Curry

Art Kell liked to travel in big cars. Seen here, his 1923 Studebaker Big Six was packed and ready to go. In the late 1940s, he and his wife drove to Florida in a new DeSoto, had a nice time and drove home. He got a speeding ticket in Williamsport when almost home. It is remembered that he was really mad about that.

Photograph courtesy of Bud and Tim Corwin Collection

Seymore Lindsey painted a wonderful mural of an eagle with an American flag background on the Kell Hardware building. It might still be there, hidden behind modern siding. To the right was a one-horse plow in a circle with the Kell name and advertising. No clear photograph of this artwork has ever been found. The truck in front was Kell's coal delivery truck, driven by Howard Wagner for many years. This photo dates from the 1930s.

In 1961, Art decided it was about time for him to retire. The business had been in the same family for nearly 65 years. Lloyd Curtner, a hardware salesman who used to call on Art, took the helm.

It was Curtner, along with *Tribune-Courier* Editor Frank Stumbo, that came up with the slogan "99 to one we have it" in his advertising. Curtner also used to joke with customers that if he didn't have it, they didn't need it anyway. After Lloyds's untimely death, his wife Betty and their son ran the place for awhile.

In 1993, the Lloyds sold Kell Hardware to Mr. Art Meyers. Meyers expanded the business into the adjoining brick building and made other improvements over the next ten years.

Then in 2003, the business was sold to Jeff Carter. It is now Carter who manages the nuts, bolts, pieces, parts, paint and patches that helps everybody keep home and hearth together. Several longtime employees know most customers by name. Although ownership has changed over the years, Kell Hardware remains the oldest continuous business in Lexington.

John L. Garber Materials Corporation

There was never a shortage of gravel in the Clear Fork Valley. The town gravel pit was next to the cemetery and the railroad opened one near Hanley Road. Harvey Fleck had a gravel pit on Cockley Road in the 1930s, which became a successful venture with the move to improve area roads and lift drivers out of the mud.

Fleck was a good businessman with a wide circle of friends. For quite a few years he led a group of deer hunters to northern Canada each fall. They drove as far as they could go. Then a camp owner met them with a caterpillar and hauled their equipment eight miles further, while they walked. It was a regular sojourn with men like Jay Walker, Cliff Sherrod, Paul Schindler, Ora Yoah, William Ingram, Homer Grant, Dr. Lee from Lucas, Dr. Myron

Art Kell (center), part-time employee Dick Cochran (right) and longtime Kell employee Virgil Bachelder (left) are shown in this picture taken in the 1950s.

Photograph courtesy of Homer Wagner Collection

Seen in this 1935 photo, Wagner's 1929 Chevrolet truck could haul three ton of coal.

Reed from Mansfield and undertaker Ora Snyder and a few others. A couple took their dogs along. While deer were not plentiful in the Lexington area at that time, one Canadian trip netted 18 deer in eight days. Mona Schindler told her husband Paul that she wouldn't have to worry about him on these trips. With a doctor and an undertaker along, if one couldn't take care of him the other would.

The gravel firm became Harvey Fleck and Son when Harold joined the firm. After his father's death, Harold didn't have the drive to sustain the business and went bankrupt.

John Garber had worked for Fleck for 11 years and bought the business from Richland Bank. With his experience, John knew how to turn things around and did so. In 1958, he started a trucking business and rather than sit behind a desk, he was behind a steering wheel.

Newer and bigger equipment kept pace with area road building and construction. Business was so good that finally the Cockley Road pit was nearly exhausted. Part of that pit was graded to create a beautiful lake next to the bike trail. A second source was opened up on Kocheiser Road, near the Route 97 and 71 junction.

Some folks wonder when Garber will ever retire, but he keeps on trucking.

Ed Wagner was involved with at least two business ventures during the 1930s and 40s. During the depression, he hauled coal from the mines and delivered it to folks in town. In that era, nearly everybody heated their homes with coal. Gas furnaces didn't come into much use until after World War II.

Ed's son, Homer Wagner, recalled that his dad had a 1929 1½-ton Chevy truck, which could haul about three ton of coal. Homer went along sometimes and remembered they would leave at night, so they could get to the mine, near Warsaw in Coshocton County, by 4:00am. That way Wagner could be the first in line when the mine opened. (This gave them time to get back to Lexington and make deliveries before the day was over.) They slept in the cab of the truck.

Coal was dumped in at the mine and shoveled out when delivered back home. Homer recalls that they got about $5 or $6 a ton for the coal. They had a set of truck scales in the floor of the family garage on First Street to weigh the amount delivered.

The second money maker involved Hollywood. Ed built an enclosed two-wheeled trailer with a movie projector and concession counter inside. He would show outdoor movies during summer. A canvas screen was stretched between trees or whatever, with the audience seated on the ground or on folding chairs they brought along. The movies were free to the public and Wagner was paid by local merchants that sponsored the shows.

Wagner made a nightly circuit each week. Bellville, Butler, Johnsville, North Lake Park each had their own movie night. In Lexington, they were shown at Orchard Park. Later, the movies were shown in town at Whitney's Mobile Station. At another point, they were shown in the middle of Mill Street. (They just closed the street at dark. After the Farm Bureau mill closed at 5:00pm there wasn't much traffic anyhow.) Kids looked all forward to movie night.

The pictures were the "B" movies, mostly of the western variety, with such stars as Hopalong Cassidy, Gene Autry, Tim McCoy, Roy Rogers and Tex Ritter. Tarzan was another favorite. Good always triumphed over evil, in a hail of bullets or a fistfight, to the cheers of the audience. Wagner always played music before it was dark enough for the show. One of his favorites, played weekly, was Tex Ritter singing a tune. Part of that song went "Whiskey, dry whiskey, dry whiskey I cry, if you don't kill me I'll live till I die." It was a puzzling song for a bunch of kids.

The age of drive-in movies and television finally ruined the movie business. Kell Hardware and the Farm Bureau both got their coal by railroad car, had unloading means and they delivered. Gas conversion units for furnaces eventually replaced the coal business in Lexington. These changing events put Wagner out of business, but he is still fondly remembered by old-timers.

Mid Ohio Sports Car Course was the brainchild of Lester Clever Griebling or "Les" as he was known. As a youngster, Les won the first Soap Box Derby held in Mansfield, back in 1937. He had a passion for cars and loved anything with four wheels. So naturally he opened a repair garage in 1954.

Three years later, the garage became the Suburbanite Motors Foreign Cars dealership. There he started selling the German made Isetta, with a door that opened the whole front of the car. Next the popular MGs, Morris, Sprite, and Austin lines of British cars were added and became a fast selling success. Les and his brother,

Photograph courtesy of Homer Wagner Collection
Ed Wagner's movie trailer was a welcome sight to local youngsters. During weekly visits, the outdoor movies were free and he sold popcorn and candy from the rear door.

Photograph courtesy of Robert Snyder Collection
Les Griebling started small, with a garage. In this photo he had moved on to selling cars like this Isetta. Eventually he went on to start the nationally known Mid Ohio Race Track.

Photograph courtesy of Marilyn Linton Miller

When Harry Linton squeezed the remote shutter release on his camera, he captured wife "Maggie" and their six children. Unknown at the time was that there were four more children yet to be born.

Carroll, not only sold the cars, but could keep them running. If there was a problem, they were there to repair.

With the sports cars came a dream of a race track. After finding a few investors, and selling the idea, construction began in 1961, with the track opening in 1962. The original track had a few tight twisting turns that had some drivers using second gear. These were by-passed after several years as track improvements were made.

More than a few local people were skeptical about Mid Ohio's success, but as the town became a traffic jam on race days, the doubts disappeared. Les Griebling's attention to detail and laying out a race course that was both challenging and spectator friendly, brought national attention to Mid Ohio. Live TV broadcasts and several appearances by the Goodyear blimp were a sensation.

Big name drivers like Peter Revson, Jackie Stewart, George Folmer, Mario Andretti, Bobby Rahall, and a host of others were watched closely at the track in the daytime. Folks also looked for them to make an appearance at Bucks in the evening.

Griebling was a member of the Kiwanis Club, to which was given the job of selling programs at the gates. Money earned at the track supported their programs at the depot, Boy Scouts, school age sports, and leadership programs for years.

Les sold the track to Jim Trueman in 1981 and retired. The Trueman family continued to make improvements and the track has brought a tremendous amount of business to the area, and national attention to Lexington. Who could have imagined that a kid in a Soap Box Derby would someday create a race course from a weed and brush covered field…and accomplish what he did in his lifetime. Les Griebling, a much honored local man, died in February 2003. He was 78.

Harry and Margaret Linton were a rather remarkable couple. They were married in 1898, and had moved to Lexington in 1909. Harry was a skilled machinist with the Smith Gas Power Company. They were to have ten children, the largest family in Lexington. With that growing bunch of mouths to feed, there was always a need for extra income and they found it in photography.

Photograph courtesy of Marilyn Linton Miller Collection
The Linton camera captured many family outings with classic pictures of the era. This was taken at what is now Lexington Park.

Photograph courtesy of Linton Family Collection
An arrival at the Linton home was an opportunity for a snapshot. The building (in the background) across the street is now part of the Lexington Moose Lodge.

Harry was the energetic type and became the Smith company photographer, in addition to his machinist work. He took pictures for Smith sales and installation brochures and the like.

The town's longtime photographer, Gilead Mansfield, had died in 1897. So as a sideline, Harry took his bulky camera, with glass plate negatives, and snapped pictures of street scenes, the railroad, factory, church groups, and business places around town. Then he printed them on postcards and sold them for a little extra income.

Wife "Maggie", as she was known, picked up the craft. Family members recall that she helped develop the negatives and prints and took a good many photographs herself. Most of these were family or neighborhood pictures, but they also reveal her skill as a photographer. Daughter Marilyn still has a wooden box, full of Maggie's wonderful glass negatives.

Maggie was a remarkable woman. Raising ten children and helping Harry kept her busy. Son, Richard, and daughter, Marilyn Miller Linton, recall the time their sister Helen came down with polio. When the prescribed treatment didn't help, they said their mother treated Helen by instinct. Maggie exercised and rubbed her legs daily with "skunk oil." Helen recovered for the most part, even though she always walked with a

Photograph courtesy of Marilyn Miller Linton Collection
Mother must have had a hand in this classic picture of young Bill Linton photographing his sister Helen.

slight limp. She later married and raised four children. It wasn't until years later that the "Kenny Method" of rubbing and exercising polio patients was developed.

The Linton children also laugh about the time they started a fire on the vacant lot next door. (It's now the middle of First Avenue.) The smoke spooked a man's horse and he angrily called them names and started to throw rocks at them. That's when Maggie came out on the front porch carrying a rifle. That ended that… and its just as well, they said she was a crack shot with a gun.

Linton worked for Harry Smith until the plant closed. Then he worked at the Ohio Brass, until he was laid off by Burt Parker, a man that he had helped get a job there. It made him mad and he never went back. He worked for the village as marshal and street commissioner, then was hired to head the water department when it was created.

When he was marshal, a bunch of boys went on a toilet tipping spree one Halloween night. It didn't take a genius to figure out who the culprits were and Harry rounded them up. Faced with arrest, he took the boys around and made them upright and reset the toppled privies. That was a much tougher task than tipping them. When they finished, he took the whole bunch downtown and bought them ice cream. Harry knew how to handle kids. The boys always respected him when they became men.

During World War II, Harry got an old Model A Ford. He shortened the frame, installed a heavy truck rear end, added lower gearing, and made his own tractor. He plowed a lot of "Victory gardens" for people during the war and made a little extra money. Having a garden helped with the war effort (freeing up crops from large farms for the troops). It was the patriotic thing to do.

In Linton's later years, he sold insurance and tinkered in the well-equipped machine shop he kept in the barn behind his house. He was 83 when he died in May of 1958. His beloved Maggie joined him a few years later.

Their legacy to Lexington would be their part-time photography business. Through the lens of their camera were captured the scenes of Lexington that words alone could not match. If the Linton photos were deleted from this book, not much would be left of early 1900 Lexington.

Carl Brumenshenkel was a hard-working man, if there ever was one. Men who till the soil for a living seldom know an eight-hour day and fewer still worked as hard as farmer Carl.

He was born in Mansfield, in 1899, to immigrant parents. His father was German, his mother Swiss and he learned the greenhouse trade from his father and uncle while growing up in Mansfield. He had to quit school in the eighth grade to go to work. On a trip back to Germany to visit relatives, he met his wife Linda. In 1926, they were married.

His new wife had always lived in the city and was dismayed when she saw the 49-acre farm Carl bought north of Lexington. A one-story brick house, originally built by Asahel Watson, the son of Amariah Watson, had burned in 1913. Using the brick walls that remained standing, a new home had been built. It was brick on one end, frame on the other, with a new second floor. It turned out to be a nice home and six children grew up on that farm.

Forty-nine acres would be too small for a conventional farm, but Carl saw a business opportunity. The land was level and good. So he built greenhouses. He started out farming with a team that was one horse and one cow.

The Clear Fork used to flood part of his farm with a degree of regularity. In the 1959 flood, the water almost got up to the house. So he had the channel dredged, straightened.

Carl kept farming with horses until 1942, when he bought his first tractor. Over the years, Carl expanded the farm and added to the greenhouse and buildings as Lexington grew. By the 1980s, it included 271 acres. However, Carl still oversaw the greenhouses, hired

Maggie and Harry Linton, seen on their 50th anniversary.

help, and guided farm operations. He was everywhere from dawn to dusk.

Photograph courtesy of Rosie Brumenshenkel Hoffner
A younger generation learned about farming from grandpa.

Photograph courtesy of Rosie Hoffner Family Collection
Helmut Schumacher, who spoke no English, worked for a man that left him in an unheated barn in winter. A mailman, who spoke no German, noticed he was missing one day and found him. A hurt Helmut said only "Brumenshenkel" over and over. The mailman retrieved Carl, who interpreted, and they rescued Helmut. He had lost his toes and nearly froze to death, but he found his place. After that day, Carl gave him a job and home. Here Helmut works for Carl, as he did for years, stooped over due to crippled feet and poor eyesight.

His greenhouses were always busy in summer and Carl was a master with crops and vegetables. It seemed that he alone could have fresh sweet corn from midsummer to nearly October. He knew what types to plant and when. The couple was also always willing to give their customers advice on cooking or canning.

Though born in Mansfield, Carl had a slight German accent, which was understandable considering the background of his parents and wife. So, although they were proud American citizens, he and his wife suffered verbal abuse and a few threats, during the dark days of World War II. Some of their regular customers spoke mostly German. When these folks came in, Carl and Linda talked to them in their native tongue. Because of this, they were viewed with suspicion by a few non-thinking individuals. Although the abuse hurt, Carl and Linda took it in stride.

He was a life member of the Mansfield Liederkranz and a longtime member of the Jugs Grange. He and his wife Linda liked to dance. In addition to her household chores, Linda helped take care of the greenhouse, but not the field work. There were six kids, four boys and two girls, to raise. That was enough. Sadly, Linda died of cancer in 1960.

It was a bit of an education to be at the greenhouse when Carl and a customer from a Scandinavian country were present. They each spoke various dialects of their native languages and made comparisons translated to English. It was fun and educational just to listen to them.

Brumenshenkel often told what foods were good for you and what to avoid. He stopped smoking when his wife became ill and his lifestyle worked. Carl died in 1993 at age 94. He had remained active until the last ten years or so. When no longer able to do the heavy field work, Carl became what he called "a tractor farmer." He only drove a tractor or waited on customers in the shop.

The popular and expanding farm market is still in the family, now being run by grandson Gary Levingston and his wife.

Mohican Valley Dairy can trace its beginning back to 1918 when brothers Robert and Samuel Kisling started a small dairy operation on Orchard Park Road. In 1921 Sam moved his family to the 144-acre farm on Route 97 south of Lexington and lived in one half of the big

Photograph courtesy of Vivian Van Cura

Sam Kisling and son Richard in the late 1920s. The Kisling children grew up in the business.

double farmhouse with brother Robert's family living in the other half. A short time later Robert moved to a farm east of Mansfield.

Sam and Ruth had six children. They started with twin girls, Audra and Majora, then another girl, Vivian, before they had two boys and then another girl, Nancy, was born. The oldest girls became the family farmhands and milkmaids until the boys, Richard and Dale, were big enough to help. Even then it was a seven-day-a-week operation for the whole family.

Sam Kisling's milk route was in Mansfield. It started on Lexington Avenue and went down to Sixth Street. Daughter Vivian Kisling Van Cura, a petite energetic former schoolteacher, remembered going with her father in the days when milk was dipped from a can and poured into the customer's container. She later recalled that one day when she was nine, *"Pop stopped the truck along the road, came around to my side and said, "Get over there Vivian, you're going to learn how to drive this truck."* She did, and helped run milk in glass bottles to some customers or followed Sam down the street with the truck which saved him many steps. She drove horses and tractors, chased cows, milked and washed bottles along with the rest of the family. She and her brothers and sisters did this even in high school, working weekends and summers. Kids that grow up on a farm develop an early work ethic. *"We never resented it because we had good parents."*

"Gib" Shaffer was an early milkman in Lexington, followed by Jenner McBride. Sam Kisling bought McBride's route sometime around 1937 and dropped part of his Mansfield route. The milk was delivered in glass bottles and was not homogenized, so the natural cream rose to the top. By the time Dick and Dale Kisling took over the dairy, they had 150 customers and made three routes every day. In summer, bottles were placed in customers insulated boxes so it wouldn't spoil. In the 40s, milk was 10 cents a quart, six cents a pint. Payment was by cash or a milk ticket often left in the empty return bottles.

The Kisling girls were to record some of the hazards and events growing up. Vivian recalls running her head through the windshield when "Pop" stopped quickly for a fire truck. At a young age, *All of us had to get up real early and milk three cows apiece before going to school while mother fixed a wonderful breakfast. Bacon and eggs, sausage and pancakes etc. During rabbit season she'd have pancakes with rabbit and rabbit gravy - delicious! The milk was put in five- or 10-gallon cans and cooled in the spring run while we ate and was bottled after breakfast. Pop, Dale, Richard and a hired hand would milk the rest.*

Many Sundays after our noon meal Pop, Mom and we five kids would get in our Buick and Pop would drive us around on scenic country roads until evening milking. How beautiful the open country was at that time.

Nancy was not born until Vivian and her twin sisters were in high school, but like the others was part of the family business. She was to write, *Sometime in the late 1930s my father took me with him on a train to Springfield, Ohio to the International Harvester factory where we picked up and drove home a brand new milk truck. My brother Richard by that time did nearly all the delivery of milk. He was 13 years older than I to the very day. I started helping him on weekends and in summer. He took one side of the street and I the other. On some streets when he got back he started up and I ran and hopped on. I wondered what my mother would think if she saw me.*

The customers were nice and I learned to say 'good morning' and 'thank you.' I also learned to make change, it was fun and we didn't have to have a calculator. My brother loved to visit when we hit Main St.; he talked to the guys at Crep's Meat Market, Derrenbergers Pharmacy, Krogers and out in the country Corners Restaurant and Kinton's Market. While he visited I had to wait in a hot truck in summer and freezing cold in winter.

Sometime around the 7th grade my mother bought me bib overalls and plaid shirts to wear on the milk route. A boy who was in my class came out of his house one

Photograph courtesy of Vivian Van Cura

(L to R) Richard, Sam and Dale Kisling are seen in this 1946 picture. The motorcycle was used when calls for extra milk came in while the only truck was away on a route.

morning. He hooted and laughed at how I looked. That did it! I was so embarrassed; I didn't want to go on the route any more. I stayed in bed in the morning as long as possible to keep from going. One morning my father made me walk to Lexington to help.

During those years of growing up, I lots of time had to rinse the bottles in summer. My brother ran them through the washer and I had to rinse them and put them in the crates. It was not a hard job but it was so hot in the boiler room I didn't like it. Meantime I roamed the fields and streams, picked wildflowers, and watched fish, turtles, snakes and frogs along the banks of the Clear Fork. I always watched which pasture the bull was in so I could go to the other one. My bad dreams of my childhood were always about the bull chasing me.

All in all, it was a good time to grow up.

Richard Kisling's daughter Janice Levy remembered another episode. At age five she and cousin Dale Jr. were riding on a tractor with Grandfather Sam when it went over a big rock and completely overturned. Janice was sitting on the battery box and was pinned under the tractor as was Sam. She cried and both hollered for help until some men passing by on their way home from work heard them. Sam couldn't hear Dale Jr. and figured he was dead. He wasn't. The little kid had simply walked back to the house unhurt and didn't tell anybody. Sam was laid up for a few days. Janice was unhurt by some miracle.

She too, helped with the farm work, helped her father deliver, worked in the milk house, fell down the hay chute, rode cows from the pasture to the barn, (got bucked off a few times and once broke her glasses), stepped in fresh cow manure in her bare feet, climbed up to the top of the silo to pitch silage and ran behind a tree and yelled for help one time when the bull chased her. As a young girl delivering milk she had another memory; *There was another place, a hotel, down in the basement was a beer joint. I was a kid, I was afraid and the place smelled like beer.*

The Kisling kids played basketball on the barn floor, helped feed the thrashers, and watched apple butter and ice cream making. She also fondly recalls that it *was a good life.*

At one time, the dairy farm supported three families and produced 800 quarts of milk a day, seven days a week. As Richard and Dale's own families grew, they too would help out. The two boys and their wives took over the dairy operation and delivery routes when Sam retired.

The Kisling family operated one of the last four independent home delivered dairies in the state. Other area dairy farms sold their milk to companies like Pages, Isalys, Carnation, and others who would run trucks to the farms. The now highly collectable Mohican glass bottles that once cost Kisling eight cents had risen to 50 cents each and caps were also much more expensive. It was harder to compete with the big stores.

The blizzard of 1978 ended home delivery. However, customers could still pick up milk at the farm and a surprising number did. Their cream on top milk was what folks wanted, rather than the homogenized stuff that came in a cardboard box or plastic jug at the store. It all finally came to an end in 1985 when Dick and Dale decided to retire. At the time, the family's Mohican Valley Dairy had been serving the area with good milk and friendly service for more than 60 years. It was the end of an era.

Vidonish Studios is a unique business, which brings both color and art to a town that is in need of both. Vinyl siding, fake shutters and plain glass windows can only go so far.

Bill and Cherri Vidonish had a hobby working with colored glass, the kind often seen in church windows. During family gathering years ago someone suggested that they should go into business for themselves. It was a big step.

However, in 1981, starting in a rented room of the old bank-post office building, they took that step. The business has grown over the years to the point where it now occupies parts of two buildings. The portion once used by the Lexington Savings Bank decades ago gives them the distinction of being the only retail store in town with its own walk-in vault. They leave the vault door open and use it as a closet.

The colorful art glass panels and windows they sell are custom made to suit a buyer's design or preference. It is the added touch that gives architectural distinction to area homes. Tiffany style lamps are displayed and old ones can be repaired.

The workshop is an amazing place to observe the craft.

Photograph courtesy of Peggy Jo Carpenter Collection
The Lexington Soy Products Company plant, shortly after World War II.

One can see artisans turning out leaded glass creations, each one different, each one a lasting work of art.

Lexington Concrete & Supply

William (Bill) Baker bought the coal yard business next to the railroad station from the A. C. Kell Hardware in 1954. Prior to that time, Bill had operated trucks hauling coal from mines in southern Ohio and hauling gravel and stone. He began adding a line of builder supplies and block to his business.

In the spring of 1957 with three partners, construction began on a ready mix concrete batch plant on Mill Run Road. Completed in the fall of that year, they started delivery with a couple of used six-yard trucks. They sold concrete to the booming housing construction industry underway in town. The office and yard were consolidated on Mill Street in April of 1958.

Baker left after seven years. John Henry Fuhrer became the principal owner and the name changed to Lexington Concrete & Supply. At this writing an entirely new plant and office are nearing completion. The fate of the old plant is unknown. The old truck wash out area must have concrete 40-feet deep, offering a great foundation for some future building.

Lexington Soy Products Co.

The old Cockley Mill went broke sometime in the late 1920s or early 30s and later the property housed a pickle factory. Nothing has been found of this business, but apparently it too failed. In 1943, the Berea Milling Co. moved to Lexington. The machinery in the old plant was very suitable for milling soy beans and the manufacture of soy bean oil.

Four gigantic steel storage silos were built and a railroad siding extended to an unloading pit between them and the mill. The plant became one of the biggest customers for the local B&O Railroad as many box, hopper and tank cars moved in and out of the plant. Side track shortage caused dozens of cars to be stored at the Shaffer Siding near Bellville at harvest time. The oil extracted from beans was shipped by tank car.

Harold Carpenter was manager and his son, Robert, along with others kept the "bean plant" going day and night. A noon steam whistle announced lunch for the whole town and slamming railcars and locomotive noise were not always appreciated at night. But folks got used to it. The mill used a World War II Army halftrack to move rail cars until one day it reportedly got squished between two cars. After the Clear Fork Reservoir was built, they bought Bill Volz's army halftrack and used the other one for parts. They were something for a kid to watch and play on.

The old mill burned in the summer of 1951 and the fire department could do little. A loss to the town, a few housewives were not too unhappy to see it burn because of the airborne dust it created. A petition to close the mill had been circulated earlier. Later, with the milling equipment destroyed, the plant went to a chemical extraction operation.

A spectacular fire in July 1959 halted that production for a while. As demand fell for oil, one by one a number of soy oil plants in Ohio went broke after the war. The Lexington plant was eventually forced to close too. The huge silos were dismantled and moved to Marengo, Ohio. Cement contractor Andy Walker and his sons have constructed new buildings on the site.

Lexington Industrial Park

At this time there is a surprising amount of business and employment on the east side of town. The industrial development was first planned by realtor Robert Davidson and Fred Bechtel. They saw the need for an expanded manufacturing, rather than just residential growth, for

a village tax base. In 1989, Bob Wolf bought them out and expanded the park.

Richland Screw Machine (now Mansfield Screw Machine Products), which moved from Mansfield and Buckeye Educational were the earliest business buildings on Industrial Drive. Then Chet Delong moved his glass and tool rental business into his new building on the corner in 1989. Chet's brother, Curry Delong, was with him and still has a growing furniture refinishing business. Chet had started a tool rental business on the north side of East Main in 1972. He then built a larger building of his own on the south side of the street in 1976. The Lexington do-it-yourselfers kept him busy.

Bob Wolf developed, and later sold, several local commercial businesses. Richland Products, Argus

Next Generation Films (background) and Mansfield Screw Machine Products (foreground) are two of the larger companies in the growing Lexington Industrial Park.

Images and Argus Silkscreen were among his numerous successful local ventures. There were others. Wolf had a management gift for being able to see potential by buying, revitalizing, and modernizing stagnate firms.

Other concerns have also made the park their headquarters. Most notable of these is Next Generation Films. With David Frecka as CEO, he has rapidly developed his plastic film and bag manufacturing line. At this time the business has expanded into several buildings and is still growing.

Hi-Stat Manufacturing Company. Inc. is an amazing success story and the largest employer in the Lexington area.

C. John "Jack" Hire was an exceptional man. A former Eagle Scout, he grew up in Ashland and earned an Electrical Engineering degree at Purdue University. During the Korean War, he served as a cryptology officer aboard the USS Missouri.

In 1955, he moved to Mansfield and worked at Therm-O-Disc. Hire had good entrepreneurial instincts and knew to surround himself with good people. He started out on his own running Hi-Fi Haven, a retail TV and music store. In the 1960s he sold the store and founded radio station WVNO.

In a small Mansfield shop on Distl Avenue, Hire founded Hi-Stat Manufacturing in 1969. They made quality electrical controls and sensors for truck, farm and automotive equipment manufacturers. With a contract from Chrysler for electrical switches, the infant company quickly outgrew that facility.

They moved to their new building, on Mill Street in Lexington, in 1971. By 1977, that also proved to be too small, as business exploded and a new larger plant was built. It has been expanded several times since then and another factory was added in Sarasota, Florida.

In December 1998, Hire sold Hi-Stat to Warren, Ohio based Stoneridge Inc. for $362 million dollars. That firm, founded in 1965, had bought several electrical manufacturing companies over the years, but Hi-Stat with 1,700 employees (nearly 500 in Lexington) was its largest acquisition at that time. Stoneridge has continued to grow in the automotive electrical field and now owns plants in Sweden, England, India, and is entering China at this writing.

After a long illness, "Jack" Hire died in January of 2004 at 74. He was a distinctive leader who wasn't afraid to take a chance and left a legacy in the Lexington area that will be long remembered.

Moved to Lexington in 1971, Hi-Stat, now Stoneridge, is the town's largest employer. They employ almost 500 people in Lexington.

Historic Building Mourned

One day it was there, the next it was gone.

Without a whimper from village officials or the historic preservation society, Lexington's last truly personal historic building was carted away. No one at the Richland County Museum so much as raised an eyebrow. No brass plaque denoting its place in history ever adorned its walls.

The old outhouse behind the ancient brick home of the Chalfant family on East Main was sold to a farm family on Kings Corners Road. Long retired from active duty in town, it would serve standby duty in semi-retirement in a peaceful country setting. These trusty privies are sometimes necessary during prolonged rural power failures, which leave indoor plumbing nearly useless.

A careful 1985 survey by the writer revealed it to be the only remaining example of a necessary structure that once was found behind every home and business in Lexington. By some miracle, it had been spared from Halloween vandals.

However, in the blink of an eye, on August 4, 1992, it was gone. Another page of history had been turned.

The last outhouse in town, semi-retired, left for a life of country leisure in 1992.

Schools and Education

School kids that may be coerced into reading this book may wish to skip this chapter, but there are some interesting bits they'll miss if they do. Fear not because it's rather short.

In 1989 former Lexington student Elsie Simon compiled and published A Scrapbook of Lexington School History, which is an excellent and detailed history of the educational system in the Lexington area. It took her a dozen years to collect and put it all together. It's a collector's item and copies are available at the local library. It's an excellent book and there is no need to repeat her work here.

Look for it at a library. You'll enjoy it. It's very interesting reading.

This is the 1889 Lexington High School picture. Professor John Miller is in the front row (third from right). However, none of the student body (18 of them) are identified. This picture was takenin front of the 1850 school on Church Street (now the County Museum)

The 1894 Lexington school building was located on Frederick Street. The yellow-brick part of the current Junior High was added onto the front during 1930. At present (117 years later), classes are still held in this venerable building every day of the school year.

Women Drivers

Sandy Hill, August 1903:

An exciting accident was that which took place on Sandy Hill last Wednesday. Two ladies from Columbus were on their way to Cleveland in an automobile when the auto became uncontrollable and went backwards instead of forward. The ladies became frightened and jumped from the auto and it backed into a ditch where it was left until Mr. Dir was called and hitched his horse to the auto and hauled it up to Mr. McCartney's yard where it was left. Two gentlemen from Mansfield were called and upon examination it was found to have run out of gasoline. Mr. Dir conveyed the ladies to Mansfield where they expected to board a train for Cleveland. The auto was taken to Mansfield the next morning. No damage was done except one wheel was bent a little.

Considering the dirt roads, fragile tires and chance of bad weather this was a risky trip for the two women.

Men had "parking" problems too. Lexington, April, 1895: *John Shauck's horse broke its fastening on the park and ran down Main St. with terrific speed and after making a circuit the foaming steed collapsed at Johnson's shop. Mr. Shauck's vehicle was totally wrecked and in its mad flight had nearly collided with passing teams. In breaking loose, Shauck's horse frightened Robert Richey's horse which ran a few yards and careened on the park and the mettle steed broke loose from the trills and annihilated time at a dizzy rate. Mr. Richey's vehicle was also wrecked.* The seat behind the steering wheel would not be the domain of men. Women quickly mastered the art of driving and the invention of the self starter opened the world to them.

Young Jeanette Wirick was learning to drive in the 1920s. The Model T Ford seems to have had a hard life, although she was not entirely to blame for its condition. Jeanette is well remembered for her 41 years as dietician and manager of the Lexington School Cafeteria.

Photograph courtesy of Helen Griebling

Driving an open car in winter was either by necessity or love of adventure. The word stupidity also comes to mind. Here Louis Griebling, with suitcase on the fender, prepares for a trip to college.

The unhappy faces of the women in the back seat indicate that men were going to be in for different seating arrangements soon. Women could drive a car just as well as men in this 1913 picture.

A Little Church History

Reverend Henry George

The first minister to preach in Lexington was Rev. Henry George, a missionary from the American Baptist Society of Philadelphia, who settled three miles south of Chesterville. Rev. George was born in Talgarth, South Wales, in 1761, and came to America sometime around 1800. In 1811 he, along with his family, was sent as a missionary to Ohio.

George established the Chester Baptist Church and traveled a wide area, as a missionary to the Indians. He preached in the cabin of Amariah Watson during the spring of 1814, which was Lexington's first recorded church service.

In a letter George wrote to the Society in 1818, he detailed some of his efforts with the Indians. The letter was published in *The Latter Day Luminary,* a publication of that denomination:

I have been twice out with them about three weeks each time. We had a meeting that lasted three days and three nights with the greater part of the Wyandot and some of the Delaware tribes, preaching, praying and singing most of the time. I went down river to the Seneca tribe; but for want of an interpreter could do nothing with them. From thence I went to Lower Sandusky (note, present-day Fremont) and preached three times among the whites. Thirty two or three were buried this fall. It is a place almost without the preaching of the Gospel. I passed down the bay (note, Sandusky Bay) preaching almost daily; and up the Huron River through Richland County, a country near the Indian lands, where I found some scattered Baptists and others in need of Gospel ministry. When I had done preaching where I could conveniently find an open door, I returned home

One of Rev. George's letters ended with this:

Dear brother, I rejoice in the Lord, by his providence, has brought a poor unworthy dust such as I am, near 4,000 miles from my native country to preach the unsearchable riches of Christ among the Idolatrous gentiles of America. This I am resolved to do as long as I am supported by the Lord and his people. Dear brother, pray for me without ceasing.

On his way back home to Chesterville from these preaching trips, Lexington would have been one of his stops. Speaking with his broad Welsh tongue, through an interpreter, it's hard to imagine a red-headed Rev. George had much luck. The Indians of each of these several tribes already had their own language or dialect and native religion. What tremendous odds he faced. He was truly a dedicated man of God.

George also farmed, worked as a brick and stone mason, and attended to civic duties in Knox County. He died in 1821 at age 61 and is buried next to the Chester Baptist Church on Route 314, south of Chesterville. A very large, old stone marker, laid flat identifies his grave. It's an interesting and a moving piece of history to see. Also interesting is the fact that the Welsh language was used in that congregation until it was dropped in April, 1832. Some members left because of the decision.

Noah Cook

Noah Cook was a Revolutionary War soldier who came to this area with his family in 1814. Cook had served six enlistments in the Pennsylvania militia from 1776 to 1782. This included once serving as chaplain of the Fifth Regiment of Continental troops under General Sullivan.

Cook was also with the troop of volunteer militia at Mingo Bottom near Steubenville, when Col. William Crawford was chosen to lead them on an ill-advised raid. The raid was to be against Indian villages in northwest Ohio, along the Sandusky River. That 1782 attack against the Indian villages was without justification. As Crawford's army advanced, it met and was outnumbered by, a confederation of Indians and British troops. Crawford's army fought well, but was forced to retreat at night. During the confusion of that retreat, Col. Crawford was captured near Leesville just north of Galion. Days later he was tortured and burned at the stake by the Indians.

Of the 480 men, about 400 escaped and Noah Cook was among the lucky ones. He lost his horse and was on foot, but he had his life. Perhaps this part of Ohio appealed to Cook as the army had marched west through the wilderness of what is now Lucas and Mansfield. Or maybe the area caught his eye during the retreat, which may have been along the Clear Fork Valley. No one knows for sure. However, he would one day return.

Lexington's first church is the building on the right. Built by the Presbyterians in 1832-33, it was sold to the United Bretheren in 1836. William Lutz bought the structure in 1893 and moved it across town to Walnut Street for use in his lumber yard.

A religious man, perhaps his war experience deepened his faith in God. Having acted as chaplain, he evidently felt a calling to hold a church service in the valley where no church existed. As the story is told, he advised neighbors of his intentions. However, at the appointed time only his family was present. Undaunted, he spoke, prayed, and they sang. A passerby heard and word was spread. At the next calling, a good attendance was noticed. From this humble beginning the seed of a church was planted.

Cook was present in Richland County as early as 1813 and by 1824 owned a total of 830 acres of the valley, in both Washington and Troy townships. His children; Daniel, Jabez, Henry, Jacob, John, William, Amos and Rachal Cook owned another 1,340 total acres in the county. Noah had thirteen children.

Irregular church services were held by itinerant preachers in cabins, barns, and a rough schoolhouse starting in 1816. Baptist Rev. George, Presbyterians Rev. George Van Eman and Summerville labored here. On September 10, 1822, Amariah Watson made his home available for the first meeting of the Universalists Society in the county. He was of that faith.

The first church building was built by the Presbyterians sometime in 1831-32, on land donated by Amariah Watson. Noah Cook was the leader promoting its construction, offering Mr. Bell 70 acres of land in exchange for timber and erecting the structure. The congregation was constituted as a Presbyterian Church, March 29, 1832. Noah Cook, a former soldier; Jacob Cook, a former tavern keeper; and Andrew Barnett, a former Elder, were elected to the posts of Ruling Elders. The new congregation welcomed Rev. Adam Torrance as its first regular pastor the following year.

As the only denomination in town with a building, the Presbyterians grew in numbers and their members reflected the leadership of the area. However, they were not alone in God's work.

The Universalists

The Universalists built a church at the top of the hill on the west side of Plymouth Street in 1842. Not much is known of this congregation. At one time it was quite large, but the county history relates that a week-long debate between their Rev. Biddlecome and a Methodist minister, Rev. Powers, must have been the death knell for its future. By the 1870s, the church building had been converted into a home. In later years, the building was moved to Short Street and a second floor added. At this writing it's the home of Bud Corwin next to the post office.

The Methodists

The Methodists also organized and built a church on Delaware Street in the early 1840s. In early days, several prominent ministers drew many followers and, at one time, the Methodists became the leading congregation in Lexington both in size and stature. Adam Poe,

The old Methodist Church on Delaware Street was remodeled and converted into a home after the church failed. It was the home of the Maxwell family for years.

who went on to found Ohio Wesleyan University, and Russell Bigelow, who once served as missionary to the Wyandot Indians, were gifted preachers who could fill a room. The congregation even established a small country chapel on Bell Road.

But as with any denomination the church declined for reasons unknown. No records have been found. Perhaps it was the Methodists involvement in the temperance movement or bickering members. In August 1884 newsman Al Moore commented,

That quaint old structure, the Methodist Church, built in the early era of our ancient village, is revered by many for its old time associations. Membership of the church has rapidly diminished by death and removals and the gospel benefices are no longer dispensed from its pulpit. We are informed that the ancient edifice will soon be for sale.

It was remodeled and converted into a home for the Maxwell family for many years.

The Presbyterians

The Presbyterians grew rapidly in their infancy, and needing larger quarters, sold their church building to a new United Brethren congregation in 1836 for $422. They built an impressive new brick church. In that era, there was a lack of engineering principals relating to masonry buildings. Inadequate foundations below the frost line and unacceptable cement mortar mix formulas were factors that often led to unhappy results. Seymore Conger had his new brick house west of town fall down before he ever got the roof on. So it was with the Presbyterians. After 12 or 13 years, the building was declared unsafe to use and a new frame church was built on Grange Street. It was dedicated in February, 1850.

The Lexington Presbyterian Church is unique in that all its session and membership records have been preserved. They paint a word picture of the good works, the enduring faith, and dedication of pastors and members. They also record the struggle for change, the discord, and the well-intended but ill-advised actions by both pastors and laymen. Every denomination goes through these trials.

In the 1830s, any Presbyterian who strayed off the path of the denomination rules was charged and put on trial by a Session of Elders. A trial by one's peers was an ordeal to be avoided, but deemed necessary to keep folks in line. Otherwise, their sinful ways might embarrass

Fire In 90-Year-Old Lexington Building

MAY 1, 1941

Volunteer firemen, shown above, battle flames which destroyed a three-apartment building in Lexington Wednesday afternoon. An oil stove explosion in the apartment of Mrs. Ia Devine while she was absent was blamed for the blaze. The explosion was heard, and fire discovered by Mrs. Arthur Sherman, who resides in an adjoining apartment. The 90-year-structure, formerly a church, is owned by Jesse Clark, who occupied one of the apartments. The fire destroyed the building and most of the household goods owned by the three families. The loss is partially covered by insurance.

This newspaper photo is the only known picture of the 1850 Presbyterian Church. No other photograph exists with church records or members. Shortly after this 1941 fire, the building was torn down.

the whole membership. If found guilty, a person was sometimes "removed from fellowship," that is to say, "kicked out."

In 1836, Jacob Beckley was charged with deception of his neighbors and making promises he knew he couldn't keep. He got the boot. Thomas Patterson, the local blacksmith, was seen intoxicated on several occasions and at his trial, witnesses told of seeing him stagger and "appeared to have difficulty of utterance." At his trial Patterson explained he had been afflicted with a bowel disorder and diarrhea medicine prescribed had little effect. He had been advised to try brandy. He did. The more he took, the better he felt. He must have been feeling really, really good on several occasions. He confessed his actions and promised to quit the cure. They let him off the hook.

The ruling Elders fielded another rumor at a session meeting in March of 1838: *Whereas it has been ru-*

mored that the Presbyterian Church is in favor of slavery and particular allusion being made to the Church of Lexington, therefore resolved that the session view the American system of slavery as it now exists a flagrant transgression of the Law of God contrary to every principle of our holy religion consequently a flagrant sin, that ought to be eradicated from every branch of the Christian Church."

William Campbell was involved in another trial, where he was accused of withholding a subscription paper where members pledged support for the church and minister. This, along with other member infractions, the slavery issue, and bickering by other members led to the founding of the "New School Presbyterian Church" next door in 1844. They lost their minister Rev. Evans and quite a few good parishioners.

What happened here was typical of what happened to many Protestant churches. It was a reluctance to change. There were many folks resisting anything new in their staid, rigid old church. A choir first had to be voted on by the Presbyterians. A musical instrument, a piano or organ raised eyebrows when introduced in some churches. We never needed one before! God gave us voices! Sunday school was another radical idea, which the New School members wanted and they got it, starting with a clean slate and leaving the old traditions behind. Today we see the same situation with some congregations resisting contemporary worship services with modern hymns and music. An example is found in the Presbyterian record July 6, 1895:

We would state as public information to all our people the law of our beloved church in these matters;

The 1905 Presbyterian Church was the newest and largest in town.

1. Promiscuous dancing calls for faithful and judicious discipline

2. Dancing, card playing, theaters, operas, gambling, lotteries, are condemned by our church courts.

3. Social dancing and dancing schools are to be prohibited among church members.

4. Dancing parties permitted by Christian heads of families may be subject to church discipline.

Other denominations had similar rules. It was a tough rule to enforce as regular dances and parties were being held by the young people in the Lexington Odd Fellows Hall, the tavern and the grove at the cemetery.

This left the area with three Presbyterian churches. The "Old School" as the original became known was in competition with the "New School" and there was also the "Associate Reformed Presbyterian Church" at Troy, near present-day Gass Road and Route 97 under the preaching of Rev. Richard Gailey.

Abolition and the Underground Railroad

The 1838 anti-slavery declaration of the Presbyterians was not just confined to their denomination. The movement to abolish southern slavery practices was becoming an issue in all the normally quiet congregations in the area. Not many ministers or laymen felt the same about the issue. Some wished to ignore the subject, while others felt the southern states should continue their own ways. And then there were those opposed to slavery and the Abolitionist movement was gaining strength.

The Underground Railroad in the Lexington area knew no particular denomination or political party. The Samuel McClure farm on Texter Road and the George Mitchell home and water-powered mill west of town near the Buckhorn Tavern (Route 97 and 314) were known stations. Sterling Green, of Indian ancestry, on the upper Clear Fork and members of the Gass family north of town along Lexington-Springmill Road were also active in the Abolitionist movement. There were others. Fugitive slaves were generally moved through the country rather than run the risk of capture in cities. Some "conductors" on the railroad movement felt it was their religious duty.

No one in Lexington kept a written record, but a clue is found in the Presbyterian records of February 8, 1843, when charges were filed by William Lyon against William Campbell, one of the ruling Elders:

I charge Wm. Campbell a member and ruling Elder in said church with the crime of first circulating a scandalous report against me by showing a letter to different persons in and out of the bounds of the church, which letter stated or conveyed the idea that I had in a clandestine manner conveyed away a negro or colored man on a stolen horse.

The long, controversial, church trial was finally dropped, due to lack of evidence. However, it is highly probable there was something going on. There was a stiff legal penalty for helping fugitive slaves and the case was best swept under the rug. Hear no evil, see no evil.

Some slaves came from the Quaker settlements in Morrow and Knox counties. Others arrived from Iberia. Benjamin Gass once delivered five runaway men along with five or six women and children in one wagonload to Robert Finney. Finney fed and hid them in his Springfield Township home. Later, they were passed along to the next station towards Oberlin. Finney helped hundreds on their way to Canada.

The Congregationalists

The "New School" church became a Congregational denomination in 1862. Their building was built in 1846 for $835, indicating the rapid growth and financial well-being of membership. It is most unfortunate that the early records of this congregation have been lost. Nothing remains before 1915, except from a Women's Missionary Society.

In 1873, the prospering congregation expanded the existing basic building, adding new windows and a beautiful steeple and bell tower. The bronze bell was a gift from merchants in New York, where Bloomer Sowers bought stock for his general store. It was a used bell, cast in 1848 by the New York and Brooklyn Brass & Bell Foundry and weighs nearly half a ton. At one time, it was used as the town fire bell and of course to announce Sunday church.

The building has always been a beautiful historic landmark and has been well-maintained. In 1959, the congregation bought the old house that had formerly been the Methodist Church and after using it for class rooms tore it down for expanded parking. In recent years, an addition was built in keeping with the original architecture.

The United Brethren

Very little is known of the United Brethren flock. They were still active in the early 1880s, but closed their doors a short time later. The denomination sold the old church building to William Lutz in the summer of 1893 and in November he hooked up a couple of his steam engines and pulled it down through town to Walnut Street for use as a planning mill and wood shop. Once again, no local records of this congregation, which was a longtime part of the village have been found.

The Baptists

The same holds true for the Baptists. An early 1837 record of the Chester Baptist church mentions a member moving to the "Baptist Church called Lexington in Richland County." Nothing more has ever been found. Perhaps it was a rural church. The Baptists did return in 1960, when a mission church was started in an old house east of town. In 1965, ground was broken for a new sanctuary building next door with plans for future additions. They never seemed to gain membership after that and finally closed their doors in 2006.

The Mormons

The Mormons were to have an early effect on this area. Jacob Myers, a prosperous millwright and mill owner near Butler in the 1820s, joined the Mormon Church in 1833, severing his Methodist connection.

Myers owned considerable land and a busy mill operation, which made him a well-known businessman. He was a popular miller, until he joined the Mormons and then he was viewed with some suspicion. He quickly became a presiding elder in the Worthington branch of the Mormon Church and three congregations were formed in southern Richland County, one each in Green, Worthington and Perry townships. The members became clannish, supported one another and their strange new religion didn't set well with the mostly Protestant area churches that began losing members. There were hard feelings and family divisions that often developed when someone joined their faith.

Joseph Smith, the Mormon Prophet and founder, had gathered his followers at Kirtland in northeast Ohio and established his church there. Building a temple had nearly emptied the treasury. As troubles and violent persecution erupted, Smith received a revelation to move his flock to Missouri. The 800-mile trek would be an expensive undertaking and financially well-off Jacob Myers was pressured to respond with what funds he could give and borrow. He was nearly broke when the Mormon wagon train left Kirtland. It passed through Mansfield on July 16, 1834, and stopped for the night near old Ontario. The men on the train were well armed in case of trouble. It was to be a long tiresome journey.

Two years later, Jacob Myers would lead his own wagon train west to the "New Zion" in Missouri. Most of those in his care came from southern Richland and surrounding counties. Francis Boggs, a founding member of the Lexington Presbyterian Church, and Desdemonia Fullmer from Perry Township went along with their families. Desdemonia would someday become one of Joseph Smith's 28 wives as he promoted polygamy. The practice was strongly blasted by other denominations as clergymen pounded their pulpits and denounced all Mormons, their lifestyle and manner of worship.

The Myers wagon train left Richland County in the early fall of 1836 amid bittersweet feelings. One estimate places the number at 50 or more wagons. It was to be a rough trip after a late start and not all would make it. They were unwelcome in Missouri when they arrived. Since Mormons heavily settled in one area and dominated the politics and economy, they were hated by non-Mormons. In the fall of 1838, an armed mob attacked and murdered 17 Mormon men and an 8-year-old boy. Another 13 men and one woman were wounded at a settlement called Hahn's Mill, which had been built by Myers. All Mormons were later driven out of the state by order of the Governor. Three of the dead and 11 of the wounded were from Richland County.

Many Mormons, shunned and denounced by family and friends, had severed a bond that perhaps would never heal. There had to have been tears shed. Others, including the clergy, were happy to be rid of them and the ruckus caused by Smith and his new religion. Ironically, there were good, honest, hardworking, God-loving people on both sides. All that separated them were their religious beliefs. It was to be one of the greatest religious divisions the United States had ever seen.

Reverend Richard Gailey

Reverend Richard Gailey was a truly remarkable man. Born in October 31, 1806 in Letterkenny, Ireland, he came to America as a tourist when he was 21. To learn about the country, he walked from Philadelphia to Pittsburgh. He came to Mansfield and spent a year at the

Lorin Academy, a private school there. He went back to Jefferson College at Pittsburgh, graduated in 1835, and then entered a theological seminary in Allegheny, Pennsylvania. Gailey was ordained a Presbyterian minister and called to Richland County in 1849 to take a three point charge at Monroe (near Lucas), Pine Run, and the Troy church, just west of Lexington. The cemetery along Route 97 was the church location.

It must have been a humble start. The Troy congregation had held their first services in the shed house of Ichabod Clark's distillery. When Gailey arrived, the Troy church was a log building. In 1853, after a fire burned the log structure and the lumber stored inside for a new building, they succeeded in finishing a new church building next to the cemetery.

Rev. Gailey lived at Hastings, a crossroad community about three-and-a-half miles southeast of Lucas and a short distance from the Monroe Church. He was a good preacher and during his ministry noticed there were no educational opportunities for students in those one-room schools beyond the 8th grade. On May 5, 1851, he opened the Monroe Seminary as a private high school in the church building. Students attended six days a week and, in spite of its remote location, attendance began to grow. Two of the students were his daughters, Jane and Mary. Gailey was a busy man with school six days and three church services on Sunday.

His students received good instructions. "The education, moral and intellectual, of everyone, must be chiefly his own work," or "You are aware my young friends you live in an age of light and knowledge." And then

Reverend Richard Gailey

this, "Articulate very distinctly, just imagine old Mr. Robinson (who was known to be quite deaf) was sitting in the farthest corner of the church and speak so that he could hear every word." So efficient was his training in this respect that his students upon entering college were not surpassed by many and a number often took first honors in their class.

However, there were problems as other schools opened. Gailey's remote location, coupled with the limited boarding available outside Lucas, made it difficult to house students. So, in 1854, Gailey moved to Lexington to be near the railroad.

However, owing to family illness and the lack of a suitable house (they evidently used the old octagon brick school nicknamed "the Ark"), the school was moved back to Monroe that fall. In Monroe, a small house was built for use instead of the church. Still, the seed had evidently been planted in Lexington, with the result being a community stock company was formed. The company built a two-story brick school building for Gailey on Delaware Street. Rev. Gailey had moved his first classes into the uncompleted building in the fall of 1860.

In 1866 problems arose between the trustees, and the building was sold at half its value to Gailey. The Troy Presbyterian congregation moved into the upper floor, with the Lexington Male and Female Seminary using the lower.

The good minister did most of the teaching and it is recorded that his "hour" consisted of 120 minutes. He was joined by his daughters when they graduated from college. Jane, the oldest, was first assistant and taught music, vocal and instrumental. Mary Elizabeth taught drawing, painting, and ornamental needle work. The private school was a great asset to the area and students paid $1.12 to $1.50 a week to board in local homes. The first year, more than 100 students were enrolled and enrollment increased in succeeding years. Some students arrived from far away places by railroad. More teachers were employed for a variety of classes.

History has never fully recorded the effect Rev. Gailey and his students had on the social and cultural activities of the community. The school instructors molded attitudes and provided leadership much needed in the quaint old village. The music taught, books read and lessons learned in the school filtered into the whole area. The seminary was a blessing envied by other towns.

In 1868, Mary Gailey married former seminary student Robert C. Brown, which ended her teaching connection, although other teachers were still employed. In that era, married women were not supposed to teach school. The husband was to provide support, the wife was to stay home.

On July 4, 1870, Rev. Richard Gailey made out his will, which read in part, "Being about to visit my native land, knowing the uncertainly of life, especially on a sea voyage, I do hereby dispose of my Estate, real and personal, by this my last will and testament." A long awaited visit to his family and homeland must have been a dream come true.

In August of that year he sent a letter from Killeylasten, Ireland, to his son-in-law, Col. Robert C. Brown, in Lexington, which in part follows:

I have arrived once more in my old play ground. The scenes of my youth seem to rise up before me, in every direction, and when I view them, I seem to forget all the time since and fancy myself a sprightly youth as when I left them. But alas, when I look around for the fathers, they have long gone to the silent tomb. When I enquire for the boys and girls that once ran playful through thru streets, many have died. Many have gone to America, and some are still here but how changed! Youth has turned into old age, and the rosy cheeks are faded as the leaf of autumn. I am very agreeably surprised at the great kindness I every where receive. A party every day. At present six engagements are made and an indefinite number postponed.

....I have made arrangements by which (no preventing province) I will be home about the 9th or 10th of Sept. and hope to find you all well....David Gregg wrote to his mother, that I had started for Ireland. She had her carriage on the road in a few minutes with her daughter and son-in-law, and reached my brother's a little before sunset. They are very fine looking people. I am to dine with them tomorrow at one o'clock.

The seminary students from both Monroe and Lexington were to attain success beyond imagination. At a reunion held in 1880, with an estimated 250 in attendance, speakers noted that 18 alumni had gone into the ministry, 16 became lawyers, 12 had taken up medicine, and an uncountable number had become teachers.

Among the notable graduates was John Peter Altgeld, who became the governor of Illinois. Altgeld was born

The Lexington Seminary, run by Reverend Gailey was a great asset to the town. This photograph dates from the 1880s.

in Germany in 1847, one of seven children, and came to America when only a few months old. A poor farmboy, he attended the Methodist church near Newville to learn English. At sixteen, he lied about his age and served in the Civil War. Afterwards, poorly dressed and nearly broke, he begged and pleaded Rev. Gailey to let him attend his school, promising to repay every penny even if it took years. Gailey could see something in the young man and let him enroll. In 1860, the small Altgeld family farm was near Little Washington, and in his poverty he carried food from home and ate in his boarding room to save expenses. He recalled Mother Gailey was aware of his circumstances and helped him. With Gailey's help he qualified for a first teaching job at the Woodville School south of Mansfield.

From there he studied law, practicing first in Ohio, and then he moved to Chicago, where he was active in law and politics. A few weeks after being elected governor of Illinois, feeling their trial had been unfair, he pardoned the men involved in the 1886 Hay Market riots. The pardons gained national recognition and strong condemnation from the press. It was once said that he was so powerful politically that were it not for his foreign birth, he could have been nominated for President. When he died in March of 1902, 50,000 people braved a snowstorm to pay their respects. Thousands more attended memorial services. Among those who eulogized him were William Jennings Bryan and Altgeld's law partner, Clarence Darrow. The press that once vilified him now praised his many achievements.

Local graduates of the Gailey Seminary included members of the Sherman, Brinkerhoff, Beverstock, Cockley, Conger, Sowers, Galbraith, Lawrence, Englehart, Frye, Betchtel, Andrews and Maxwell families. Most would become successful leaders wherever they lived.

Reverend Richard Gailey died on April 2, 1875, of heart failure. He was buried on Sunday, April 4, at 1:00pm, and the procession that followed him to his final resting place was the largest ever seen in Lexington. Hundreds walked behind and alongside the hearse. His wife, Catherine, daughters, and two sons, Richard Jr., a lawyer, and Rev. John Gailey, along with a host of others said a tearful last farewell. Those who knew him saw to it that the one of the largest monuments in the cemetery was erected in his honor. It's on the right, at the top of the hill.

The leadership of the Lexington Seminary fell to daughter Jane until March of 1880, when she was married to Rev. Thomas Dysart in the seminary auditorium in front of her scholars. For years many students carried a vivid memory of the wedding. The couple went to Olathe, Kansas, where he preached and she started another school in 1883. Jane died in 1899. Her husband had preceded her in death in Kansas in 1882.

The seminary continued for a few years under Prof. James Wilson, but eventually closed due to declining enrollment. The result was the establishment of the Lexington Public High School. The old Presbyterian congregation evidently dissolved or merged after their leader's death. Except for his trip to Ireland, Gailey had missed only three Sundays in 26 years, a record that locally has never been matched. The seminary building was used for William Lindsey's harness shop until 1896, when J. H. Sherer bought the property and tore it down. Sherer used some of the bricks to build a new house, which years later became Snyder's Funeral Home. The only remains of the seminary are a section of garage wall.

The Church of Christ

The Church of Christ was started by a member of the Cook family. Noah Cook and son, Jacob, were the first two founding members the Presbyterian Church. Jacob Cook's son was Carter Cook and he was an early member of the New School, later known as the Congregational Church. Carter's son, Orville Cook, became an evangelist and came back home.

In a few years, Orville founded what became the Lexington Church of Christ. Rev. Cook was a good, forceful preacher. He was invited to speak in the Congregational Church, at meetings outdoors and in the town hall, which was used after the church was organized in 1900. In May of 1901, the new building on Delaware Street was dedicated and the membership grew under Cook's able leadership. Old-timers interviewed years ago fondly remembered his common sense, excellent sermons. He was an outstanding preacher and lived on the old family farm on Route 42 south, where he grew up. Cook stayed until 1908, when he left for the evangelist field for which he had a calling.

The Presbyterians built their second church building of the new century in 1905-06, at a cost of $7,960. It was the most beautiful and substantial edifice in town. Members dug into their pockets, and some helped dig the basement. Everybody pitched in. The stained glass windows and memorial bell in an ornate tower set it all off.

For the next half century the Presbyterian, Congregational, and Church of Christ were the only three in town. The Methodist Church at Steam Corners was the closest rural church. Of these, the Presbyterian was the largest and most influential. In 1960 the Presbyterians tore down a house next door and built a two-story educational wing, the first church construction in over half a century.

1950s - Present

As the building boom began in old Lex, so did the prospects rise for various denominations to start new mission congregations. In 1957, the Lexington Church of The Nazarene was formed by Rev. Cecil Rice and built a new sanctuary near the high school. They were the first. In 1961, Rev. Don Shilling knocked on doors and soon founded the Evangelical United Brethren Mission Church, which later became the Church of the Cross. Founded as a EUB, through a denominational merger in 1968, it became a United Methodist Church.

Other denominations quickly came into the area. In 1964, Rev. George Billman started what became the Christ Lutheran Church and in 1968 his flock moved into a new building on Frederick Street. After Billman finished serving as pastor, he remained here as a dedicated worker in school and community events until his death in 2006.

The Grace Brethren Church got its infant start in late 1965 and moved into their first building in 1969. Two years later an addition was finished. Also in 1965 the Church of Christ outgrew their 1901 building and moved into a new larger complex on Delaware Street.

The old building was used as a Church of God, but has undergone a couple of name changes since.

The Catholics had land donated by Ruby Campbell in 1969. By April 1971, the Resurrection Parish, under Father Weithman, moved into a new modern building, designed by local architect Paul Shuler. This is by far the largest congregation in the Lexington area, which was established for Catholics in southern townships of Richland County.

At this time (2007) the writer counts twelve different congregations in the immediate Lexington area, with plans afoot to build yet another. Go out a few miles and four or more can be counted. Except for Resurrection Parish, which celebrates numerous Masses, all the others have one thing in common. If one shows up late for services, there is always an empty seat. Were Lexington to just have one or two giant churches, most folks attending services would feel like a number rather than a useful part of their faith. The fellowship, a most important factor in any religious gathering, would be missing. Smaller congregations have that, although there is always the financial struggle to maintain missions, staff, and properties.

The women of the new Church of Christ were dressed in the latest style. If those hats were still in church fashion, a man might be able to sneak a short nap behind one during a long-winded sermon without the preacher noticing.

The End of the Rails

Albert "Rudy" Gore was a railroader, as was his father before him. He was best remembered for his time on the "helper" engine stationed at Lexington. Starting work as fireman with his engineer father in the 1890s, he worked his way up to engineer on the B&O. It was his lifelong career.

Rudy was a lucky man for a quite a while. He lived on the east side of Plymouth Street partway down the hill and could walk to work at the depot. When the need for a helper engine stationed at Lexington ended, "Rudy" went to the main line. A granddaughter remembers standing on the back porch waving to a passing train. She could tell it was grandpa by the way Rudy blew the whistle.

For a mainline crewman, it was down the line one day and hopefully a return trip the next, unless the trainmaster had other plans. Time at home was often limited and irregular.

To some, being an engineer on a steam locomotive was a glamorous career. Interesting, perhaps, but the searing heat inside the cab of a standing or slow moving engine was more than most would want to endure in summer. The smoke, dirt and soot were also always with the crew. In winter, backing an engine any distance in zero degree weather was pure hell. The hood over the cab was like a giant air scoop and a cold blast of air and coal dust penetrated the crew. The B&O had a heavy canvas curtain at the rear of the compartment in winter, but it offered little protection. Raking hot coals out of the firebox onto the cab floor was one solution. However, with the heat came smoke and fumes. Slippery steps and handrails were a danger, as was bad weather and night operation visibility. Railroading was a dangerous job and schedules must be kept no matter the conditions.

Old age and bad health caught up with Rudy. He was forced to leave the job he loved. During his last years, he became terribly crippled, and with bowed legs, had great difficulty getting around. He knew his time was near and requested that he be buried on the far west side of the Lexington Cemetery, just across the Clear Fork from the B&O tracks, where he once worked. His wish was granted in 1948. The day of his funeral was memorable.

As the funeral procession came down the hill on East Main a locomotive was standing on the side track in front of the station. As the hearse approached the rail crossing, the bell on the engine started to ring, a signal to warn the crew and bystanders the engine was ready to move on. The funeral procession nevertheless continued on to the cemetery. All during the final services the steam activated engine bell continued its rhythmic ding, ding, ding from across the way. It continued as family and friends exchanged handshakes and hugs offering words of sympathetic memories afterwards. As those attending finally left the cemetery and re-crossed the tracks to a family gathering, the engine bell still continued its rhythmic sounds. During the whole time the engine never moved.

The brotherhood of the railroaders went far beyond union membership or company loyalty. Out on the road, away from family, they had to look after and take care of one another in times of illness, accident or injury. They worked together, and laughed together. It was a bond much deeper than most could comprehend. "Rudy" Gore would never again have to endure the heat, the smoke and the dirt of a locomotive cab. The engine crew, on duty unable to leave a live engine, had turned on the bell as a way of saying farewell to a brother and friend who had reached the end of the rails. He was moving on to a far better place.

Photograph courtesy of Mary Kay Gore Leedy
Albert "Rudy" Gore

Photographs of Lexington's Past

Clarence "Spike" Lutz is standing in front of a Spanish-American War Gatling Gun that once stood on the northeast corner of the town square. It was donated to the Smithsonian Institution in Washington D.C. and was replaced by a scroll in honor of our servicemen.

Boy Scout Troop 131 built a Revolutionary War period cannon in 1976. (Yes, a fully functional field artillery piece, circa 1776.) With uniforms sewn by their mothers, the troop paraded and fired their magnificent cannon at many local events over the years. The cannon still exists and is in storage in one of the village buildings. (Your writer is that character on the far right.)

Leaning badly in this photo, the Mercer-Griebling mill was the last water-powered mill in Troy Township. It collapsed on a warm summer day in 1920.

A Lexington baseball team, sometime around 1920. Seen here are: (Back row, L to R) Clyde Boe, Bert Parker, Carl Maul, John George – Manager, Henry McKee, Claude Horn, "Micey" Wagner. (Bottom row, L to R) Reverend McCormick, Paul Applegate, Sid Earhart, ? Guidenberg, Jim Biddle

Photograph courtesy of Linton Family Collection
The first house on the north side of First Avenue looked rather lonely in 1909. The small buildings to the right were necessities of life. The fields in the distance are now Templeton Terrace.

Photograph courtesy of Harry Linton Collection
There weren't many white collar jobs in Lexington in the early 1900s, but there was plenty of work if you didn't mind a little dirt and sweat.

Jim Fellows (left) and Orva Day had a flour mill, which was powered by a Buick automobile engine. Day's horse ran off one time and caused a major train wreck. (Fortunately there was no horse insurance, so his rates didn't go up.)

The newly organized town band was photographed sometime in the 1890s. Gilead Mansfield took this picture in front of his house, which stood where the Lex Beverage Center drive through is now.

John George is seen here standing in front of his "Big Store." The Big Store sold ice cream and ham sandwiches. It was located in the old "Odd Fellows" building. Later the Odd Fellows portion of the building (third floor) was torn down and the building was used as both a roller rink and movie theatre at one time.

Adrian Young (left) and Erwin "Butch" Castor ran Castor's Economy Garage from the 1920s to the early 1950s. They kept customers' cars running during World War II.

The William Cureton and Son Foundry, which was also identified as the Smith Foundry at one time, burned down around 1916.

Music in the Park? When the piano craze swept the country, this store was set up in the rear of the William Bonham Funeral Home, located adjacent to the town square park. The Embarq phone building sits there now. Unknown is whether the crates still contained new instruments. Does a piano sound any different at 10 degrees.

The 1934-35 Basketball team was well supported by the town. They traveled to far-off places such as Adario, Shiloh, Plymouth and Weller to get a good game.

An envious Lexington often referred to the Bellville Street Fair as "the drunk's reunion." Efforts to have our own (without the drunks) have been held on Frederick Street, West Main and the Plymouth Street Village Park over the years. The latter is the venue of our growing and successful annual Blueberry Festival.

Left to right are:
(Back row) Fred Gore, Duane Wirick, Don Lehman, Cloyd Hulver, Dale Wentz, Art McLaughlin, Paul Fisher, Don Jesson.
(Second row) Roger Jesson, Ronald Bender, John Wirick, Gene Wirick, Richard Beighley, Jim Wentz, Marvin Bender.
(Front row) Donald Prosser, Rob Rinehart, Otis Kinton, Don Hurrell, Fred McLaughlin, Rob Wentz, Wayne Detrow.

Lexington's Boy Scout Troop 1 won the Hillier Trophy, which was given by the Johnny Appleseed Council to the best troop for outstanding advancement. This picture was taken sometime in 1947. Troops 131 and 152 were formed when Troop 1 became too large and was divided in the late 1950s.

The Gass Family

William Gass was a truly remarkable pioneer. Born in Pennsylvania in 1769, he worked his way west over the years settling just east of Mt. Vernon in 1806. The Mt. Vernon area could only boast of "five or six inhabitants" and the Gass family consisted of a wife and four boys, Benjamin, James R., John, and William Jr. A daughter Elizabeth, born in 1800, was kicked in the forehead by a colt in 1805 and died a month later.

The second son, James R. Gass, would in later years write a detailed account of the family history and their eventual move to Troy Township, which was then known as the "New Purchase." A copy of this account was given to the writer by Mr. and Mrs. Russell Cline, Gass family descendents, in 1966, just before they moved to Arizona. Gass was to write:

In October 1811, Father, Uncle Francis Mitchell and Joseph Mitchell prepared for camping out a few nights and determined to explore part of the new purchase. They were gone three or four days and were so well pleased with the wild country that father selected the west half of section 12, township 20 (Note, Troy) and range 19, and Francis Mitchell the south west quarter of section 11. The land office was then at Canton to which place father hurried and entered his half section and also the quarter section for Francis Mitchell. These were the first land entries in this township.

We were all anxious to see our land in the new purchase, so on the last day of October, 1811, brother Benjamin and I each mounted on a two year old colt, father riding an older mare, all furnished with a few

Photograph courtesy of Helen Steiner Smith
The log two-story home of William Gass was built in the 1813-1814 era. Years later a frame addition enlarged the home, doubling its size. The log portion was torn down in 1947, leaving the present day half a house.

Photograph courtesy of Helen Steiner Smith

This house on the corner of Cook and Lexington-Springmill roads is the remaining half of the William Gass 1813 home. The log portion was to the left before it was torn down in 1947. The 1812 blockhouse was located on the front lawn.

days rations, blankets, axe and guns, and posted off to the Mohican. Night overtook us soon after crossing the creek where Bowers grist mill stands. We struck our fire, tied up our horses and camped out for the night in an old vacated Indian Wigwam. Early in the morning of Nov. 1, 1811 we pursued our journey through the woods but along an Indian trail and halted to warm, as it was a cold cloudy morning, at an Indian village of some six or seven families. An Indian trail from there to Upper Sandusky passed through our land so we followed it until we arrived at our premises, then built up a large fire some two or three rods north of where A. O. Eastman's saw mill stands. Father was desirous of seeing the south east quarter of section 11 so he tied the fore feet of our mare closely together and turned our ponies out to pasture in the run bottom – left me to keep camp while he and Benjamin steered off west to view the land. The day seemed long and dreary to me as it was cold and snowy. They returned in the afternoon much pleased with the land so we brought up our horses and camped for the night.

Saturday morning, Nov. 2, 1811 a clear frosty morning, after feeding our horses a few ears of corn which we brought with us, we took an early start for home well pleased with our premises. We steered east into what is now Washington township until we reached the State road from Mt. Vernon to Mansfield, which was opened so that wagons could barely pass then south to where Bellville now is.

Their campsite was just north of the west end of Hanley Road next to the present bike trail.

After selling their Knox County farm in the spring of 1812, the Gass family prepared to move to Troy Township. William Gass with sons Benjamin and James R., a hired hand, a three-horse team, and a wagon load of tools and provisions, made the three-day trip to the new land. They cleared off a site at the present-day southeast corner of Cook and Lexington-Springmill Roads and built a rough log cabin 14 feet square. Two young cousins were hired to start clearing a field and split 2,000 fence rails.

After some delays they left Knox County with two borrowed Pennsylvania wagons loaded with household goods hitched with five-horse teams. The trip from Mt. Vernon took three days and the last few miles they had to cut a road for the long teams to pass. They arrived at their new home April 23, 1812. They continued to clear land and make improvements until the war with Great Britain broke out that summer and after the Copus and Ruffner Indian massacres they, with others, fled back south to Knox County.

James R. Gass was to write:

Father with us were back to see our premises every few days. So he got a number of our old neighbors who were soldiers to assist in transforming our cabin into a block house, which was accomplished by taking logs we had provided for a larger house and with them building the upper story of the cabin two feet wider than the lower, having the logs extend out a foot in all corners leaving a space all around and affording a chance to shoot down the outside of the lower wall and affording numerous port holes for firing out at a foe.

The block house was never attacked and after the Indians were removed from this area the larger log cabin was no doubt completed sometime in the 1813-14 period. The dark brown house that now stands on that corner was in reality a later addition to the two-story log cabin. They shared a common roof line and an opening or "dog trot" was between the two. The 1813 log cabin portion to the north was torn down sometime around 1947. The block house stood, according to James R. Gass, about 50 or 60 feet in front of the house now standing on that corner. Hastily built of round logs for temporary shelter it was no doubt used as a barn until decay ended its useful life. Its existence was never recorded in the early Richland County histories.

The site was selected by Gass due to a free flowing spring just a few feet to the north along present-day Cook Road. Until the age of the automobile, water was piped down to a watering trough at the corner for the use by those passing by. The water then flowed into a small stream in the valley called Isaac's Run which was named after an Indian who once lived along its banks.

In that rough pioneer era, William Gass was elected to the State Legislature in 1813 for Knox and Richland counties and re-elected again the following year. He and his children became influential leaders in what was once known as the "Gass Settlement." William gave each of his sons a quarter section of his land and they prospered. The families were deeply involved in the Underground Railroad prior to the Civil War.

William's brother, Patrick Gass, was a remarkable character. Born in June, 1771, he grew up to be a rough frontiersman, carpenter, and soldier. He knew Daniel Boone, was fond of whiskey, and was known for fighting and riotous behavior. He was also a sergeant on the 1804-1806 Lewis and Clark expedition from St. Louis across the Rocky Mountains to the Pacific and back.

Patrick Gass kept a journal of the expedition that was first published in 1807. It was an immediate hit, although he received only 100 copies for his share of the venture. During the War of 1812, Patrick enlisted and lost an eye in the battle of Lundy's Lane. Afterwards, he returned to the family home near Wellsburg, West Virginia.

The frontier area around Wellsburg had changed, so he left. He came to Mansfield and, no doubt, the Lexington area where he worked as a carpenter and chased down stray horses. His father, Benjamin, died in 1827 and he returned to Wellsburg, where in 1831, at age 60, he took a 20-year-old wife and fathered seven children. In 1858, he found religion and was baptized in the Ohio River before a good sized crowd, who must have wondered if his past sins could be washed away. From booze to preaching, he became an exhorter for the Campbellite church and was an attention-holding speaker, who traveled for that denomination. He was well-remembered for being in this area and for the change of character from those who knew him previously.

His wife died in 1849 leaving him with six children to raise, one just an infant, and a different lifestyle than in his early years. The mellowed old soldier died in April

The James R. Gass home, built in 1843, was a station on the Underground Railroad.

of 1870 at the home of his daughter. He was 99 and had outlived every member of the Lewis and Clark Expedition. The heroic Patrick was laid to rest beside his wife Maria in a Brook County, WV cemetery in graves that were unmarked until a century later.

Ironically, the mother of William and Patrick Gass is believed to be buried in an unmarked grave in the Troy cemetery. She came here after her husband died in 1827. She died in 1831. No grave marker has been found, possibly lost in the years the place was not maintained.

In the family history, written by James R. Gass, he recorded this event while the family was still living in the Mt. Vernon area:

I think it was in December, 1806 that Uncle Patrick called on us on his way home from his long journey up the Missouri and down the Columbia rivers with Captains Lewis and Clark. This is the first time I can remember seeing him. He was riding on an elegant red and white spotted horse and was steering for his parent's home in Brook Co. W. Va., and remained with us some eight or ten days.

James R. Gass built the beautiful sandstone house on Lexington-Springmill Road in 1843. Sadly, his wife Jane would not enjoy its beauty. She died, on August 28, 1843, during childbirth and the newborn infant died six weeks later. The home was always a landmark and once served as a station on the Underground Railroad.

His lengthy family history is well written. It was republished in the Biographical History of Richland County Ohio 1983, by the Richland County Genealogical Society. It is most interesting and recommended reading.

Sgt. Patrick Gass, 1771-1870, was a member of the famous Lewis and Clark Expedition and worked in the Lexington area for awhile.

Those Daring Young Men

Lexington once had an airport of sorts. It was Wright Armstrong's cow pasture at the top of the hill on Delaware Street. Lexington Court and the Church of Christ now sit where airplanes once buzzed low to get the cattle out of the way so they could make a reasonably safe, but bumpy landing.

Russell Gledhill from Galion was among the first to land his open cockpit WACO "F" biplane in that pasture. This was sometime around 1938. Gledhill was a barnstormer, that is, he landed all sorts of different places so he could earn a little money taking passengers aloft. The pilot sat in the back, passenger in the front.

Gledhill, from Galion, started flying in 1929 after he graduated from Park's Air College in St. Louis. He did a lot of barnstorming and was a really good pilot. After gaining the required 200 hours, he was licensed to haul passengers.

When the barnstormers showed up in Lexington, it took a real thrillseeker to be among the first customers. An aerial view of Lexington was something to brag about, but there was a lot of danger. The planes were old, the skill of the pilot was unknown, and there was no insurance on airplane, pilot or passengers. Heck, it had only been 30 years since the Wrights first flight.

A 10-year-old kid named Lloyd Whitney was one of those early 1938 daredevils. One trip aloft with Gledhill and he knew he had to learn how to fly! And he did just that, qualifying for a pilot's license in 1944 at age 16.

Lloyd took lessons at Gages' field near Ontario, a site now occupied by General Motors. Gages was a grass field with two small buildings and no airplane hangers. Out in farm country, it wasn't much to look at as far as airports go.

On practice flights Whitney used to fly low over a house near Waterford Road south of town. A pretty girl named Shirley lived down there. He would toss out a weighted note as he passed. None of these missiles of affection ever hit the young lady, but she got the message. Mrs. Shirley Whitney later claimed it was the first airmail she ever got.

Jeff Treisch and Al Mulberg owned this 1929 Keith Ryder biplane. Treisch was a barnstormer, hauling passengers for a penny a pound when this 1938 photo was taken.

Gledhill's friend Jeff Treisch, also from Galion, hauled passengers at county fairs, air shows, and soon in a 1929 Keith-Ryder biplane. The cost of a flight was a penny a pound. Treisch later bought a 10-year-old, 1929 Curtis Robin OX-5 for $450, did his own mechanical work, and made money.

Several other pilots from Galion and Jim Bender from Bellville were all familiar with the Lexington's "cow pasture landing field." Bender, a World War II B-17 pilot, became a part-time salesman for Piper Aircraft. He later bought a 1946 Piper Cub J3, which he flew from his farm field near Bellville. In 1948, he built a Quonset-hut type hanger that could hold five planes. The 60' x 1,500' grass runway Bellville field was a regular stop for local pilots until recent years.

But times caught up with those daring young men. Gledhill had a family to support and spent more and more time running the Gledhill Lumber Company in Galion. Treisch too, had to sell his beloved Robin for $900 at the end of World War II. Federal regulations mandated insurance, and higher gas prices made the cost of ownership too expensive. Bender operated an airfield of sorts to survive. Whitney still delivered the mail - by Chevrolet - out of the Lexington Post Office.

Whitney recalls renting Bender's Piper Cub J3 and landing in Lexington's cow pasture airport during the summer of 1947. It may have been one of the last if not the last airplane to do so. New houses, trees and the march of progress had slowly closed the curtain on Lexington aviation. Evidently, no one had ever asked for permission to land there anyway

Photograph courtesy of John Gledhill Family
Russell Gledhill was the first to land an airplane in Lexington. This photo dates to World War II, when he was training pilots.

A Future History

Some day someone will set down another chapter of this area we call Lexington. Perhaps that person will record some of the many things this book missed or had to pass by and take a look at the people and historic events still to come. This is an interesting place to live, full of just plain folks, some of which have that oh so special trait of character or genius that will make them memorable. Who will the future leaders be?

In the writer's opinion, in the past there have been four men who greatly impacted this place. Quite naturally Amariah Watson the founder is one. Local genius Harry Smith and homegrown Cleveland lawyer – farm owner William "Bud" Cockley both steered the town to a lake and water supply while helping to oversee the future town growth. John Morley had a vision of what a planned community should look like and brought it into being. All had support and problems to overcome along the way.

There were the business and industrial leaders who left their mark along with the preachers, teachers and elected officials. Hard work and taxes gave us the best school system in the area and good parks. But our forefathers built wooden buildings on Main Street which burned down leaving us in the present day with a mishmash of architecture that lacks the charm of a Bellville. That will be hard to improve. Traffic will be another problem.

Lexington will soon have grown from a village into a city. To continue to be a great place to live, it will need an employment base. Lexington is fortunate to have the firms now located and growing in its industrial areas. More opportunities for expansion must be available and encouraged.

However, a town is known by its people. Lexington has a wonderful character of its own and within its bounds are to be found some real characters. One may be reading this book.

Index

102 Ohio Volunteer Infantry,, 99
1850 Lexington Schoolhouse, 15
1878 History of Wayne County, 132
1904 Curved Dash Oldsmobile, 120
1929 Keith Ryder biplane, 238
1934-35 Basketball team, 231

A

A Scrapbook of Lexington School History, 209
A. B. Beverstock and Moses Sowers, 112
A. C. Kell Hardware, 205
A. O. Eastman's saw mill, 234
Abernathy, Dr., 92
Abernathy, Maylor, 54
Ackerman's journalism class, 40
Adams, John F.,111
Allis Chalmers, 162-163, 186
Alspach, A., 25
Alta Greenhouse, 83
Alta Hill, 83
Alta Rifle Club, 83
Altgeld, John Peter, 220
American Baptist Society of Philadelphia, 212
American Pie Pizza, 149
Amish country, 132
Ammon, Jacob, 132
Anderson, Dr., 92
Anderson, Wm., 108, 110
Andretti, Mario, 197
Andrews family, 221
Andrews, D. K., 56, 109
Andrews, Mayor, 50
Applegate, Harry, 179
Applegate, Paul, 226
Appleseed Shopping Center, 159
Appleseed, Johnny, 114
Arehart, Robert, 154
Argus Images, 207
Argus Silkscreen, 207
Armstrong, Delaware Chief Thomas, 8
Armstrong, Leland, 154
Armstrong, Mayor Emery, 165
Armstrong, Richard, 149, 158
Armstrong, Rolla, 1
Armstrong, Wright, 48, 153
Armstrong's Royal Blue Market, 119
Associate Reformed Presbyterian Church, 217
Aten's Meat Market, 149
Atmosphere, 153
Auer, Jacob, 28
Auditor of State of Ohio, 174

B

B&O Cedar Point Excursion Special, 76
B&O Railroad, 2, 47, 71, 83, 102, 143, 176, 185, 205
Bachelder, Ella, 191
Bachelder, Virgil, 194
Bachelors Club, 36, 191
Bailey, Capt Daniel, 107, 109
Baker, Col., 98
Baker, Gen. L. C., 98-99
Baker, Isaac, 108, 110
Baker, Ray, 33
Baker, William *Bill*, 205
Baldwin, 13
Baldwin Class Q1, 73
Baldwin, Harvey, 22
Baptists, 218
Barber, Tom, 159
Barnes, Joseph, 110
Barnes, Simon, 108, 110
Barnett, Andrew, 213
Barney Kroger's stores, 149
Barney, T. C., 109
Barnum, Dr., 92
Barr, Oliver, 108, 110
Barr, R. P., 107, 109
Battle of Lundy's Lane, 235
Baughman, A. J., 27
Baughman, Jacob, 22
Baughman, Josias, 114
Baughman, Mrs., 22
Baughman, Wilson, 108, 110
Bauman's Pool Room, 129
Baumgard, Mr., 187
Bechtel, Fred, 206
Bechter, Charles, 95
Bechtoll, Solomon, 110
Beckley, Jacob, 215
Bectel, A. E., 84
Bectel, Adam, 84
Becthell, Solomon, 108
Beighley, Richard, 232
Bell Family, 28
Bell Tavern, 28
Bell, Deputy Sheriff Tom, 49
Bell, Robert, 27
Bellville Star, 25
Bellville Street Fair, 231
Bellville's first tavern, 33
Bender, Jim, 239
Bender, Marvin, 232
Bender, Ronald, 232
Berea Milling Co., 205
Berry, Mark and Barb, 115
Berzzarins, Dr. Val, 92
Betchel family, 221
Beverage, Ira, 179
Beverstock family, 221
Beverstock General Store, 118-119
Beverstock, A. B., 56, 117-119, 121-122, 149, 169
Beverstock, Allen, 30, 118-119
Beverstock, Barney, 108, 110
Beverstock, Frank, 44, 110
Beverstock, Fred, 107-108, 110

Index

Beverstock, Rollin, 121
Beverstock, Silas, 107-110
Bezzarins, Dr. Val, 93
Bicentennial Park, 17
Biddle, Jim, 226
Biddlecome, Rev, 213
Big Store, 229
Bigbee & VanBusirk, 68
Bigelow, Russell, 214
Bikar, Pete, 141, 145
Billman, Rev. George, 222
Biographical History of Richland County Ohio 1983, 236
Bishop, Red, 156
Blair, Deputy Marshall, 36
Blair, James, 47, 54, 107, 109
Blair, Mayor, 146
Blair, Melvin, 49
Blair, Samuel, 108, 110
Blair, William, 107, 109
Blann, Brubaker, 10
Bliven, C. E., 56
block house, 235
Blueberry Festival, 231
Boals, Daniel, 107, 109
Boals, Joseph, 107, 109
Board of Public Affairs, 5
Boe, Clyde, 226
Boggs & Son, 191
Boggs Tinware Shop, 115
Boggs, Ezekiel, 107, 109
Boggs, Francis, 218
Boggs, James, 191
Bogner, Bertha, 103
Bohham & Ritchie, 127
Bonham, Bill, 127
Bonner, Issac, 110
Boone, Daniel, 235
Boosters Club, 188
Booth, John Wilkes, 99
Boston Coolers, 157
Bowers Road bridge, 187
Bowland, Thomas, 108
Bowser, Martin, 108, 110
Boy Scout Troop, 131   225
Boyce, Harold, 68
Brannon, Patrick, 110
Brickcrete, 164
Brinkerhoff family, 221
Bromfield, Louis, 132
Brooker Brothers Trucking, 100
Brooks, B&O Detective, 49, 50
Brotherhood of Electrical Workers union, 168
Brown family, 158
Brown, Col. Robert C., 94, 108, 110, 220
Brown, Corporal Aaron Moses, 143
Brown, Mary (Gailey), 47
Brown, Walter, 155
Brownie, 143, 144
Brumenshenkel, Carl, 200-201
Brumenshenkel, Linda, 200
Bryan, William Jennings, 221

Buckhorn Schoolhouse, 33
Buckhorn Tavern, 30, 32, 217
Bucklew, Leland, 62
Bungtown, 85
Bureau River, 13
Burkepile, Buck and Betty, 152
Burkhart Lumber Co., 83
Bush, Ray, 28
Butch Castor's Sohio Service Station, 149
Butler, 8

C

Cable TV Company, 33
Caldwell, Samuel, 22, 116
Callender, Jack, 50
Cambell, Mary Ann, 105
Cambell, R. B., 108, 110
Camel Back locomotives, 72
Camp Reynolds, 160
Campbell, Ruby, 105, 223
Campbell, William, 216-217
Canterbury, Robert, 62
Canton Workhouse, 50
Carey, Dr. Cora, 92
Carey, Dr. George, 92, 107, 109
Carey, John, 110
Carey, Mason, 92
Carpenter, Alonzo, 108, 110
Carpenter, Harold, 205
Carpenter, Justice, 107, 109
Carpenter, Robert, 205
Carrothers, John, 107, 109
Carter Tavern, 33
Carter, Ed, ix
Carter, grandfather, 174
Carter, Jeff, 194
Carter, Miller, 108, 110
Carter, Richard M., 60
Carter, Robert, 33, 154
Carter, Samuel, 18, 116
Cashell, Walter *Mick*, 153
Cass and Cousins, 128
Cass, James, 108, 110
Castor family, 102
Castor, Bill, 53
Castor, Charles, 100
Castor, Irwin *Butch*, 58, 150, 229
Castor, Nelson, 49
Castor, Robert, 100, 102
Castor, Sgt. Robert L., 101
Castor, William, 100, 102
Castor's Economy Garage, 150, 229
Catholics, 223
Centennial Exposition, 138
Certified Oil Company, 155-156
Chalfant Family, 208
Chalfant, Charles, 50
Chalfant, Chester, 50-51, 179
Chalfant, Ruth, 50-51, 106

Index

Charlie Hartenfelt's High Speed Bulk Plant, 149
Chase, Silas, 108, 110
Chatterton, Mr., 179
Chester Baptist Church, 212, 218
Chindler, Wm., 108, 110
Christ Lutheran Church, 222
Christian Klink distillery, 114
Church of Christ, 56, 222
Church of God, 223
Church of Lexington, 216
Church of the Cross, 93, 222
City Berberton, 56
Civil War veterans, 95
Clark, Ephraim, 12
Clark, Ezekiel, 113
Clark, Ichabod, 66, 113
Clark, Jesse, 215
Clark, Joe, 156
Clear Fork Dam, 2
Clear Fork Hills, 159
Clear Fork Reservoir, 185, 188, 205
Clear Fork Valley, 7-8, 212
Cleland, Harvey, 107, 110
Cleland, Hoyt, 139
Clever, George, 59, 104, 149
Clever, Kenny, 149
Clever, Lloyd, 59, 153
Clever, Sam, 83
Cline, Jack, 61-62, 66, 72-73, 75
Cline, Mr. and Mrs. Russell, 233
Clover Hill School, 19
Cloverleaf Community Club, 85
Clymer, Betty, 93
Clymer, Dr. David, 92-93
Cobey, Herbert T., 40-41
Cochran, David, 138
Cochran, Dick, 194
Cockley & Galbraith, 121, 149, 177
Cockley family, 221
Cockley farm, 155, 184
Cockley Mill, 56, 77, 118-120, 122, 126, 128, 205
Cockley Road pit, 195
Cockley Steam Roller Mill, 116
Cockley, Allen B., 110
Cockley, Benjamin and Fannie, 117
Cockley, Capt. W. W., 108, 110, 118
Cockley, Katherine, 48, 184, 188
Cockley, Mary U. (Beverstock), 117, 147
Cockley, Rollin, 48, 123, 153
Cockley, W. B., 109
Cockley, W. W., 117, 119-120, 122, 147, 149, 184, 190
Cockley, William *Bud*, 120, 154-155, 165, 184, 240
Cockley's Mansion, 184
Cockley's Wiliben Farm, 165
Coffman, John H., 110
Colckley, W. W., 177
Coleman & Alexander, 21
Coleman, Adna, 21, 107, 109, 111
Coleman, George, 13, 22, 108, 110
Coleman, Obediah, 110
Coleman, P. T., 116

Coleman, Tom, 30
Collins, Jim, 68
Columbus and Lake Erie Railroad, 71
Columbian Grange #1393, 15
Columbus Dispatch, 139
Columbus Grove, 170
Colwell, Mrs. John Maggie, 141-142
Colwell, Samuel, 107, 109
Company C, 15th Regiment, OVI, 81
Company C, 86th OVI, 117
Company D, 45th Regiment, Indiana Calvary Corps, 94
Company D, Ohio Veterans Reserves, 94
Company G, Ohio Volunteer Infantry, 94
Company L, 10th Ohio Volunteer Calvary, 94
Conger family, 221
Conger Post of the 85, 81, 94, 97
Conger, Col. Everton J., 97-99
Conger, Major Seymore Beach, 97-98, 108, 110
Conger, Rev. Enoch, 97-98
Conger, Seymore, 214
Congregational Church, 55, 126
Congregationalists, 217
Cook, Amos, 213
Cook, Carter, 222
Cook, Daniel, 213
Cook, Henry, 213
Cook, Jacob, 10, 12, 21, 111, 213, 222
Cook, John, 213
Cook, Logan, 108, 110
Cook, Lt Jessie J., 108, 110
Cook, Mrs. John, 35
Cook, Noah, 212-213, 222
Cook, Orville, 222
Cook, Rachel, 213
Cook, Thomas, 112
Cook, William, 213
Cook's Tavern, 22, 111
Coon, Jacob, 107
Coonses, 10
Cooper, Col., 190
Corbett, John, 107, 110
Corners, 90
Corners Restaurant, 143, 157, 164, 203
Cornman, Robert, 108, 110
Corwin, Bud, 213
Cottage Reading Circle, 83
County Museum, 209
Courtney, Elzy, 108, 110
Cover, Asa, 33
Covered bridge, 17
Coyner, Harness, 108, 110
Coyner, Wm., 108, 110
Cracraft, Charles, 108, 110
Craig, Beva, 56
Crain Mill, 120
Crawford, Col. William, 212
Crawford, Colonel, 8
Crep's Meat Market, 155, 203
Creps brothers, 155
Cring Reality, 153
Cromwell, Rev., 158

Index

Crooks, General, 10
Croxton, General John C.,117
Cullen, Michael, 139
Cullen, Paul, 90-91, 164
Cully, Lee, 32-33
Culp Building, 149
Culp, C. D., 108
Culp, Cliff, 68
Culp, Columbus D., 110
Culp, George, 107, 109
Culp, Jefferson, 108, 110
Culver, Calvin, 7, 10, 48
Cunitz, George, 189
Cunningham, John, 107, 110
Cunningham, William, 49
Cureton, Samuel, 128
Cureton, Tom, 179
Curtis, Col., 69
Curtner, Better, 194
Curtner, Lloyd, 194
Custer Hotel, 35
Custer House, 23-25
Custer, George, 24-25
Custer, Justice (of the Peace), 146
Cyclone, H. Williams, 35

D

Dailey, 13
Dailey potato storage building, 133
Daily Sanduskian, 71
Damsell, William, 107, 109, 111-112
Darrenberger's pool room, 133
Darrow, Clarence, 221
Dauch, Philip, 67
Davidson, Robert, 206
Day, Cyrus, 108, 110
Day, Orva, 75, 228
Dayton Electrical Engineering Laboratories Company, 182
Decker, Max, 156
Decker's, 155-156
Deeds, Edward, 181
Deems, Lewis, 107, 109
Delamater, Harriet, 24
Delamater, James, 108
Delaware Indian villages, 8
Delaware Road (now US 41), 17
Delco, 182
Delco Farm Lighting system, 182
Delmater, James, 110
Delong, Chet, 206
Delong, Curry, 206
Dennis, Charles, 107, 110
Dennis, Jacob, 97, 107
Dennis, Jake, 95
Derrenberger Pool Room, 151
Derrenbergers Pharmacy, 149, 203
Detrow, Wayne, 232
Dial, Harvey, 56

Dickson, Louie, 1-2
Dickson, William, 25
Dill, Carl, 87
Dill, Wynonia, 105
Dill's Café, 87
Dillon, Denny, 27
Dilly, Samuel, 108, 110
DiSalle, Governor Michael V., 50
Dollar Kodak, 53
Drivers Club, 91
Dunlap, Jan, 189
Dunshee Family, 33
Dunshee, Mr. , 139
Dunshee, T. E., 15
Durant, Charles, 182
Dye, Daniel, 110
Dyeart, Rev. Thomas, 222

E

Eagle Scout, 207
Earhart, Myrtle, 53
Earhart, Sid, 53, 67-68, 86, 95, 97, 139, 143, 179, 226
Earhart, W. H., 190
Earhart, William, 48
Eastern Elementary, 168
Eastgate, John, 108, 110
Easton, Mr., 113
Eaton, E. S., 186
Eckert, Arthur, 84
Eckert, Ermina, 84
Eckert, Orlando, 84
Edge, Tom, 155
Eggert & Weldon's general store, 85
Ehrlich, Toby, 164
Eller, Harvey, 22
Embarq phone building, 30
Engine 389, 77
Englehart family, 221
Englehart General Store, 67
Englehart, President A. G., 37
EPA, 167
Erb, C. F. *Old Erb*, 83
Essex Wire Corporation, 166-167
Evangelical United Brethren Mission Church, 222
Evans, Rev., 216
Eyerly, Jacob, 108, 110

F

Farm Bureau, 196
farm vacation service, 86
Farmers Hotel, 23-24
Farquhar, Wm., 10
Farst, William, 90
Faust, Barb, 96
Fellows, Jim, 228

Index

Fergeson, James, 108, 110
Ferrell brothers, 86
Ferrow Bros., 67
Fighler, John, 179
fighting Winbiglers, 85
Fillings, Calvin, 52
Fillings, Lexington Marshal Calvin, 50
Finkbeiner, Pettis and Strout, 189
Finney, Bill, 33
Finney, Robert, 217
Fire Fighter's Club, 58
Fires, 54
first bridge in Lexington, 16
First National Bank, 122, 158
First non-Indian child, 8
First Postmaster of Lexington, 12
First road tax, 16
Fisher, Paul, 62, 151, 232
Fisher's Mobile station, 62
Fix, Robert, 108, 110
Fleck, Harold, 195
Fleck, Harvey, 194-195
Fokner, Hugh, 132-133
Follen, Deputy Marshal, 47
Folmer, George, 197
Foltz, Augustus, 84
Ford and Studebaker dealership, 57
Ford, Charles, 147
Ford, Doc, 171
Ford, Emma, see Smith, Emma (Ford)
Ford, Robert, 146-147
Fox, Georgia, 9, 13
Fox, Vincenz, 67
France, Mr., 59
Frecka, David, 207
Frederick Street, 2
Freiheit, Greg, 25
Freisch, Jacob, 109
Frigidaire Division of General Motors, 182
Frush, Dr. Riley England, 92
Frush, Dr. Wertz, 93
Fry, G. M., 22, 48, 54
Fry's three-story frame candy factory, 55
Frye family, 221
Frye, G. V., 126
Frye, George, 128
Frye, Kathryn, 127
Frye, Mayme Carey, 127
Frye, Rev. Geroge V., 126
Frye's candy factory, 126
Frye's Caramel factory, 126-127
Fuhrer, Dan, 162-163
Fuhrer, John and Mary, 79
Fuhrer, John Henry, 205
Fullmer, Desdemonia, 218

G

Gages' field, 238
Gailbraith family, 221
Gailey Seminary, 84, 115, 191
Gailey, Rev. Richard, 219, 220-222
Gailey, Catherine, 222
Gailey, Jane, 219-220, 222
Gailey, John, 108, 110
Gailey, Mary, 219-220
Gailey, Rev. John, 222
Gailey, Rev. Richard, 47, 108, 110, 217-218
Gailey, Richard Jr., 190, 222
Galbraith, *Buzz*, 66
Galbraith, George, 121, 149, 174
Galbraith, Robert, 121
Galion Airport, 86
Gambles' Lunch Room, 100
Garber, D. W., 30, 113, 139
Garber, John L., 194-195
Garber, Les, 84
Garfield, President James A., 118
Garret, Ed, 37
Garrison's Mill, 17
Garver, Samuel, 109
Garver, Sherm, 48-49
Garverick, Ada, 134-135
Garverick, I. W., 149
Garverick, Maurice *Boots*, 59, 133-136
Garverick, Max, 135
Garverick's welding shop, 135
Gass family, 217, 233, 235
Gass Settlement, 235
Gass, Benjamin, 233, 235
Gass, Elizabeth, 233
Gass, James R., 59, 233, 235-236
Gass, Jane, 236
Gass, John, 233
Gass, Patrick, 235-237
Gass, William, 7, 110, 223, 233-236
Gatton, Cy, 141
Gcraig, Beva, 56
General Motors, 182
George Carter farm, 133
George, Jacob, 33
George, John, 226, 229
George, Mayor William, 47
George, Reverend Henry, 212
Georgia Institute of Technology, 164
Gerhart, Wade, 50
Gibson, Sally, 143
Gilt Edge Terpsichorean Club, 35
Girl Scouts, 52
Gleckner, Jack, 115
Gledhill Lumber Company, 239
Gledhill, Russell, 238-239
Glen, Dr., 92
Goff, John, 108
Goon, Jacob, 110

Index

Gore, Albert, 72-73, 224
Gore, Claude, 4, 77-78
Gore, Fred, 232
Gore, Richard, 5-6
Gorman Nature Center, 29
Gorman, Jim, 160
Grace Brethern Church, 112, 222
Graham, J. J., 108, 110
Graham, John, 145
Graham, Morris, 1-2, 145
Graham, Morris and Jenny, 146-147
Grand Army of the Republic, 94
Grange Library, 83
Grant, Homer, 194
Grasshopper pie, 88
Graves, Clarisa (Watson), 14
Graves, Sterling, 12, 14, 66, 113
Great snake, 169
Green, Francis, 64
Green, Sterling, 158, 217
Green, Tom, 158
Green's Hatchery, 64, 149
Greentown, 8
Gregg, David, 220
Grice, Matthew, 108, 110
Griebling, Anna, 139
Griebling, Carroll, 197
Griebling Family, 113
Griebling, Frank, 38, 114, 139, 158
Griebling, Jacob, 113
Griebling, John and Jennie, 137
Griebling, Lester Clever *Les*, 196-197
Griebling, Louis, 211
Griebling Gristmill, 83
Griebling's Troy Mill, 114
Gristmill, 8
Groff, John, 110
Grubb, Henry, 107, 110
Grubb, President, 37
Guidenberg, 226
Gulf Oil station, 50

H

H. P. Maxwell grocery, 34, 49
Habitat for Humanity, 93
Haflic, Phillip, 108, 110
Hahn, Benjamin, 92
Hahn, Dr. David, 92, 116
Hahn, Rev. Benjamin D., 116
Hahn's Mill, 218
Hainer, Carrie, 177
Hainer, LuDella, 9, 188
Hainer, Margaret, see Smith, Margaret
Hainer, Mr. and Mrs. John, 177
Hainer, Mrs., 105
Halderman, John, 12, 21-22
Hall, C. J., 77

Hamilton, Mayor, 47
Hanawalt family, 115
Hanawalt, John, 114
Hancocck Albert, 44
Hand, Avery, 164
Hardee restaurant, 88
Harding, George, 84
Harding, President Warren G., 84
Harry Smith Collection, 1
Harry Smith's factory, 126
Hart Brothers, 151
Hartman Electric Manufacturing Company, 164, 168
Hartman, Albert W., 168
Hartman, Lew, 164
Hartzlers, 84
Harvey Fleck and Son, 195
Haynes, Joe, 132
Heatherington, Florence, 84
Heatherington, Wilbur, 84
Heidlebaugh, Gloria (Ferguson), 104
Heidlebaugh, LT Rollin, 103-105
Helltown, 8
Henderson, Dr. James, 130
Hendrickson, Walter 82
Henry J Custom Roadster, 134
Henry, Roger, 84
Herring, John, 114
Heskett, A., 124
Heskett, Al, 75
Heskett, E., 124
Hethrington, Wesly, 108, 110
Heyser, Artie, 105
Heyser, Charles Russell Speed, 102-103
Heyser, Elias, 108, 110
Hi-Fi Haven, 207
Hi-Stat Manufacturing Company, Inc., 207
Hickok Oil Co., 77
Highway Patrol, 165
Hildebrand, Bonne, ix
Hill, George, 120
Hill, William H., 110
Hillier Trophy, 232
Hire, C. John *Jack*, 207
Hirth, Bill, 58
Hirth, William, 1
Hiser, Hugh, 156
Hiser, Hugh and Marie, 156-157
Hiser, Marie, 86, 156-157
Hiser, Mert and Hugh, 157
Hiser's Sandwich Bar, 65, 156
Hiskey Alice, 84
Hiskey, Albert, 84
Hiskey, George, 84
Hiskey, Henry, 108, 110
Hiskey, Leroy, 84
Hiskey, Samuel, 108, 110
Hiskey place, 112
History of Seneca County, 132
History of Wyandot, 132
Hively, Adam, 72, 83
Hochstetler, Elias, 132

Index

Hoffman, Frederick, 110
Hoffner, Ed, 164
Hoffner, Jack, 164
Hoffner, John, 164
Holiday Hill, 159
Holton, P. L., 108, 110
Home Savings and Loan bank building, 26
Homerick, Sam, 128, 179
Hook and Laddar Company Number One of Lexington, 54
Horn, Claude, 226
Hoverstick, May, 105
Howe Fire Wagon, 56
Howell, William, 33
Hugh Hiser's Sandwich Bar, 143
Hughes, Art, 128
Hughinart, Mr., 1
Hulbner Brewing of Toledo, 66
Hull, Brigadier General William, 8
Hull, Harley, 72
Hull's Surrender, 10
Hulver, Cloyd, 232
Hurrell, Don, 232
Hyser, Tod, 102

I

Iberia College, 84
Icabod Clark's distillery, 66, 219
Indiana Condensed Milk Company, 124
Indiantown, 14
Ingram, William, 194
Ink, Charles, 153
Ireland, David, 149
Isaac's Run, 235

J

J. E. Slaybaugh & Assoc., 23
J. Lortchen Hotel, 33
Jackson, Frank, 108, 110
Jackson, Mrs., 158
Jacob Cook's Tavern, 16
Jagger, John, 151
James McClure's Tavern, 21
James, Frank and Jessie, 145, 147-148
James, Perry, 147
Jarvi, Nicholi, 35
Jennings-Lawrence, 185
Jerome, John Baptiste, 8
Jerome's Town, 8
Jesson, Don, 232
Jesson, Roger, 232
John F. Adams and Willaim Damsell drygoods partnership, 112
John John's Hotel, 33
John Newcomer's school bus garage, 134
Johnny Appleseed Council, 232
Johnny Appleseed Shopping Center, 40
Johnson, Delos, 107, 109, 174

Jones & Brown, 154
Jones, Al, 145
Jones, Day, Cockley & Reavis, 184
Jones, Dr. Johannes, 132
Jones, Harlen, 44
Joslin Hotel, 23, 25
Joslin, C. C., 83
Joslin, Charles, 25
Joslin, S. B., 118
Jugs Corner, 84-85
Jugs Grange, 84-85, 201
Jugs School, 85

K

Kaiser, Henry J., 134
Kaschates, 130
Kell Brothers, 192
Kell Brothers Hardware, 191
Kell Hardware, 55, 122, 149, 153, 158, 174, 176, 191, 193-194, 196
Kell, Art, 193-194
Kell, Arthur C., 192
Kell, Marshall, 191
Kell, Martin, 191-192
Kell, Thad, 191-192
Keller, Daniel, 107, 109-110
Keller, James, 108, 110
Keller, James, 11
Kenny Foundry, 128
Kettering, Charles, 128, 181-183, 188
Kiinton, Officer Raymond, 52
Killigan, John, 107
King, D. L., 108
King, David L., 110
King, Jacob, 114
Kinton, Eddis and Dorothy, 87-88
Kinton, Harold, 159
Kinton, Otis, 232
Kinton's Market, 203
Kinton's Orchard Park Market, 87
Kirkwood, Governor Samuel J., 23
Kirkwood, Samuel J., 118
Kirschenheiter, John, 42
Kisling, Audra, 202
Kisling, Dale, 202-204
Kisling, Dick, 202, 204
Kisling, Majora, 202
Kisling, Nancy, 202-203
Kisling, Richard, 202-204
Kisling, Robert, 201-202
Kisling, Ruth, 202
Kisling, Sam, 201-202
Kisling, Vivian, see Van Cura, Vivian (Kisling)
Kiwanis Club, 5, 93, 197
Klink, Christian, 66
Knapp, Alex, 179
Knox, George, 108, 110
Koheiser, Clarence, 179

Index

Koogle, Charlie, 149
Koogle's Grocery, 149
Krogers, 203
Kunkle, Lawrence, 58
Kunkle, Polly, 88, 153
Kyner Bros. orchestra, 35

L

Ladies of Lexington, 46
Lake Shore Gang, 49
Laman, Benj, 108, 110
Langworthy, Cyrus, 13
Lantz, Frank, 107
Larsen, Carl, 179
LaSalle, 14
Laubie, Fred, 151
Lawrence family, 221
Lawrence, Wilbur, 179
Lebarre, Dr. I. H, 92
LeClair, Harry, 62
Lee, Dr., 194
Leedy, Jim and Mary Kay, 84
Leedy, John and Ida, 86-87
Leevering, Haddie, 179
Lehman, Deputy Carroll, 51
Lehman, Don, 232
Leppo, Jim, 176
lever, Lloyd, 153
Levy, Janice (Kisling), 204
Lewis, 13
Lewis and Clark Expedition, 235-237
Lewis, Amariah, 30
Lewis, Cynthia (Watson), 13-14, 30
Lewis, Geo., 108, 110
Lewis, Levi, 32
Lewis, Mary, 32
Lewis, Nelson, 76
Lewis, Stationmaster Nelson, 76
Lewis, William, 13-14, 113
Lex Beverage Center, 228
Lex-Gate Village, 155, 159
Lexian Restaurant, 62-63, 159
Lexington Advertizer, 38
Lexington Asphalt Paving, 145
Lexington Band, 122
Lexington Board of Education, 93
Lexington Boy Scout Troup 1, 232
Lexington Cemetery, 79, 82
Lexington Chamber of Commerce, 5
Lexington Church of Christ, 222
Lexington Church of The Nazarene, 222
Lexington Class of 1916, 5
Lexington Class of 1927, 4
Lexington Concrete & Supply, 205
Lexington Courier, 42
Lexington Directory, 113
Lexington Emigration Club, 116

Lexington Equity Exchange, 77
Lexington Fire Department, 59
Lexington Hardware, 129
Lexington Hotel, 23
Lexington Industrial Park, 168, 206
Lexington Kiwanis Club, 76, 86
Lexington Ledger, 41
Lexington Male and Female Seminary, 220
Lexington Men's Service Club, 164
Lexington Moose Lodge, 198
Lexington Odd Fellow Hall, 217
Lexington Pictorial, 38
Lexington Police, 51, 165
Lexington Presbyterian Church, 214, 218
Lexington Public High School, 222
Lexington Savings Bank, 123, 149, 183, 204
Lexington school building, 209
Lexington School Cafeteria, 210
Lexington Seminary, 221-222
Lexington Shopper News, 38-39
Lexington Soy Products Company, 59, 77, 122, 205
Lexington Times, 38
Lexington town band, 106
Lexington's 175th birthday celebration, 81
Lexington's Senior Center, 76
Linco Restaurant, 88-89
Linco station, 89
Lindley Tavern, 23-25
Lindley, Elizabeth, 22-23
Lindsey, Florian, 138-140
Lindsey, Mary (Miller), 139
Lindsey, Mrs., 136
Lindsey, Ralph, 1-2, 139
Lindsey, Rex, 139
Lindsey, S, 35
Lindsey, Seymore, 2, 18, 25, 127, 135-136, 140, 191-193
Lindsey, Verda (Smith), 139
Lindsey, William, 107, 109, 139, 222
Linton family, 198
Linton, *Bill*, 199
Linton, Harry, 58, 60, 133, 197, 199
Linton, Margaret *Maggie*, 197, 199-200
Linton, Marilyn, 133, 199
Linton, Marshal Frank, 50
Linton, Richard, 133, 199
Locke, Mayor William J., 184
Lockhart, 13
Logan, Barbara, 56
Logan, Charles, 25, 49
Logan, Gladys, 143-144, 149
Logan, John, 80
Logan, Mr. & Mrs. Lee, 139
Logan, Mrs. Lee, 141
Lorin Academy, 219
Lots number 1 and 4, 21
Louis Bromfield Farm, 88
Loveland, Augustus, 147
Lucas, 8
Ludwig, Dr., 92
Lutz Bros. steam engine, 18
Lutz Lumber Company, 5, 77

Index

Lutz, Clarence *Spike*, 5, 225
Lutz, Fred, 125
Lutz, Henry, 124
Lutz, Ralph, 5, 48, 53, 59, 164
Lutz, Ruth (Derrnbrger), 5
Lutz, Ruth and Ralph, 5
Lutz, William, 68, 124-125, 213, 218
Lyon, William, 217
Lyons, Tom, 130-132

M

M&S Railroad, 71
Mahon, Thomas, 114
Main Street Disaster, 55
Main Street repaved, 18
Maher, Lawrence, 83
Malabar Inn, 88
Mann, Dr. A., 92
Manner, W. G., 113
Mansfield and Newark Railroad, 67
Mansfield and Sandusky City Railroad, 69
Mansfield General Hospital, 50, 93
Mansfield Herald, 32, 34, 46, 68, 169
Mansfield Liederkranz,, 201
Mansfield News Journal, 30, 34, 41, 59, 139
Mansfield Public Library, 40
Mansfield Savings Bank, 122
Mansfield Screw Machine Products, 206
Mansfield Telephone Company, 142
Mansfield, Gilead, 199, 228
Maple, Chief Joe, 59
Maple, Joe, 60
Mark IV partnership, 164
Markley, Charles, 50, 68
Marks, Abraham, 108, 110
Marsh, Henry, 107, 109
Marshall, James, 107, 109
Marshall, Mr., 17
Mason's Refrigeration, 67
Mast, Dr. Earl, 92
Mast, Dr. Ester, 92
Mast, Drs., 93
Maul, Carl, 226
Maxwell, 13
Maxwell family, 214, 221
Maxwell, George, 25, 149-150
Maxwell, Hugh, 149-150
Maxwell, Miss Effie, 120
Maxwell's, 149
Maxwell's garage, 56
Mayor's Court, 47
McBride, 87
McBride, Jenner, 202
McCarrick, Mayor William, 189
McCartney, Mr., 210
McClain, J. W., 77
McClure, Chalmer, 25
McClure, James, 10
McClure, Samuel, 10, 217

McClurg, Albert, 110
McClurg, Hamilton, 108, 110
McCormick, Reverend, 226
McCune, James, 108, 110
McCune, Mrs. C., 35
McCune, Robert, 110
McCune, Thomas, 110
McEwen, Francis, 31, 113
McEwen, John, 31
McEwen's Cross Roads, 3
McFarland, Robert and Georgia, 185
McFarlands, 186
McIntere, James, 107, 109
McIntere, Thomas, 107, 109
McIntire, Jess, 59
McIntire, Laura, 105
McIntire, Lee, 62
McIntire, Lowell, 4, 154
McJunkins, W. W., 108, 110
McKee, Dillian, 14
McKee, Henry, 226
McKee, Tim, 131
McLane, Charles, 116
McLaughlin, Art, 232
McLaughlin, Fred, 232
McLaughlin, Jim, 62
McLean, Arthur, 12
McLear, 72
McMillen, Dr., 92
McNaul, Alan, 129
McNaul, Albert *Poose*, 49
McNaul, John, 149
McNaul's Meat Market, 149
McWilliams, Dr. Watson, 85
Meece, Hanna, 84
Meece, Jacob, 84
Melodeon, 170
Memorial Day - May 30, 1906, 108
Memorial Day - May 30, 1916, 109-110
Men's Service Club, 5, 93, 188
Mennoite Church, 85
Mentzer, Raymond, 58
Mercer-Griebling mill, 226
Mercer, B. F., 113
Meredith, Fred, 88, 90
Meredith, Ray, 90
Methodist Church, 214
Methodists, 213
Meyers, Art, 194
Meyers, Bentley, 108
Mid Ohio Race Track, 85
Mid Ohio Sports Car Course, 196
Midwest Fabricating Co., 83, 154
Midwest Houses, 154, 159
Midwest Staff Architect, 155
Miles, Dr. L. B., 92
Miller Professor John, 209
Miller, D. P., 108
Miller, Daniel, 27, 43
Miller, David P., 110
Miller, Ed, 62

Index

Miller, George, 114, 118
Miller, Harry, 139
Miller, Henry, 141
Miller, Lester, 89-90
Miller, Samuel, G., 32
Millers War of 1884-1885, 119
Milligan, John, 109
Minnear Hotel, 26, 102, 149, 153, 175
Minnear, B. F, 25, 107, 109
Minnear, Belle and Benny, 26-27
Minnear, Beulah, 26,-27
Minnear, Mabel, 26
Minnear, Paul, 26, 27
Minnear, Waynon, 26
Mishey Family, 30
Mishey, Styrl, 33
Mitchel, Francis, 233
Mitchell, Charles *Pappy*, 25
Mitchell, George, 31, 217
Mitchell, Joseph, 233
Mitchell, Nathaniel, 32
Mizer, Jacob, 132
Mobile station, 63
Mohican Division, Number 212, 45
Mohican House, 22
Mohican Valley Dairy, 201, 204
Monroe Seminary, 219
Mont's West Main Mobile Station, 151
Moon, John, 108, 110
Moore, Al, 26, 34, 37, 120, 147, 169, 174, 177, 190-191
Moore, H. S., 34, 108, 110
Moravian missionaries, 8
Morley, Adelle, 155
Morley, John, 83, 154-155, 159, 184
Mormons, 218
Morrison, Jack, 155
Mount, J. P., 108, 110
Moyer, Robert, 159
Mrs. Lee's Home Cooking, 149
Mulbert, Al, 238
Mull, William, 179
Murphy, Carl, 139
Murray, Thomas, 108, 110
Myers, Bentley, 110
Myers, Clyde, 94
Myers, George T. *Monkey*, 94-96, 109
Myers, Glen, 59
Myers, Jacob, 218

N

Narience, Joseph, 108, 110
Narrance, James, 110
National Cash Register Company, 181
Neely, James, 116
Neer Manufacturing Company, Inc., 168
New Purchase, 233
New School Presbyterian Church, 216
New York and Brooklyn Brass & Bell Foundry, 217

New Zion, 218
Newcomer, John, 93, 145, 152-153, 164
Newel, Capt., 10
Newlom, Charles, 108, 110
Newmam, Charlie, 82
Next Generation Films, 206-207
Numbers, Alice, 147
Numbers, Enock, 108, 110
Numbers, Wm., 108, 110

O

O'Doud, Charles, 49
Oak Hill Cottage, 132
Oakes, Dr. Milton, 92-93
Oakwood Rockwell Cemetery, 14
Oberlin College, 132
Oberlin, John, 37
Ogg, Ray, 19, 179
Ogle, Enoch, 33
Ohio and Erie Canal, 69
Ohio Brass, 200
Ohio Gauge, 73
Ohio General Assembly 76th District, 122
Ohio Governor Meigs, 8
Ohio Medical Collage, 170
Ohio Power Company, 128, 182
Ohio Register, 21
Ohio State Legislature, 5
Ohio State Liquor and Brewers Assoc., 68
Ohio State University, 176
Ohio Temperance League, 47
Ohio Wesleyan University, 214
Old Cook Tavern, 22, 55
Old Fellows, 229
Oldfield, Jonathan, 10
Ontario Cemetery, 80
Ontario Tribune, 42
Orchard Park, 86-88, 155, 196

P

Palm, Dwight, 179
Palm, James, 108, 110
Palm, William, 108, 110
Park Hotel, 23, 25
Park's Air College, 238
Parker, Bert, 200, 226
Patterson, Thomas, 171, 215
Paxton, Donald, 77
Pearson, Drew, 40
Penelton, H. B., 50
Pennel, James M., 43
Peoples Bank of Bellville, 121
Perry Victory, 10
Perry, *Cub*, 48

Index

St. Peters, Joseph, 72
Pharis, William, 107
Phelps, H. H., 56
Philip, Wm., 108, 110
Philips, Rev. Geo., 108, 110
Pierce, Jessie, 105
Pipe, Captain, 8
Plank Mill, 119
Poe, Adam, 213
Poff, Bill, 159
Poland, Emma, 84
Poland, Scott, 84
Poland, Simon, 107
Pollock, Charles *Runt*, 48-49
Pollock, Oris, 37, 125
Portner, Fortney, 85
Post, J. M., 107
Powers, Rev., 213
Presbyterian Church, 46, 141, 170, 216
Presbyterians, 213-214
President Madison, 8
Proctor, John Jr., 34
Proctor, Rev and Mrs., 34
Proctor, Rev. A. E., 38
Prohibition, 68
Prosser, Spoke, 86
Prosser, Bob, 36
Prosser, Bonnie, 86
Prosser, Donald, 232
Prosser, Mary Eva, 86
Prosser, Nancy, 86
Prosser, Natalie, 86, 138
Prosser, Sherrilyn, 86
Prosser, *Spoke*, 86
Proto, Larry, 152
Public Square, 20
Pugh, John and Florenda, 32

R

R. R. Company, 169
Radio Station WVNO, 207
Rahall, Bobby, 197
Railroad, 124
Ramsey, Alice (Numbers), 147
Ramsey, Captain, 146-147
Rat Cellar, 27
Rathskaller, 27
Ray Cashell's bakery and lunch room, 129
Red Crown gasoline, 150
Reed, Dr. Myron, 195
Reel, Nelson and Tillie, 100
Reel, Robert, 100
Reel-Swigart Field, 100
Remy, Edward, 121
Republic Motor Car Co., 182
Republican Newspaper, 190
Resurrection Parish, 223

Revson, Peter, 197
Rhodes, Governor, 166
Rice, Rev. Cecil, 222
Richey, Mr., 210
Richey, William, 107, 109
Richie, Morris, 68
Richland County Genealogical Society, 236
Richland County Museum, 208
Richland County Sheriff's Department, 165
Richland Foundation, 6, 167
Richland Mall, 42
Richland Products, 206
Richland Report, 40
Richland Screw Machine, 206
Rider, Levi, 108, 110
Riggle, Harrison, 107
Riggle, Henry, 110
Rinehart, Alvin, 62
Rinehart, Rob, 232
Ritchie, B. F., 43
Ritchie, Ed., 59
Ritchie, Sherriff, 37
Ritter, Jerry, 110
Ritter, Levi, 107
Robbins, Elisha, 13
Robbins, Elizabeth (Watson), 13-14
Robert Beaty Tavern, 33
Robert Castor Post of the VFW, 144
Robert Davidson farm, 138
Roberts, Dick, 90, 156
Roberts, Richard, 10
Robins. Elisha, 10
Rocky Fork Valley, 184
Rogers, G. G., 186
Roll of Living Soldiers, 109
Ross Field, 85
Ross, Alice, 142
Ross, Clarence, 85
Ross, Frank Gee, 142
Ross, Frank Jr., 142
Ross, George, 85
Ross, Jay, 142-143
Ross, Verna, 85
Route 314, 1
Route 97, 1
Rowland, Thomas, 110
Royal Blue Super Market, 158
Ruhl, Agnes, 84
Ruhl, Cassie, 84
Rummel Mil, 119
Rumsey, Captain Levi, 145, 147
Rusk, Charles, 49
Russell, 132
Rutherford, J. A., 19
Ryan, Louie, 133, 153

S

Sager, Dr. J. F., 92
Samsell, Dr. I. S., 92

Index

Sanderlin, W. R., 186
Sanders, Squires, 108, 110
Sandusky & Monroeville, 69
Sandusky, Mansfield & Newark Railroad, 32, 72, 112
Sandwich Bar, 158
Sandy, 165
Sandy Hill, 210
Satterfield, John, 61, 76, 177
Satterfield, John, 83
Satterfield, Nellie, 76
Saunders, O., 23-24
Schindler farm, 176
Schindler, Isa (Lindsey), 139
Schindler, Mona, 90, 105, 195
Schindler, Paul, 59, 194-195
Schroeder, Charlie, 86
Schroeder, G. F., 87
Schumacher, Dwight, 155
Schumacher, Helmut, 201
Scott, James M., 110
Scott, Robert, 62
Scott, Thomas, 110
Searls, Mrs., 82
Secony Mobile, 151
Secretary of the Interior, 118
Section gangs, 124
Seif, Simon, 154
Seither, Edward, 108, 110
Serles, Robert, 107, 109
Seward H. Mott, 154
Sexton House, 79-80
Shafer, Walter, 79, 154
Shaffer Siding, 205
Shambaugh, Jacob, 108
Shambaugh, Thomas, 108, 110
Shauck Cemetery, 85
Shauck, John, 210
Shauck, William, 32
Shelby Seamless Tube, 174
Shelenbarger, Jane, 170
Shellenbarger, John, 107, 110
Sheppard, Delbert, 74
Sherer, J. H., 222
Sherman family, 221
Sherman, Jim, 155
Sherman, John, 23
Sherman, Mrs. Arthur, 215
Sherman, Phyllis, 157
Sherrod, Cliff, 194
Shew, Jacob, 110
Shilling, Rev. Don, 222
Shingler, Clarence, 68
Shoppers News, 40, 48
Shortess, Jess, 116
Shuler, Carrie, 84-85, 136
Shuler, Paul, 223
Shuster, Chris, 179
Siege of Atlanta, 94
Siley, George, 108, 110
Simon, Elsie Moore, 50
Simon, Elsie, 209

Sinclair Station, 153
Sloverine Salve, 130
SM&N locomotive, 70
SM&N Railroad, 112-113
Smaltz, A., 124
Smaltz, Jane, 22
Smaltz, Michael, 52
Smarts Music, 143
Smith barbershiop, 129
Smith Bridge Company, 18
Smith Clean-Gas Producer Plants, 180
Smith Electric Light Company, 176-177
Smith Family, 2
Smith Foundry, 124, 230
Smith Gas Engine plan, 56
Smith Gas Power Company, 19, 124, 197
Smith Gas Producer plant, 77, 177-179, 182
Smith, Boyd, 173, 176
Smith, Carrie, 177, 180-181, 188
Smith, Dr. Henry H., 18, 92-93, 124, 170, 172, 174-175, 177, 180
Smith, Ed, 129
Smith, Edward Malcolm, 180
Smith, Emma (Ford), 170
Smith, Harry, 1-2, 9, 23, 56, 92, 124, 128, 139, 153, 158, 164-165, 170, 173-175, 177, 179-180, 182- 185, 187-189, 200, 240
Smith, Helen, 188
Smith, Henry,   67
Smith, Henry Ford, 180-181
Smith, Howard Wayne, 180
Smith, John, 86
Smith, Joseph, 218
Smith, Margaret (Hainer), 171, 173, 181
Smith, Mrs. Dwight, 139
Smith, Special Deputy Emory, 50
Smith's whiskey, 67
Snyder Family, 81
Snyder Funeral Home, 81
Snyder Print Shop, 41
Snyder, Bob and Dorothy, 143
Snyder, Dave, 164
Snyder, Dorothy, 40
Snyder, J. Todd, 81
Snyder, Ora, 195
Snyder, Robert, 38, 40,-42, 48, 59, 143, 144
Snyder, Robert and Dorothy, 81
Snyder's Funeral Home, 40, 59, 222
Soap Box Derby, 196-197
Socialist party, 174
Soldiers Buried in Lexington Cemetery,109
Soldiers of the Rebellion, 108, 110
Soldiers of the Revolution, 107, 109
Soldiers Reunion, 96
Sons of Temperance   45
Sowash, Marshal Ira *Mike*, 50-52, 61
Sower's grain warehouse, 74
Sower's Grove, 35
Sower's warehouse, 76
Sowers & Bevertock's general store, 149
Sowers Building, 55, 191

Index

Sowers family, 221
Sowers grain warehouse, 70
Sowers, Art, 149
Sowers, Bloomer, 35, 55, 217
Sowers, Charlie, 149, 153
Sowers, Frank, 153
Sowers, Gary, 153
Sowers, George M., 55
Sowers, Lucile, 105
Sowers, Moses, 107, 109, 115, 118
Sowers, Vi, 49
Sowers' General store, 149
Spanish-American War, 108, 110
Spaulding, Alma, 171
Spaulding, I. A. L., 24
Spoolman's saloon, 47
Springtown, 85
Spurgeon, Samuel, 132
St. Nicholas Magazine, 170
St. Peters, Joseph, 72
Standard Oil Company, 181
Star Telephone Company, 141
Steam Corners, 85, 104, 138, 142, 145
Steam Corners band, 85-86, 106
Steam Corners International Airport, 85
Steiner, Helen Emma, 180
Steiner, Helen Smith, 1, 92, 173
Steltzes, 10
Stemco, 165
Stevens Manufacturing Company, 151, 164-165
Stevens Plant, 167
Stevens, Chan, 167
Stevens, George, 109
Stevens, Mrs., 165
Stevens, Robert Hutch, 165, 167
Stevens, Walter Chandler, 164-167
Stewart, Henry, 107, 109
Stewart, Jackie, 197
Stewart, William, 107, 109
Stiffler, Calvin, 179
Stober, Dr. John, 92-93
Stone, John, 83
Stoneridge, Inc., 207
Stough, David, 54
Stough, Samuel, 95, 108, 110
Stough, W. C., 108, 110
Strasbaugh, John, 114
Strasbaugh, Samuel, 99
Strausbaugh, Jacob, 110
Streib, Walter, 186
Struble, Dan, 177
Stumbo, Frank, 194
Stumbo, Frank and Betty, 42
Stump Mill, 120
Suavely, Mildred, 89
Suburbanite Motors Foreign Cars dealership, 196
Sunoco Station, 155
Sutliff, Lathrop, 12
Swank, Ethyl, 105
Swigart, George, 100, 151, 153
Swigart, George and Jean, 152

Swigart, Jack, 151
Swigart, Jean, 153
Swigart, Laola, 142
Swigart, Roy, 68, 151
Swigart, Roy and Leola, 151
Swigart's Café, 76, 79, 100, 134, 145, 151
Synder, Ora, 81

T

Tales of the Mohican County, 30
Tanley, 68
Tanneyhill, Zachariah, 108, 110
Taylor, Monroe, 130
Taylor, W. H., 121
Teegarden, James, 72
Temperance, 66, 68, 85-86
Temple, Fuller, 1, 179
Templeton Terrace, 155, 164, 227
Templeton, Bill, 79, 155, 160-162
Templeton, Lillian, 160
Terpsichorean Club, 24
Texaco Gas Station, 151
Texter, George, 48, 153
Texter, Theron, 140
Texter, Wesley, 84
The American, 30
The Atmosphere, 88
The Bell Tavern, 27
The Butler Times, 38
The Club, 86-87
The Corners, 88
The Eagle, 30
The Forty-Niner, 133
The Green Bay Tree, 133
The Latter Day Luminary, 212
The Lexington Times, 41
The Minute Man 38
The News of Lexington, 38, 40
The old town hall, 43
The Phoenix Brewery, 67
The Red Bull, 30
The Sultana, 99
The Troy congregation, 219-220
The Truck Drivers Club, 90
The Village Council 46
Therm-O-Disc, 207
Thomas Logan gristmill, 113
Thomas, E. W., 186
Thomas, Orland, 155
Thuma, Sam, 83
Thuma's Meat Market, 49
Timanis, Lemuel, 108, 110
Timanus, James, 140
Times Publishing Company of Butler, 38
Tobin, Brad, 72
Tolhelm, Peter, 108, 110
Torrance, Rev. Adam, 213
Touby, Martin, 192
Town Marshall, 48

Index

Town square, 20, 24
Traxler, Jim, 166-167
Treisch, Ed, 1-2
Treisch, Jeff, 238-239
Treisch, Peter, 85
Tribune-Courier, 41, 194
Trimble, Charlie, 79-80
Troy Presbyterian Church, 66
Trueman, Jim, 197

U

Underground Railroad, 217, 236
Union strikers, 167
United Brethern, 213-214, 218
United Implements, 77, 79, 161, 164
United Technologies, 167
Universalists, 213

V

Van Cura, Vivian (Kisling), 202
Van Eman, Rev. George, 213
Vanderbilt, John, 33
Vanderbilt's repair garage, 158
Vermillion Institute, 170
Veterans of Foreign Wars Post, 100
Vidonish Studios, 122-123, 204
Vidonish, Bill and Cherri, 204
Village Council, 47
Vine Hill School, 174
Voltz, William Sr., 186, 206
Volz, Bill Jr., 186-187

W

W. P. Nutter Coal Co., 83
Wade Family, 25
Wade, Nellie Gatton, 139
Wade, Robert, 25
Wade, Wilbur, 90, 156
Wages, William, 56
Wagner, *Micey,* 226
Wagner, Ed, 195-196
Wagner, Flora, 105
Wagner, Homer, 89-90, 194
Wagner, Howard, 193
Wagner, Les Sr., 185
Waldo, Thayer, 40-41
Walker and Kell Hardware, 139, 191-192
Walker settlements, 217
Walker, Andy, 206
Walker, Capt. Joseph, 10
Walker, Garver, 110
Walker, Jay, 194
Walker, John G., 191
Walker, Lisa, 157
Walker, Rev. 109

Walker, Walter, 68, 174, 191-192
Walnut Hills, 155
Walter, Ed, 25
Wappner Funeral Home, 30
War of 1812, 8, 107, 10
War of the Rebellion, 108, 110
War with Mexico, 107, 109
Washburn, Chas. P., 110
Washburn, H. P., 108
Water Wheels and Millstones, 113
Watson family, 113
Watson Tavern, 29-30, 33
Watson, Amariah Jr., 7, 9-11, 14, 21, 27, 62, 66, 82, 107, 109, 112-113, 116, 200, 212-213, 240
Watson, Amariah, Sr., 13
Watson, Asahal, 12, 14, 113, 200
Watson, Avery, 108, 110
Watson, Chole, 13
Watson, Cynthia, 8-9, 13
Watson, Dr. Noah, 30, 92
Watson, Eleanor, 13
Watson, Hanna, 13
Watson, Hugh, 13
Watson, Major Samuel, 10
Watson, Michael, 12-13
Watson, Noah, 8, 11, 13, 28-29, 107, 109
Watson, Phoebe, 13
Watson, Rachel (Drake), 14
Watson, Riley, 14
Watson, Sallie, 8
Watson, Sally (Leonard), 13
Watson, Samuel, 8, 10-11, 13, 107, 109
Watson, Theory, 14
Watson's Mill, 12-13, 21
Watson/Graves/Lewis mill, 116
Wayne's Country Market, 28
Weirick, Deputy Wayne, 50
Weirick, Earl, 186
Weirick, Marshall Wayne, 40
Weirick, Wayne, 52
Weithman, Father, 223
Welch, John, 58
Welch, Loren, 62
Welch, Ted, 58, 154
Wentz, Bill, 179
Wentz, Dale, 232
Wentz, Jim, 232
Wentz, Lonie, 179
Wentz, Rob, 232
Werrick, Charles, 49
Wertz, Dr. K. G., 92
West, Claude E., 50
Westinghouse, 164
Whited, Linda, 157
Whitford Cornelius, 107, 109
Whitney, Bob, 135
Whitney, Lloyd, 51, 151-152, 238
Whitney, Mont, 151-152
Whitney, Mrs. Shirley, 238
Whitney, Robert, 151
Whitney's Mobile Station, 64, 149, 158, 196

Index

Wiles, Dr. Otis, 92-93, 186
Wiles, Dr. W. H., 48
Wiles, Harmon, 179
Wiles, Loren, 187
Wiliben Farms, 155
William Bonham Funeral Home, 230
William Cureton and Son Foundry, 230
William, Samuel, 25
Williams, Charlie, 81
Williams, David, 12, 108, 110
Williams, Elizabeth, 80-81
Williams, John, 35, 80, 107, 113, 140
Williams, Mary, 136, 139
Williams, Mayor F. L., 47
Wilson & Hamilton's drugstore, 115
Wilson Creamery, 125
Wilson, Ed, 60, 154
Wilson, George, 108, 110
Wilson, Joe, 153
Wilson, Lowell, 124
Wilson, Major General James H., 117
Wilson, Prof. James, 222
Wilson, Professor Jasper, 47
Wilson, Wallace, 34
Wilson, Wm., 108, 110
Winters, Mrs., 35
Wirich, John & Peter, 10
Wirick, Gene, 161-164, 232
Wirick, Duane, 232
Wirick, Jeanette, 210
Wirick, John, 232
Wiseman, Phil, 41
Wittmer, D. K., 186
Wittner, J. A., 186
Wolf, Bob, 206
Wolf, Carole, 41
Wolf, Terry, 41
Wolford, Samuel, 108, 110
Women's Bachelors Club, 37
Worley, Jeff, 82
Worley, Lewis, 161
Worley, Lottie, 82
Worley, Martin, 82
Worley, Richard, 82
Worthington Branch, 218
WPA labor, 58
Wright, Catherine, 183
Wright, Wilbur and Orville, 183

Y

Yarger, Wm., 107
Yeager, Balinda, 84
Yoah, Ora, 194
Young, Adie, 150
Young, Adrian, 229
Young, Howard, 189
Young, R. G., 107

The Author

Robert A. Carter was born in Mansfield, Ohio, in 1935, and graduated from Lexington High School in 1954. Married with 5 children and 10 grandchildren, 3 great grandchildren. He currently lives in Mansfield with his wife Jackie. He is a member of the Richland County Chapter of the Ohio Genealogical Society, the Ohio Historical Society and the Society for Preservation of Old Mills (SPOOM). Since 1964 he has written six local area history books, including *1964 Lexington Sesquicentennial booklet; The Sandusky Mansfield & Newark Railroad* (2002); *Tom Lyons The Indian That Died 13 Times* (2003); *Tales of the Old-Timers – The History of Lexington* (2007); *The Mansfield Riots of 1900* (2009), and *Water-Power Mills of Richland County* (2016).

As of 2023 he continues to write articles for the *Tribune-Courier*.

Also Available from Turas Publishing

Water-Powered Mills of Richland County

by

Robert A. Carter

$29.00

https://turaspublishing.com/product/water-powered-mills-of-richland-county/

www.ingramcontent.com/pod-product-compliance
Lightning Source LLC
Chambersburg PA
CBHW081105080526
44587CB00021B/3461